US CHESS FEDERATION'S

OFFICIAL RULES *of* CHESS

7TH EDITION UPDATED FOR 2020

Tim Just, Chief Editor

National Tournament Director
FIDE National Arbiter

US Chess Federation's Official Rules of Chess
Tim Just, chief editor

National Tournament Director.—Seventh Edition.

ISBN: 9781797716909 (paperback)

Printed in the United States of America
Seventh Edition

Contents

I. An additional set of scholastic rules, developed by the Scholastic Committee for scholastic tournaments, may apply instead of the rules in this book. The scholastic rules are updated often and are available from US Chess.

II. The current FIDE laws of chess can be viewed at:

http://www.fide.com/fide/handbook.html?id=32&view=category

TD TIP: *Tournaments submitted to FIDE must use FIDE rules, even if the event is held in the United States and is also US Chess rated. In those events FIDE rules trump US Chess rules.*

III. ***Fischer 960 Chess:*** *US Chess adopts appendix F of the FIDE Laws of Chess (for Chess 960 (Fischer 960).*

Please note that within chapters some pages have large areas of blank space. This is to avoid the splitting of important material over two pages.

Acknowledgments

The editor could not have succeeded without the help of many others and appreciates the efforts of former US Chess Director of events Francisco Guadalupe for taking steps in making the publication of this 7th Edition possible. The editor also expresses his appreciation to Franc, Ken Ballou, Boyd Reed, David Kuhns, Dan Lucas, the Tournament Directors Certification Committee, and the Rules Committee for providing invaluable input and devoting many hours in proofreading the book. Dan Lucas also contributed invaluable technical expertise in the publication of this edition. IM Ron Burnett provided essential copy-editing services.

Thanks also to the past editors, Kenneth Harkness, Martin Morrison, Tim Redman, Bill Goichberg, Carol Jarecki, Ira Lee Riddle, Dan Burg, and Tim Just.

I also appreciate the efforts of past US Chess Executive Directors Gerry Dullea and Al Lawrence for their contributions to earlier rulebook editions.

Rulebook edition 6 would have been impossible to publish without Francisco Guadalupe; furthermore, his efforts made the online version of the 7th edition possible.

Introduction: The Evolution of Chess Rules

The earliest printed rules of modern chess appear in a book by the Spaniard Luis Ramirez Lucena. The book is believed to have been published in 1497, shortly after the moves of the queen, pawn, and bishop were changed to what they are today.

Lucena's rules are sketchy, but he describes the difference between the old and new styles of chess, as well as the various moves, while providing some definitions and advice. One bit of advice states:

> *If you play at night, place your candle on your left-hand side, if by day, place your opponent facing the light. It will be worse for your opponent if you play him when he has just eaten and drunk freely. During a game drink water, not wine. Play for a small stake, so that the thought of it may not trouble you.*

The trick of placing your opponent with the light in his eyes was apparently an old Spanish custom, for it is repeated by Ruy Lopez in his text published in 1561.

Chess literature in the sixteenth and seventeenth centuries records the rules followed in various countries. In those days there were considerable differences, including castling, pawn promotion, stalemate, and the en passant pawn capture. Some of these differences were still being debated in the nineteenth century.

In the eighteenth and nineteenth centuries, codes were adopted by chess clubs and eventually by national chess associations, but there was no general agreement on the rules. The first international tournament, in London, 1851, was played under "the rules of the chief European Chess Clubs." In the first national tournament held in this country, in New York, 1857, play was governed by the rules published in *Staunton's Chess Player's Handbook* (London, 1847). In 1860 a revised code published by Staunton in his *Chess Praxis* became generally recognized for English and American tournaments.

Although basic chess laws were fairly well standardized by the mid-nineteenth century, the rules governing competitive play were in a state of confusion. The rules committee of the 1880 American Chess Congress refers to its "delicate and difficult task of dissecting the mass of disordered and conflicting codes of chess laws at present in operation." The congress adopted a revised code, but it was copied largely from Staunton. This code was generally recognized until 1897, when New York's Manhattan Chess Club obtained the American rights to laws that had been officially adopted by the leading chess associations and clubs of Great Britain and published them as *The American Chess Code*.

Old chess rules may die hard. Some eighteenth-century chess rules stated that a promoted pawn could only take the place of a captured piece. Even though no book in English has restricted promotion in this way since before the Lincoln presidency, chess clubs and organizations still receive many calls asking whether such a rule exists. Likewise, even some tournament players believe a player who touches a piece that cannot move must move the king, a rule abandoned at least one hundred years ago.

When the World Chess Federation (*Federation Internationale des Echecs*, or FIDE) was founded in 1924, an early priority was the formation of a uniform international chess code to supplant the variations practiced in different countries. Such a code was adopted by FIDE in 1929. These rules governed play in most tournaments in the United States and other nations until 1952, with the addition of some supplementary regulations and interpretations by national or local organizations. In 1952, FIDE published a new edition of the *Laws of Chess*.

Before the mid-1950s, US Chess had no official set of rules. The need to supplement the FIDE rules was growing, primarily because of the popularity of Swiss system tournaments. FIDE rules were written for Master round robins, with few participants, in which directors could provide close supervision. Swisses of over a hundred players would be costly to organize on the same basis.

A US Chess Tournament Rules Committee was formed in 1953 to write the rules, but its members were unable to devote the necessary time to their task, and its chairman resigned. Kenneth Harkness, the US Chess business manager (a position similar to today's Executive Director) was then appointed acting chairman of the US Chess Tournament Rules Committee. He submitted several drafts to the members of the committee, but none responded. Finally, Harkness submitted his draft to Hans Kmoch of FIDE, who provided some additional ideas.

Authorized by US Chess president Frank Graves, Harkness's work appeared as the *Official Blue Book and Encyclopedia of Chess* in 1956. David McKay published this edition and subsequent US Chess rulebooks. The book included a US Chess rule requiring a player to maintain a "complete and legible record of all the moves of the game" to win on time, a more efficient way to run a Swiss than the FIDE practice of having directors count moves. The book established that either descriptive or algebraic notation (both long and short form) was valid, provided a table of chess symbols in various languages, and included a US Chess rating system regulations.

In 1962 FIDE reinstated an old but rarely noticed prohibition on draws by agreement before the thirtieth move, this time with real intention of enforcement: the penalty was to be loss of the game by both players. The rule was tried for two years, but players ignored it or circumvented it with agreed repetitions of position, and directors were unable or unwilling to enforce penalties. It was abandoned in 1964.

Harkness issued the *Official Chess Handbook* in 1967. He included the laws of chess, supplementary rules, chess notation, and some ideas on "how to run a chess tournament." The adjustment of players' ratings by the director after every round, included in the 1956 book, was abandoned as "an unnecessary refinement." Some FIDE rules which were also FIDE rules were changed. Rules regarding scorekeeping were expanded and clarified, and a player was allowed to ask (through the director) to borrow the opponent's scoresheet if necessary. The rule providing that a player sealing an illegal move loses the game was modified to allow the director to waive this penalty if the player's intention is obvious. The timing and consequences of draw offers and draw claims were discussed in far more detail than previously (though still far less than in today's rules).

Harkness also edited the *Official Chess Rulebook*, published in 1972, the year of his death. This volume was basically an abridged version of his *Handbook*. He added material on notation, chess clocks, and rules for blind players. US Chess tournament rules were condensed and put into the book, but current FIDE changes were not included. These 1970 - 72 modifications to the FIDE laws plus US Chess changes through early 1973 were distributed in a pamphlet edited by Martin Morrison, chair of the US Chess Rules Committee, and published privately by Paul Masson Vineyards.

Martin Morrison, then US Chess technical director, edited the next publication, *Official Rules of Chess* (1974), dedicated to the memory of Harkness. Morrison acknowledged the help of Pearle Mann and John Osness of the US Chess Tournament Direction Committee. FIDE had published a new set of rules in 1972, and these were included in this edition.

The US Chess time-forfeit rules were clarified. In order to win on time a player must have a scoresheet with no more than three move pairs omitted when the opponent's flag falls, a refinement that encouraged those expecting to win on time to keep score move after move. Also, time forfeits were no longer to be called by players or directors, but by players only. This change addressed the unfairness of directors claiming on behalf of some players but not others. Complete Swiss pairing rules were presented, rules for speed chess added, and sections on prizes and tie breaking expanded significantly. No preference was given for tie-break methods, but the following were listed and briefly explained: Median, Solkoff, Sonneborn-Berger, Kashdan, and Cumulative.

Morrison also edited the *Official Rules of Chess, Second Edition*, published in February 1978. The "corrected" version appeared in March 1979. William Abbott, Stephan Gerzadowicz, Joseph Lux, and John Osness all provided help with this edition. The US Chess rules were written as part of the FIDE rules section, although the pairing rules were separate. Cumulative was listed as the only tie-break method for Swisses. This edition also introduced the idea that a player should not be assigned the same color three times in a row. Rules for computer participants were added for the first time.

From 1979 through 1986 chess tournaments underwent substantial change, which prompted much demand for a revised rulebook. Several committees were appointed to do the job but failed to make progress. Finally, under the aegis of the US Chess Executive Board, Jerome Bibuld and Glenn Petersen wrote an initial draft of the new rules for comment by a panel of National Tournament Directors.

Meanwhile, FIDE was revising its rulebook, with two important changes aimed at making it easier to use. Interpretations were incorporated into the rules themselves, and the rules were reorganized in a manner developed by US Chess's Tim Redman and Gerry Dullea. These changes were the basis for the revision drafted at the 1983 Manila Congress.

Tim Redman was appointed by the Doyle Executive Board as editor for the forthcoming US Chess rulebook. After consulting existing drafts, he completely rewrote the US Chess rules and procedures to improve clarity, incorporate recent practice, and allow pairings to be fully computerized. Dullea continued to work as his principal assistant, drafting additional sections while Redman focused on the central game and tournament rules. Both had the benefit of expert advice from directors across the country. George Cunningham provided technical assistance in defining the statistical relation between color allocation and win expectancy.

The Redman 3rd edition was the first to include a significant rule change that has made tournaments fairer and easier to run; i.e., players with a legitimate reason were no longer prohibited from stopping both clocks. Prior to this change, a player who needed a director, when none was in sight, had to send a third party to find one. By the time the director arrived at the board, the player's game was sometimes lost or hopeless. Another important change in the 3rd edition was the separation of FIDE rules from US Chess rules. The 4th edition of the rulebook went even further by placing the FIDE rules many chapters after the US Chess rules to emphasize the differences between them.

Redman's book also added sections on the new sudden death time controls, computer memberships, handicapped players, players' rights and responsibilities, US Chess Code of Ethics, and the Crenshaw-Berger tables for round robin pairings, which correct a color imbalance caused by a withdrawal in a round robin.

Half-point byes, having become popular since the previous edition, were described for the first time. In the case of an ambiguous sealed move, instead of declaring a forfeit, a director finding two or more reasonable interpretations of the move could leave the choice between them to the opponent. Officially put into use May 1, 1987, the book was applauded as being user friendly, providing much more in the way of explanation than previous editions. A much more detailed index was also included.

A 4th rulebook edition was published in 1994, edited by Bill Goichberg, Carol Jarecki, and Ira Lee Riddle. This edition revised and updated both the rules and their explanations, and added substantial new material on topics not previously addressed, roughly doubling the size of the rulebook.

Since 1987, sudden death time controls had become extremely popular; by the end of the twentieth century most Swiss tournaments in the nation used them. Rules for sudden death have been developed and improved through actual practice and were incorporated into the general US Chess rules in the 4th edition.

A player need not have a scoresheet to win on time in sudden death, but scorekeeping was originally required for players having at least five minutes remaining, as in traditional time limits. Enforcement of this rule proved difficult; there were continual complaints about players with over five minutes not keeping score in an effort to *blitz* opponents with fewer than five minutes. This was not a problem in conventional time controls, as a player who stopped keeping score could not win on time. A new sudden-death rule providing that if either player has less than five minutes remaining, neither is required to keep score, was first used at the 1988 New York State Action Championship and met with such immediate success.

Technology in the form of time delay and increment capabilities was in its infancy when the 4th edition was published. Those clocks were developed in response to the proliferation of short sudden death time control events that allowed a player enough time in a game to create an easily winning or non-losing position; yet, many a player would still lose on time. The time delay clock allowed players to use a few extra seconds per move so they could easily draw or win those positions. The 4th edition editorial team developed the rules that would guide that era's players and directors in dealing with the fast paced and popular development of time delay clocks.

In the early 1990s many players did not use time delay clocks while playing in sudden death time control tournaments. It was felt that this gave the player using a time-delay clock a winning, or at least a non-losing, edge. The 4th edition of the rules addressed those concerns by developing the "no losing chances" rule.

The attractiveness of Quick Chess tournaments with their emphasis on short time controls, a separate rating system, and no need of score keeping made the regulations a popular inclusion in the last rulebook of the twentieth century.

The 4th edition also developed the concept of allowing a player to re-enter a tournament when that player got off to an unacceptable start.

The revised 1992 FIDE rules were included in the 4th edition. Several FIDE rules were adopted as US Chess rules; however, the U.S. was then and continues to be the world's Swiss system pioneer, and new ideas are more likely to start with US Chess and eventually to be adopted by FIDE than vice versa.

Thanks to the efforts of the US Chess Executive Director, Al Lawrence, the 4th edition took on the aura of a US Chess handbook, rather than the more rules oriented editions of the past.

The 5th edition (2003) editors, Tim Just (Chief Editor) and Dan Burg, continued the practice of improving the clarity and meaning of the rules, improved book usability, and significant cross referencing of the rules. In the past the chapters with the rules received the attention of the editorial staff while other personnel attended to other chapters, formatting issues, and indexing chores. The 5th edition was a totally hands on editing project for each chapter as well as for formatting and indexing chores.

With the development of the US Chess web site as a source for US Chess handbook information, this current 6th edition, edited by Tim Just, devotes more space to the rules and rules issues. The Internet provided the editor with a wider, more accessible, and more useful forum for discussions on rulebook improvement topics. A link to the FIDE "Laws of Chess" was included in this edition, rather than a complete reprint of those rules.

The 6th edition has many more rules in sync with the FIDE Laws of Chess than past editions. Increment time control rules were added since the publication of the 5th edition. Internet chess and blitz chess rules, with an independent Blitz rating system, are new to this edition.

The 7th edition, edited by Tim Just, is available online as well as in print at the US Chess website. Many rules updates and improvements are included in this new edition. Additionally selected sections of this edition are available as individual downloads.

Swiss System

The invention of the Swiss system has been credited to Dr. J. Muller of Brugg, Switzerland. The first Swiss system tournament is believed to have been held at Zurich in 1895.

The original Swiss tournaments around the turn of the century usually ran for four or five rounds over two days and averaged about ten participants. By 1904 the number of entries had greatly increased, and contributors to the *Swiss Chess Magazine*, who claimed that the method was too dependent on chance factors, were attacking the system. "This all sounds very familiar," said Harkness of these attacks, recalling that his innovations designed to expand the popularity of chess had also come under fire from the old guard within US Chess.

The Swiss system achieved little popularity outside its native land until its introduction into the United States in the 1940s. Occasionally, an unimportant central European tournament was conducted under the method. Brief descriptions of the system were sometimes included in the German yearbooks, in which it would be mentioned one year but ignored the next; apparently this system was considered of little significance.

Grandmaster George Koltanowski, the "Dean of American Chess," is given credit for introducing the Swiss system into this country and strenuously advocating its widespread use. In 1942 Koltanowski visited Texas and persuaded the Texas Chess Association to try the Swiss instead of the then prevailing Holland system. The 1943 Pennsylvania Championship, directed by Koltanowski, is the first known Swiss tournament in America. During the next few years, many state and regional tournaments adopted the system. It answered the problem that had long seemed unsolvable; i.e., how to handle many participants in a limited time.

The 1945 U.S. Intercollegiate was the first national tournament to use the Swiss, and its success led US Chess to consider using the same method for the U.S. Open. But instead, there was a compromise with tradition. The 1946 U.S. Open in Pittsburgh had 58 entrants, and an 8-round Swiss preliminary was used in place of the old round robin prelims. The top ten from the Swiss qualified for a round robin final for a total of 17 games, too long by today's standards.

When the 1947 U.S. Open in Corpus Christi produced a record 86 entries, it was believed that an 8-round Swiss prelim would have little meaning with such a large field. This fear now seems unjustified, but it did result in US Chess taking the fateful step of holding the entire event as a 13-round Swiss. Every U.S. Open since, and almost all other major events, have used only the Swiss system, with some turnouts far beyond what other methods could have attracted or handled. The U.S. Open drew substantial new highs of 181 players at Milwaukee in 1953,

266 at Chicago in 1963, 400 at Ventura in 1971, 778 at Chicago in 1973, and 836 at Pasadena in 1983, all playing in one section. Some multi-section events such as the National Scholastics, National Open, World Open, and New York Open have drawn even larger totals; the 1986 World Open had 1,506 players, more than the total membership of US Chess in 1953. And let us not forget that the SuperNationals V in 2013 had almost four times the total membership of US Chess in 1953 with 5,335 players in attendance.

The 5th edition of the rulebook, like its 3rd and 4th edition predecessors, had major changes in pairing methods for the ratings-driven Swiss system tournament. The United States has led the way in the adoption of the Swiss, which continues to gain worldwide acceptance. The development of the Swiss system, along with the invention and refinement of the rating system by Kenneth Harkness and Arpad Elo, have been the two major contributions by US Chess to the popularization of chess throughout the world. The 6th edition also reflects a shift of the US Chess rules towards the FIDE rules.

Changes in this edition

In addition to elaborations on both new and old topics, this book has many rules updates and new items addressed for the first time. I believe that the editors of the 3rd, 4th, 5th, and 6th editions were right to devote more of their rulebooks to explanation and discussion than past rulebooks, and the 7th edition continues this trend with the use of *TD TIPS* that provide insight to the use and meaning of a rule by experienced directors.

The editor realizes that there are those that might prefer a shorter book with rules only; however, the majority of players and directors will welcome the expanded explanations, *TD TIPS*, and cross-references. I also believe that the discussion of a rule is most comprehensible when it appears together with the rule and its cross-references.

For the first time the 7th edition will be available online at the uschess.org. For those interested in selected sections of the book, especially only the rules, individual selected sections will be made available for download.

A rulebook is not only for directors. Many players, including beginners, will read this book, and they too can learn from the rule explanations and *TD TIPS*.

Philosophy.

The editor intends for this edition, like the 5th and 6th editions, to be a guide for directors and players in their pursuit of seeking fair and equitable solutions to the challenges that naturally arise from a competitive sport like chess. The editor intends for this work to be a source for solving general problems and a model for the thinking skills used in dealing with unique and rare situations. Detailed solutions to obscure circumstances will be left for the discussion groups that deal with those uncommon topics.

Improvements.

This edition continued the use of an extensive cross-referencing system developed for the 5th edition. **See Also** will be the words at the end of many rules that indicate a list of related rules to follow. Any e-editions and online editions will contain easy to use point and click cross-references. Note that if selected individual sections are downloaded that some rulebook internal links to other sections may not be available.

Second, the 7th edition continues the use of *TD TIPS* after many rules to further explain how experienced directors and players have effectively applied the concepts of the relevant rule.

Major Rules Changes.

All relevant rules updates (Chapter 1, Chapter 2, Chapter 10 and Blitz) enacted by the Delegates since the 6th edition are reflected in this 7th edition. Policy changes happen more quickly and may not always appear in this work.

Also be aware that in this 7th edition: Chapter 6 (US Chess Code of Ethics) is completely new; while Chapter 7 (Tournament Director Certification) includes some important upgrades. Chapter 10 is new as of September 1, 2020.

There were many minor changes in the wording of rules and other materials that make them easier to understand and administer. Those changes will not be listed here; therefore, it is advisable to completely review all of the rules, not just the ones with major changes.

Summary Of Major US Chess Rules Updates
In the Seventh Edition

5B2: Advanced publicity time controls need to contain both the base time control and the delay/increment.

5C1: **Both players must have the same time control.** Addresses "Time odds" games not being ratable along with an additional TD TIP.

5E: **Recommended Increment or delay**: Old rule 5E is replaced with recommended increment and delay settings.

Table of Contents

9D: Pawn Promotion. New wording makes the procedure of promoting a pawn clearer. Now the pawn is considered touched and must be promoted to the unreleased piece touching the promotion square.

10H: Piece touched off the board. Wording changes to be consistent with rule 9D. Once the piece off of the board touches the promotion square, the pawn must be promoted to that piece.

10I2: When castling, the King must be touched first.

10I2 Variation 1: Castling is allowed if the Rook is touched first.

11A: Illegal move in last ten moves: Added wording regarding time pressure and time recovered by players.

11D1: Illegal move in time pressure: Wording defining "time pressure" was added.

11H: Director corrects illegal move in non sudden death. Rule name changed (**Director corrects illegal move outside of time pressure**) along with added wording regarding non-time pressure situations.

14G: Both flags down in sudden death: Added wording regarding the observation of the flag fall and the game result.

14H: New wording eliminating insufficient losing chances.

Variation 14H: Old rule 14H is now an unannounced variation.

14K (new): Old 14K is replaced with: The TD (tournament director) can declare a draw if the same position has appeared 5 times in a row. The TD can declare a draw if 75 moves have been made without a pawn move or piece capture

16D: Special rules for time pressure: Deleted wording replaced with added links.

16P1: Delay or increment not set: A new rule dealing with how to address the situation with clocks that are not set with the proper delay or increment.

16Q: Interruption of game: Added wording defining "interruption."

16R: Illegal moves: Rule name change with deleted wording replaced with added links.

21L1: The "good faith" deposit amount included when filing an appeal can be determined by the ED.

28L2a Variation (announced): **Giving the bye to a higher rated player**. A variation that need not be announced in advance was added to rule 28L2. The variation allows assigning the bye to a higher rated player, rather than the lowest rated player, in the lowest score group in order to improve color assignments for the entire group.

29E8: **Variation (unannounced) team pairings take precedence over color equalization.** A variation that need not be announced in advance was added to rule 28E. Variation 29E8 avoids pairing players from the same team as a higher priority than equalizing player assigned colors in team/individual tournaments.

32B1: Special prizes, above and beyond the typical prize fund, should be announced and designated.

32B3: When pooling prizes, no player can receive a prize larger than the largest amount they would be eligible for without the split.

33D1: Added wording regarding special prizes.

35F10e: Added duties of an assistant to a blind or disabled player.

35F10g: Added duties of an assistant to a blind or disabled player.

Blitz: An editor's Note: at the start of the chapter was added.

Blitz: Rule 7c: has all new wording regarding the won game.

Blitz: Rule 8: added wording after "Defining a draw" to make clear which draw claims are allowed.

Blitz: Added to rule 7d: wording regarding placing a king next to a king.

Blitz: Rule 14: deleted some wording regarding the claim of a win.

Blitz: Rule 18: added a TD Tip regarding appeals.

Digital versions of chapters 1, 2, 10, and 11 from the 7th Edition may be downloaded at no charge from uschess.org.

CHAPTER ONE

The
US CHESS FEDERATION'S OFFICIAL RULES OF CHESS

1. Introduction

1A. Scope.
Most problems concerning rules that may arise during a chess game are covered in this book. However, the rules of chess cannot and should not regulate all possible situations. In situations not explicitly covered, the tournament director can usually reach a fair decision by considering similar cases and applying their principles analogously. The United States Chess Federation (US Chess) presumes that its tournament directors have the competence, sound judgment, and absolute objectivity needed to arrive at fair and logical solutions to problems not specifically treated by these rules.

1B. Validity.
US Chess play shall be governed by these rules of chess and by all US Chess procedures and policies. World Chess Federation (Federation Internationale des Echecs, or FIDE) rules shall not be used unless specifically announced in advance. For events that use FIDE rather than US Chess rules the International (FIDE) Laws of Chess apply.

1B1. Notification.
Any variations from these published rules, including variations discussed in this rulebook, should be posted and/or announced at the tournament prior to their use, preferably before the first round.

1B2. Major variations.
A variation sufficiently major so that it might reasonably be expected to deter some players from entering should be mentioned in any *Chess Life* announcement and all other detailed pre-tournament publicity and posted and/or announced at the tournament.

1C. Types of events.

1C1. Major events.
While the basic laws of chess do not vary from event to event, some material in this book is designed principally for major tournaments and is unlikely to be relevant otherwise. For example, unethical behavior is rare in chess; many players reading this book will play virtually all their games as friendly encounters in the spirit of good sportsmanship. But there are rare occasions, especially when large prizes or important titles are at stake, when a player steps beyond the bounds of friendly competition. Rules are needed to cover these situations.

1C2. Director discretion.

In areas in which the director has discretion, it is appropriate to be strictest with rules enforcement and penalties in events that are stronger or offer larger prizes. Being harshly penalized over a trivial rules violation can be sufficiently upsetting to deter a beginner from future chess participation.

1C2a. Standard penalty.

Except where specifically noted in the rules, the standard penalty assessed by the director is to add two minutes to the remaining time of the opponent of the player not following the rules of chess.

1C2b. Non-standard penalties.

Except where specifically noted in the rules, the director may assess penalties either more or less severe than the standard penalty (1C2a). It is often more appropriate for a director to issue a warning(s) before applying 1C2a in cases involving young or inexperienced players. A director may assess a more severe penalty in cases involving players who repeatedly do not follow the rules of chess.

2. The Chessboard

2A. Explanation.
Two opponents moving pieces on a square board called a *chessboard* play the game.

2B. Description.
The chessboard is composed of sixty-four squares of identical size, eight squares by eight squares, alternately light and dark. The light squares are referred to as *white squares* and the dark squares *black squares*, even though other colors are frequently used. (For instance, in tournament play *black squares* are often green.)

2C. Placement.
The chessboard is placed between the players in such a way that the nearer corner to the right of each player is white. **For information** regarding chessboard placement for blind players see 35F1, Special chessboard. **For information** regarding chessboard placement for online boards see Rule 5C1, Graphical Display Required (Chapter 10).

2D. Files.
The eight vertical rows of squares are called *files*.

2E. Ranks.
The eight horizontal rows of squares are called *ranks*.

2F. Diagonals.
The lines of squares of the same color, touching at their corners only and running in a straight line from one edge of the board to another, are called *diagonals*; those running from one corner of the board to another are called *long diagonals*.

3. The Pieces

3A. Each player's pieces.
At the beginning of the game, one player (White) has sixteen light-colored pieces (the white pieces); the other (Black) has sixteen dark-colored pieces (the black pieces).

3B. Description of the pieces.
These pieces are as follows:

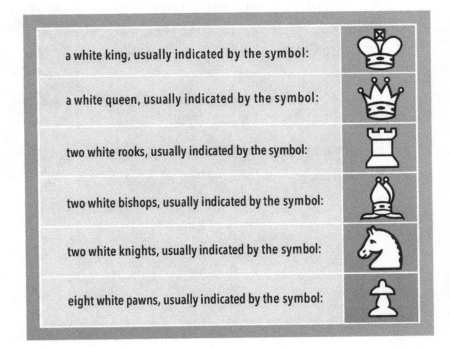

a white king, usually indicated by the symbol:

a white queen, usually indicated by the symbol:

two white rooks, usually indicated by the symbol:

two white bishops, usually indicated by the symbol:

two white knights, usually indicated by the symbol:

eight white pawns, usually indicated by the symbol:

Figure 1

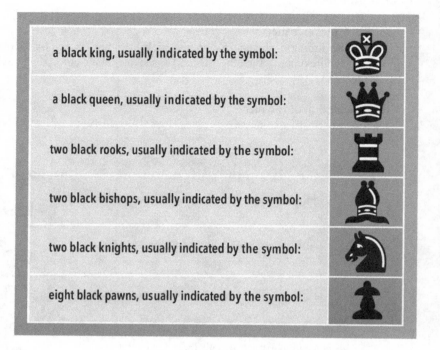

a black king, usually indicated by the symbol:	
a black queen, usually indicated by the symbol:	
two black rooks, usually indicated by the symbol:	
two black bishops, usually indicated by the symbol:	
two black knights, usually indicated by the symbol:	
eight black pawns, usually indicated by the symbol:	

Figure 2

3C. Initial position.

The initial position of the pieces on the chessboard is as follows:

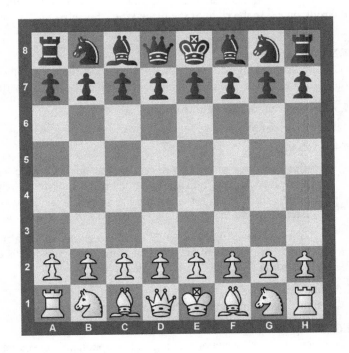

Figure 3

3D. Meaning of piece.

The word *piece* has acquired various meanings in chess jargon. When used in a rules context, a *piece* is anything on the chessboard - a king, queen, rook, bishop, knight, or pawn. This book will not subsequently use the alternate connotations of *piece*, which follow for informational purposes only.

A second meaning of *piece* excludes pawns. For instance, a chess player referring to *passive pieces* or *an attack by pieces* or *forking my pieces* is referring to pieces other than pawns.

A third and even more limited meaning: If a player is said to win, lose, or sacrifice a piece, the meaning is only bishop or knight. If a queen, rook, or pawn is won, lost, or sacrificed, it is referred to by name – *winning the queen, winning a pawn*, etc. A bishop or knight is also known as a *minor piece*, a queen or rook as a *major piece*.

3E. Other expressions involving pieces.
These are presented for informational purposes only.

3E1. Castling long.
Castling on the queenside (using the rook on a1, to the left of the white king, or the rook on a8, to the right of the black king). **See also** 8A2, Castling.

3E2. Castling short.
Castling on the kingside (using the rook on h1, to the right of the white king or the rook on h8, to the left of the black king). **See also** 8A2, Castling.

3E3. Discovered check, double check.
See Rule 12, Check.

3E4. Exchange.

    a.   *The Exchange* or *an Exchange* refers to the difference between one player's rook and the other's bishop or knight. A player giving up a rook for a bishop or knight is said to *lose the Exchange* and that player's opponent to *win the Exchange*.

    b.   *The exchange of queens* indicates the capture of each player's queen by the other player. The same language may be used regarding rooks, bishops, knights, or pawns.

3E5. Fork.
When there is a simultaneous attack on two or more pieces by one piece.

3E6. Interpose.
To place a piece between one's king and an opponent's checking piece. **See also** 12A, Definition.

3E7. Material.
Pieces other than the king.

3E8. Pin.
A piece is said to be *pinned* if either it cannot legally move because such a move would expose its king to check, or moving it would be unwise because this would allow the opponent to advantageously capture a shielded piece.

3E9. Sacrifice.
To deliberately allow the capture of a piece or pieces, receiving in immediate return no pieces, or a piece or pieces usually considered to have less value. The ultimate objective of a sacrifice is often to expose the opponent's king to attack, or to recover the sacrificed material and more.

3E10. *Zugzwang*.

A situation in which moving any piece is disadvantageous. The player in *zugzwang* would be better off declining to move (passing), but this is not permitted.

4. Objective and Scoring

4A. Checkmate.

The objective of each of the two players in a game of chess is to win the game by checkmating the opponent's king. A player's king is checkmated when the square it occupies is attacked by one or more of the opponent's pieces and the player has no move that escapes such attack. **See also** Rule 12, Check; 12C, Responding to check; and 13A, Checkmate.

4B. Other decisive outcomes.

A common way for a player to win the game is the resignation of the opponent, conceding inevitable checkmate. A player may also win in other ways, such as the opponent's exceeding of the time limit. **See also** 13, The Decisive Game.

4C. Draws.

An indecisive result or draw may be agreed upon, usually indicating that neither player expects to be able to checkmate the other. **See also** 14, The Drawn Game.

4D. Scoring.

For a won game, the winner gets one (1) point and the loser zero (0); for a draw, each player gets a half point (0.5 or ½). **See also** 22, Unplayed Games.

5. The Chess Clock

5A. Time controls and time limits.

Each player must make a certain number of moves, all moves, or all remaining moves in an allotted period of time, these factors being specified in advance. In a non-sudden death time control, if both players complete the required moves in the allotted time, a new period begins. Each such time period is called a *time control* or *control*.

Time controls appear in tournament publicity as number of moves (#), slash (/), time in minutes (mm): # / mm. For instance, if each player must make 40 moves in 1½ hours, this is abbreviated 40/90.

5B. Sudden death time controls.

For example, 40/120 SD/60 indicates 40 moves in two hours (120 minutes) followed by the rest of the game in one hour (60 minutes).

5B1. Delay and increment.

5B1a. Delay time controls. If the time control indicates a delay (pause) time, the abbreviation d/ is used; the delay time is given in seconds.

5B1b. Increment time controls. If the time control indicates an incremental (added) time, the abbreviation inc/ (or +) is used, the added time is given in seconds of added time.

5B1c. If no delay or increment is to be used then d/0 indicates no delay or increment time.

5B2. Advanced publicity required time control information.

In all advance publicity which specifies the time control, the organizer is to indicate the full time control, including the delay or increment, as minutes (mm) and seconds (ss), e.g. G/90 inc/30 (or +30); G/30 d/5; G/10 d/3; G/5 d/0. The time control must be specified in Tournament Life Announcements and should be specified in other publicity such as flyer mailings, email and on web sites. It is acceptable for abbreviated publicity to refer the reader to more complete tournament details posted elsewhere.

5C. Ratable time controls.

There are four rating systems: Regular (slow), Quick (fast), Blitz, and Online. For the purposes of rating G/minutes and inc/seconds (or d/seconds), add minutes (mm) and seconds (ss) for total playing time for each player. That is, total time equals minutes plus (seconds times 60) or mm+ss; e.g.: G/60 d/5 = 60+5 = 65 minutes total playing time for each player. Multiple time controls add all mm for each control: mm = mm(1) + mm(2) + ...

Regular only: Total playing time for each player is greater than 65 minutes (mm+ss > 65).

Dual (both regular and quick): Total playing time for each player is from 30 to 65 minutes (30 $\leq$ mm+ss $\leq$65).

Quick only: Total playing time for each player is more than 10 and less than 30 minutes (10 < mm+ss < 30).

For Regular, Dual and Quick the primary time (mm in minutes) must be at least 5 minutes.

Blitz: Total playing time for each player is from 5 to 10 minutes inclusive and the primary time control must be at least 3 minutes. $5 \leq mm+ss \leq 10$ All rounds must use the same time control. (See standard time controls table below)

Online: See Rule 2. The US Chess Online Rating System (Chapter 10).

TD TIP: Examples of standard time controls:

40/90 SD/30 inc/30	Regular
40/120 SD/60 d/5	Regular
40/115 SD/60 d/5	Regular
G/120 inc/30	Regular
G/120 d/5	Regular
G/115 d/5	Regular
G/90 inc/30	Regular
G/90 d/5	Regular
G/60 inc/30	Regular
G/60 d/5	Dual
30/30 SD/30 d/5	Dual
G/30 d/5	Dual
G/25 d/5	Dual
G/25 d/3	Quick
G/15 d/3	Quick
G/10 d/3	Quick
G/10 d/0	Blitz
G/5 d/0	Blitz
G/3 inc/2	Blitz

Figure 4

When used, standard increment is 30 seconds (Regular).
Standard delay is 5 seconds (regular or dual); and 3 seconds (quick).
Standard blitz uses no delay or increment (see chapter 11).

Although these are not all of the possible time controls, organizers are encouraged to select one of the above (or very similar) so that all participants are clear as what to expect and under which system the event will be rated.

TD TIP: Here is how the changes referred to in 5C will be implemented and administered:

Quick Chess: *A Quick Chess event is for a person who wishes to play many games in one day and not have the results affect his regular rating. The time controls in a Quick Chess tournament are designed to be a single time control of more than 10 to less than 30 total playing minutes per player, one second delay or increment counting as 1 minute playing time. 10 < mm + ss < 30. Sudden-death rules are used in Quick Chess events, except scorekeeping is not required.*

Dual Rating: *All events with total playing time for each player of 30 to 65 minutes inclusive (30 $\leq$ mm+ss $\leq$ 65) will be dual rated, that is, rated under both the Quick and Regular rating systems.*

Blitz: *Any event that the total playing time 5 minutes or greater and is 10 minutes or less (5 $\leq$ mm+ss $\leq$ 10) will be* **Blitz rated.** *(Blitz rules apply, see Chapter 11.) For clarity, it is advisable to state Blitz in the title or in the time control of the event.*

Note 1: *Game/60 d/5 is Dual Rated. If you wish for the games not to be Quick Rated, make the total basic time control at least Game in 61 minutes or longer and use a 5 second delay (61 + 5 = 66). Game/25 d/5 is also Dual Rated (25 + 5 = 30). If you do not want these games to be Regular Rated, make the time control Game/26 d/3 (26 + 3 = 29) or quicker.*

Note 2: *The TD must indicate what the time control is for all sections of all events, including the delay or increment used. If submitting by disk or paper, the time control is to be indicated. If different sections have different time controls, indicate the time control for each section. If submitting the report online, the TD is to enter the time control for all sections. The time control used indicates whether the event is regular, dual, quick or blitz.*

Note 3: *If a section has different schedules that merge, the slowest control is all that is needed, provided all games meet the criteria for the slowest time control. This applies when early rounds might fall in the dual rated group (which is regular rated, and the slower time control is regular only). All rounds will then be regular rated only.*

Example: *3-day schedule is 40/120 SD/60. The 2 day schedule plays rounds 1 and 2 at game/45 and then merges with the 3-day schedule for round 3. All that needs to be reported is the 40/120 SD/60 (120 + 60) as US Chess cannot separate the schedules at this point.*

If any games in a section use a time control that is quick-ratable only (i.e. total time greater than 10 minutes but less than 30 minutes), then all games in that section must use time controls that are quick-ratable only. If any games in a section use a time control that is blitz ratable (i.e. total time between 5 and 10 minutes), then all games in that section must use time controls that are blitz ratable.

5C1. Both players must have the same time control.

For a game to be ratable, the same time control must apply to both players. "Time odds" games (games in which the time control assigns the two players different base times) are not ratable.

TD TIP: *The director may apply penalties against a player's time before the game begins, causing the players to start the game with different times on the clock. This does not affect the ratability of the game.*

5D. Accumulation of time.

The time unused by a player during one control accumulates and is added to the player's available time for the next control.

5E. Recommended increment or delay.

For a mixed or repeating time control, or for a base time of 30 minutes or more, an increment or delay in the range of 5 to 30 seconds is recommended. For a base time of more than 10 minutes and less than 30 minutes, an increment or delay of 3 seconds is recommended. For a base time of 10 minutes or less, an increment or delay of 2 seconds is recommended.

5E1. Increment or delay with mixed time controls.

If a mixed time control includes increment or delay, the increment or delay should apply starting with the first move of the game, and the increment or delay time should be the same for all time control segments in the game.

5E2. Organizer fails to specify increment or delay.

If the organizer fails to specify an increment or delay time in the time control (which may be zero to indicate no increment or delay), the minimum recommended delay specified in rule **5E** shall apply.

5F. Standard timer.

5F1. Standard timer for increment time controls.

An increment capable clock is the standard timer for use with an increment time control.

5F1a. Increment capable clock not available.

If an increment capable clock is not available, one of the following clocks, listed in order of preference from most to least preferred, may be used:

1. A delay capable clock whose delay can be set for the increment time.
2. A delay capable clock whose delay cannot be set for the increment time.
3. A digital clock that is not delay capable.
4. An analog clock.

5F1b. Setting a non-increment capable clock for use with an increment time control.

In all cases, each player starts with the clock set for the base time. If the clock is delay capable and the delay can be set the same as the increment time, the clock should be so configured. Otherwise, if the clock is delay capable, set the delay time to the maximum possible value that does not exceed the increment time. If the clock is not delay capable, the clock is set to the base time.

5F1b1. Variation.

The organizer may specify a different time control to be used with clocks that are capable of neither increment nor delay. This must be specified in all pre-tournament publicity that specifies the time control.

5F2. Standard timer for delay time controls.

A delay capable clock is the standard timer for use with a delay time control.

5F2a. Delay capable clock not available.

If a delay capable (or Bronstein capable) clock is not available, a digital clock that is not delay capable may be used. If a digital clock is not available, an analog clock may be used. In all cases, the clock is set so that each player starts with the base time.

5F2a1. Variation.

The organizer may specify a different time control to be used with clocks that are not delay capable. This must be specified in all pre-tournament publicity that specifies the time control.

5F3. Standard timer for time controls with neither delay nor increment.

The standard timer for a time control with neither delay nor increment is a digital clock. If a digital clock is not available, an analog clock may be used.

5F4. Digital clock preferred over analog clock.

In all cases, a digital clock is preferred over an analog clock.

TD TIP: A digital clock operates silently. It can be set so that both players have exactly the same amount of time. Digital clocks time the game more precisely and are not subject to having the two sides of the clock run at different rates.

5F5. Replacement of non-standard timer in increment and delay time controls.

If either player arrives late for the start of the game, and a clock without delay or increment has already been started the player has the right to furnish and substitute a properly set delay or increment capable clock prior to the determination of Black's first move. The player substituting the delay or increment capable clock must also transfer the elapsed times shown on the original clock to the replacement clock without any additional adjustments (except to correct any errors in the display of the elapsed time).

5F6. Same clock used for the entire game.
Except as provided in rules 5F5 and Variation 14H2a, once a game starts, the same clock must be used throughout the entire game. If a defective clock must be replaced as described in rule 16O, the replacement clock shall be set in the same manner as the clock being replaced. **See also** 5F5, Replacement of non-standard timer in increment and delay time controls; Variation 14H2a, The claim is unclear and a delay clock is available for the game; and 16O, Defective clocks.

5F7. Players responsible for knowing how to set the clock.
Players, not tournament directors, are responsible for knowing how to properly set their digital clocks. In any particular game, if the player providing the clock can not properly set the clock, the opponent may choose which legal clock is to be used. **See also** 16B, How to set clocks.

5G. The flag.
Monitoring of each player's time is effected by means of a clock equipped with a flag or other special device used to signal the end of a time control; the flag falls to indicate the player's time has been used up. Some digital clocks have a beep, a light, or a display of all zeros to indicate that the player's time has been exhausted. References in this book to a flag falling or being down also apply to such *flag substitutes*. **See also** 16E, When flag is considered down; 16F, Evidence provided by flag; 16G, premature flag fall; 16H, Apparent flag fall can cause forfeit; 35F5, Special clock; and 42B, Signaling devices.

5H. Pressing the clock.
After moving, a player presses the button on his or her side of the clock, which stops that side from running and starts the opponent's side. This book refers to such action as *pressing the clock*. **See also** 6A, The first move; 16C, Removing a player's hand from the clock; 16C1, Using the clock; 16I, Starting the clock; and 16N, Beginning the round.

5I. Stopping the clock.
A player who wishes to make a claim of any sort or see a director for any legitimate reason may stop both sides of the clock before claiming and/or finding a director. This book refers to such action as stopping the clock or stopping both clocks. If the opponent's clock is accidentally started when a player tries to stop both clocks, the director will determine whether the claim is still in order. **See also** 13C6, Claimant's clock; 16Q, Interruption of game; 21F, Player requests for rulings; and 21F1, Timing of requests.

TD TIP: Players should be made aware of the fact that they should generally stop the clock on their time, not their opponent's.

5J. Further details.
See 16, Use of the Chess Clock.

6. The Right to Move

6A. The first move.
White makes the first move. The players then alternate moves until the game is over. **See also** 5H, Pressing the clock; 13D, Late arrival for game; 16, Use of the Chess Clock. ; 16I, Starting the clock; 16J, Black not present; 16M, Equipment needed to start clock; and 16N, Beginning the round.

6B. A player on move.
A player is said to *be on move* or to *have the move* when the opponent's move has been completed. **See also** 9, Determination and Completion of the move.

7. Definition of the Move

7A. Basic definition.
With the exception of castling (8A2) and promotion of a pawn (8F6), a move is the transfer of a piece from one square to another square that is either vacant or occupied by an opponent's piece. **See also** 9, Determination and Completion of the move.

7B. Crossing an occupied square.
With the exception of the king and rook in castling, no piece except the knight may cross a square occupied by another piece. When castling the king and rook may also not cross an occupied square.

7C. Capturing.
A piece played to a square occupied by an opponent's piece captures the latter as part of the move. The player making the capture removes the captured piece immediately from the chessboard. **See also** 8F5, Capturing *en passant* and 9B, Capturing.

8. The Moves of the Pieces

8A. The king.

8A1. The king's move.

Except when castling, the king moves to any adjoining square that is not attacked by one or more of the opponent's pieces.

8A2. Castling.

Castling is a move of the king and either rook, counting as a single move and executed as follows: the king is transferred from its original square two squares toward either rook on the same rank; then, that rook is transferred over the king to the square adjacent to the king on the same rank. **See also** 8C1, Castling; 9C, Castling; 10I1, King touched first, or king and rook simultaneously; and 10I2, Rook touched first.

8A3. Castling permanently illegal.

Castling is illegal for the remainder of the game for a player:

a. If that player's king has already moved, or

b. With a rook of that player that has already moved.

8A4. Castling temporarily illegal.

Castling is not presently possible if:

a. An opponent's piece attacks the king's original square (12A, 12B), any square which the king must cross over (12E), or the square the king is to occupy, or

b. There is any piece between the king and the rook with which it "is to castle."

TD TIP: In other words: (1) the squares between the king and rook have to be empty; (2) the king cannot be in check, and (3) the king cannot move through or into check.

8B. The queen.

The queen moves to any square (except as limited by 7B) on the file, rank, or diagonal(s) on which it stands.

8C. The rook.

The rook moves to any square (except as limited by 7B) on the file or rank on which it stands.

8C1. Castling.

Several restrictions on the king in castling (8A2, 8A3, 8A4) do not apply to the rook:

a. A player may castle with a rook whose original square is under attack.

b. A player may castle with a rook that crosses over a square under attack by an opponent's piece. The only examples of this are the b1 or b8 squares when castling Queenside.

c.   There is no prohibition against the rook occupying a square attacked by an opponent's piece at the conclusion of castling, but this is impossible, as the king would have to illegally cross an attacked square to bring it about.

For related information on castling see 8A2, Castling; 9C, Castling.

8D. The bishop.
The bishop moves to any square (except as limited by 7B) on the diagonal(s) on which it stands.

8E. The knight.
The knight's move is composed of two different steps. First, it makes one step of one single square along the rank or file on which it stands. It does not land on that square, as its move is not complete (9A). Then, still moving away from the square of departure, it moves one step of one single square on a diagonal. It does not matter if the square of the first step is occupied.

This move is sometimes called an *L* move, as it is equivalent to moving the knight two squares vertically, then one square horizontally (or two squares horizontally, then one square vertically). Note that the knight always moves to a square different in color than that of its starting square. A knight has a maximum of eight possible moves.

8F. The pawn.

8F1. The pawn's move.
The pawn may only move forward (towards the opponent's side of the board).

8F2. The first move of each pawn.
On its first move, a pawn advances either one or two vacant squares along its file.

8F3. Subsequent moves of each pawn.
On its subsequent moves, a pawn advances one vacant square along its file.

8F4. Pawns move vertically but capture diagonally.
The pawn is unique among chess pieces in that it captures (7C) and attacks differently from the way it moves. When capturing, it advances one square along either of the diagonals on which it stands; it attacks these same squares.

8F5. Capturing *en passant*.
A pawn, attacking a square bypassed by an opponent's pawn, the latter having advanced two squares in one move from its original square, may capture (7C) the opponent's pawn as though the latter had moved only one square.

This capture may only be made in immediate reply to such advance and is called an *en passant* (*in passing*) capture. Note that only a pawn that has advanced a total of exactly three squares from its original square is in position to make such a capture.

8F6. Pawn promotion.

On reaching the last rank, a pawn must immediately be exchanged, as part of the same move, for the player's choice of a queen, a rook, a bishop, or a knight of the same color as the pawn. This exchange of the pawn for another piece is called *promotion*, and the effect of the new piece is immediate. For instance, it may give check or serve to block a check. The promotion piece is placed on the eighth-rank promotion square it touched to which the pawn was or will be moved. **See also** 9D, Pawn promotion and 10H, Piece touched off the board.

TD TIP: Note that promotion is in no way related to other pieces remaining on the chessboard; for example, a player may have two or more queens, three or more knights, or two bishops on diagonals of the same color. The choice of the piece is not final until it has touched the promotion square on the board (See 9D also 10H).

8F7. Promoted piece not available.

If the desired piece is not available to replace a promoted pawn, the player may stop both clocks in order to locate that piece and place it on the board. A player who cannot quickly find such a piece may request the assistance of the director. It is common practice, however, to play using an upside-down rook for a second queen. In the absence of the player's announcement to the contrary, an upside-down rook shall be considered a queen. It is improper to press the clock to start the opponent's time with the pawn still on the last rank. If this is done, the opponent may immediately restart the player's clock without moving.

As soon as the new piece is placed on the board, either player should restart the clock.

TD TIP: Clocks that have a move counter may need to be readjusted if a player improperly presses the clock with a pawn still on the last rank and the opponent immediately restarts the player's clock.

9. Determination and Completion of the Move

9A. Transfer to a vacant square.

In the case of the legal transfer of a piece to a vacant square, the move (7A, 7B, 7C) is determined with no possibility of change when the player's hand has released the piece, and completed when that player presses the clock (5H).

9B. Capturing.

In the case of a legal capture (7C), the move is determined with no possibility of change when the player has deliberately touched both his or her own piece and the opponent's piece (10C) and completed when that player presses the clock (5H). **See also** 9G, Determined moves and completed moves.

9C. Castling.

In the case of legal castling (8A2, 8C1, 10I1, 10I2), the move is determined with no possibility of change when the player's hand has released the king, which has moved two squares toward a rook, and completed when that player, having legally transferred the rook to its new square, presses the clock (5H).

9D. Pawn promotion.

In the case of the legal promotion of a pawn, the move is determined with no possibility of change when the pawn has been removed from the chessboard and the player's hand has released the new appropriate piece on the promotion square, and completed when that player presses the clock (5H). If the player has released the pawn on the last rank, the move is not yet determined, but the player no longer has the right to play the pawn to another square. The choice of piece is finalized when the piece has touched the square of promotion, regardless of whether the pawn has been physically touched or placed on the promotion square. Once a piece has touched the promotion square a pawn must be promoted to that piece on that square, provided that the move is legal. **See also** 8F6, Pawn promotion and 10H, Piece touched off the board.

TD TIP: Some players thinking they are being "clever" have tried to place one of their opponent's pieces on the promotion square or inappropriately give themselves a second king; however, this is not legal, only "clever."

9E. Checkmate or stalemate.

In the case of a legal move which produces checkmate (13A, 4A) or stalemate (14A), the move is determined with no possibility of change upon release as described in 9A, 9B, 9C, or 9D, whichever applies. The move is completed simultaneously with its determination.

*TD TIP: If the final legal move produces checkmate or stalemate, pressing or stopping the clock, while recommended, is not required because checkmate or stalemate immediately ends the game. **See also** rules 13A1, The clock after checkmate and 14A1, The clock after stalemate.*

9F. Last move of the time control.

When determining whether the prescribed number of legal moves has been made in the allotted time, the last move is considered complete only after the player presses the clock (5H). The player's flag may be up after releasing the piece, it may be up while hitting the clock, but if the flag is down after the move and the opponent has not yet handled the clock, the player has failed to make the time control. **For more information** regarding analog and digital flag falls see 5G, The flag.

Except for 9E, there should never be a dispute about whether the final move of a time control or a flag fall occurred first, because a player's task is to press the clock in time to prevent the flag fall. If the flag is down, the player has not accomplished this task, and the director must rule that the move was not completed in time. If the final move of the time control produces checkmate or stalemate, then see 9E.

9G. Determined moves and completed moves.

As described in 9A through 9D above, there is a period between the release of a piece and the press of the clock during which the move is determined but not completed. The significance of this period is as follows (for information on determined moves and the visually impaired or handicapped player see 35F4, Determination of a move):

9G1. Player still on move for claims.

Claims of triple occurrence of position (14C), the 50-move rule (14F), or insufficient losing chances in sudden death (Variation 14H) remain in order during the period between determination and completion of the move. As soon as the player completes the move, it is the opponent's move, and the right to make such claims belongs exclusively to the opponent.

9G2. Determination irrelevant to time control.

In the case of 9F, Last move of the time control, whether or not the player has determined the move is of no significance in deciding whether the player has made the prescribed number of moves in the allotted time. The player's flag must remain up (5G) after the final legal move has been completed, not just determined.

9G3. Draw offers.

Except for Variation 14H2a, Resolution of Variation 14H claim, the interval between determination and completion of the move is the proper time to offer a draw (14B1). **See also** 14, The Drawn Game.

TD TIP: The first step in resolving a properly made draw claim, including an insufficient losing chances (Variation 14H) claim in sudden death, is to notify the opponent of the claimant that a claim is the same as offering the opponent a draw; however, the draw offer is proper even if a move has not been determined or completed. See rule 14, The Drawn Game, for more information on draw claims being considered draw offers.

9H. Stopping the clock.

If a player determines a move and then stops the clock to see a director for any reason, rather than pressing it, the determined move is not yet completed and the player is still on move for claims (9G1).

10. The Touched Piece

TD TIP: Without a neutral witness, Rule 10 depends on the reliability of both the claimant and the opponent. If they disagree then the TD should strongly consider denying the claim. In most cases, by denying the claim the TD shuts the door to all false claims. Upholding a false claim usually does more harm to more players than denying an accurate claim.

10A. Adjustment of pieces.

A player who is on the move and first expresses the intention to adjust (e.g., by saying *j'adoube* or *I adjust*) may adjust one or more pieces on their squares. **See also** 10E, Accidental touch of piece and 10F, appearance of adjustment.

10B. Touch-move rule.

Except for 10A, a player on move who deliberately touches one or more pieces, in a manner that may reasonably be interpreted as the beginning of a move, must move or capture the first piece touched that can be moved or captured. **See also** 10E, Accidental touch of piece; 10F, appearance of adjustment; 35F3 (the touch-move rule for blind and disabled players); Rule 12B, Touch-Move (Chapter 10)

TD TIP: The key word here is deliberately. Be especially thorough at scholastic events when investigating a "Touch-move rule" claim without a witness. After talking to the claimant and opponent, TDs will find that opponents often insist that they did not "deliberately" touch a piece. Often, after some further discussion, the TD will find that some of the opponents really did physically touch the piece in such a way that it appeared as if they intended to move it (not an accident); however, they will explain that they really intended to move another piece; therefore, they believe that since the "touch" was not literally "deliberate" (since they intended to move another piece), the rule was not broken. The TD will have to uphold the claim in this instance.

10C. Touching pieces of both colors.

Except for 10A, a player on the move who deliberately touches one or more pieces of each color, or who moves the player's piece and intentionally displaces an opponent's piece with it, must capture the opponent's piece with the player's piece, or, if this is illegal, must move or capture the first piece touched that can be moved or captured. If it is impossible to establish which piece was touched first, the player's piece shall be considered the touched piece.

10D. Piece touched cannot move.

If no piece touched has a legal move, and no opponent's piece touched can be legally captured, the player is free to make any legal move.

10E. Accidental touch of piece.

A director who believes a player touched a piece by accident should not require the player to move that piece. For example, a player's hand reaching across the board may inadvertently brush the top of a nearby king or queen, or a player may hit a piece with an elbow. **See also** 10 A, Adjustment of pieces; 10B, Touch-move rule; and 10F, Appearance of adjustment.

10F. Appearance of adjustment.

Sometimes it is clear that a player is adjusting, even when that player improperly fails to say *j'adoube* or *I adjust*. For instance, a player who uses one finger to slide a piece to the center of its square is not acting in a manner usual to the beginning of a move, and probably should not be required to move the piece. Players are warned, though, that it is wise to announce one is adjusting in advance, as a safeguard against being forced to make an unwanted move. **See also** 10 A, Adjustment of pieces; 10B, Touch-move rule; and 10E, Accidental touch of a piece.

10G. Accidental release of piece.

A player who deliberately touches a piece and then accidentally releases it on an unintended but legal square is required to leave it on that square.

10H. Piece touched off the board.

There is no penalty for touching a piece that is off the board. A player who advances a pawn to the last rank and then touches a piece off the board is not obligated to promote the pawn to the piece touched until that piece touches the promotion square. **See also** 8F6, Pawn promotion and 9D, Pawn promotion.

10I. Castling.

For description and further information of castling, see 8A2, 8A3, 8A4, 8C1, and 9C.

10I1. King touched first, or king and rook simultaneously.

If a player intending to castle touches the king first, or king and rook at the same time, and then realizes that castling is illegal, the player may choose either to move the king or to castle on the other side if legal. If the king has no legal move, the player is free to choose any move.

10I2. Rook touched first.

If a player intending to castle touches the rook first, castling is not allowed and the player must move the rook as required by rule 10B.

10I2. (Variation I) Rook touched first.

If a player intending to castle touches the rook first, there is no penalty except if castling is illegal, the player must move the rook if legal. This variation does not need to be announced in advanced publicity but should be announced at the start of the tournament.

10J. When to claim touch-move.

To claim the opponent has violated 10B, Touch move rule, or 10C, Touching pieces of both colors, a player must do so before deliberately touching a piece.

11. Illegal Positions

11A. Illegal move during last ten moves.

If, during a game, it is found that one of either player's last ten moves was illegal and neither player is in time pressure (11D1), the position shall be reinstated to what it was before the illegal move. The players do not recover the time used after the illegal move. The game shall then continue by applying Rule 10, The Touched Piece, to the move replacing the illegal move. If the position cannot be reinstated, then the illegal move shall stand. Move counters on clocks that have them may be readjusted. **See also** 11H, Director corrects illegal move in non-sudden death and 16R, No time adjustment for reinstated position.

TD TIP: When the illegal move is a king left in check, special care should be taken by the director. All moves, not just the first move, in which a player's king remains in check should be regarded as illegal. That way, an illegal move will always have occurred within the last half-move; therefore, players cannot argue that the illegal move(s) should stand. Now, go back to the first illegal move that occurred (leaving the king in check). If the moves cannot be reconstructed, go back to a position in which the king is in check, so that the king can get out of check. In complicated cases like this the director has a lot of discretion. No player should gain an unfair advantage for deliberate illegal moves, or for inadvertent ones, which were deliberately not pointed out. Remember that the clock times will not be re-adjusted; however, move counters may need to be reset to the proper move number.

11B. Illegal move prior to last ten moves.

If it is found that an illegal move was made prior to each player's last ten moves, the illegal move shall stand and the game shall continue.

TD TIP: When the illegal move is a king left in check see the TD TIP after rule 11A.

11C. Accidental piece displacement.

If, during a game, one or more pieces have been accidentally displaced and incorrectly replaced, then the displacement shall be treated as an illegal move. If, during the course of a move, a player inadvertently knocks over one or more pieces, that player must not press the clock until the position has been reestablished. The opponent may press the clock without moving, if necessary, to force the player who knocked over the piece(s) to restore the position on his or her own time. If possible, clocks with move counters should be readjusted.

TD TIP: If using increment time control it may not be to a player's advantage to start the opponent's clock if the opponent created an illegal position or accidentally displaced pieces. In that case the players may stop or pause the clock until the correct position is reinstated.

11D. Illegal move.

If a player completes an illegal move by pressing the clock, in addition to the usual obligation to make a legal move with the touched piece if possible, the standard penalty specified in rule 1C2a applies. If the opponent has completed a move subsequent to the illegal move, the standard penalty does not apply. **See also** 11J, Deliberate illegal moves.

TD TIP: A player should make sure to claim an illegal move made by his opponent before completing his next move, in order to be eligible to receive the additional time.

11D1. Illegal move in time pressure.

Time pressure is defined as a situation where either player has less than five minutes left in a time control and the time control does not include an increment or delay of 30 seconds or more. A director should not call attention to illegal moves in *time pressure*, only the players may make that claim. If, during the game, in time pressure, a player's claim that one of either player's last two moves was illegal is upheld by the TD, the position shall be reinstated to what it was before the illegal move and the procedure in rule 11A shall be followed. **See also** 11H, Director corrects illegal move in non-sudden death; and 11J, Deliberate illegal moves.

TD TIP: When the illegal move is a king left in check see the TD TIP after rule 11A.

11E. Incorrect adjourned position.

If, after an adjournment, the position is incorrectly set up, then the position as it was at adjournment must be set up again and the game continued, subject to the provisions of Rule 11A, Illegal move during last ten moves. The time on the clocks shall not be adjusted; however, move counters on clocks that have them may be readjusted. **See also** 16R, No time adjustment for reinstated position and 19I, Game resumed with incorrect position.

11F. Incorrect initial position.

If, before the completion of Black's 10th move, it is found that the initial position of the pieces was incorrect, or that the game began with the colors reversed, then the game shall be annulled and a new game played. However, the players shall begin the new game with their clocks still reflecting the elapsed time each player used in the annulled game; however, move counters on clocks that have them may be readjusted. If the error is discovered after the completion of Black's 10th move, the game shall continue. **See also** 16R, No time adjustment for reinstated position.

11G. Incorrect placement of chessboard.

If, during a game, it is found that the board has been placed contrary to 2C, Placement, which requires a white square in the nearer corner to the right of each player, then the position reached shall be transferred to a board correctly placed and the game continued.

11H. Director corrects illegal move outside of time pressure.

Except in a time pressure situation (**11D1**), a director who witnesses an illegal move being made shall require the player to replace that move with a legal one in accordance with **10B**, Touch-move rule. The time on the clocks shall not be adjusted; however, move counters on clocks that have them may be readjusted. See also **11J, Deliberate illegal moves** and **21D, Intervening in games.**

Variation 11H1. Director as witness only.

In an event in which most games are not watched by directors, a director may refrain from correcting all illegal moves he or she may notice but simply serve as a witness should one of the players point out the illegal move before ten more moves have been made (11A).

If used, this variation must be applied consistently; i.e., a director may not require players to correct illegal moves when witnessed in some cases but not in others. This variation does not need to be announced in advance.

11I. Spectators.

Spectators must not point out illegal moves (20M5), except to the director in a manner neither heard nor noticed by the players. **See also** 16Y, Assisting players with time management prohibited and 20M, Behavior of spectators.

11J. Deliberate illegal moves.

If a player intentionally makes illegal moves, the director may impose penalties. **See also** 1C2, Director discretion; 11D, Illegal move; 21F, Player requests for rulings; and 21K, Use of director's power.

12. Check

12A. Definition.

The king is *in check* when the square it occupies is attacked by one or more of the opponent's pieces; such pieces are said to be *checking the king*. Check is parried (a player gets out of check) by capturing a sole checking opposing piece, interposing one of the player's own pieces between a sole checking piece and the king (not possible if checking piece is a knight), or moving the king. The king cannot parry check by castling (8A4).

12B. Double check.

The square occupied by the king being attacked by two opposing pieces is known as *double check*, and may be parried only by moving the king. The king cannot parry double check by castling (8A4).

12C. Responding to check.

Check must be parried on the move immediately following. If a player's king is unable to escape check, it is *checkmated* and the player loses the game (13A).

12D. Check by interposing piece.

A piece blocking a check to the king of its own color, commonly referred to as *interposing*, can itself give check to the enemy king.

12E. Moving into check.

A player may not move the king, including castling (8A4), to a square attacked by one or more opponent's pieces. No move may be made by any piece which puts the player's own king in check. If a player does so, it is an illegal move. **See also** 11, Illegal Positions.

12F. Calling check not mandatory.

Announcing check is not required, and is rare in high-level tournaments. It is the responsibility of the opponent to notice the check, and a player who does not may suffer serious consequences. A player may announce check. **See also** Rule 10, The touched piece.

13. The Decisive Game

13A. Checkmate.

The player who checkmates the opponent's king, providing the mating move is legal, wins the game. This immediately ends the game. **See also** 4A, Checkmate; 9E, Checkmate or stalemate; 12C, Responding to check; and 15H, Reporting of results.

TD TIP: *This means that anything that happens* after *the checkmate move has been legally determined (see rule 9, Determination and completion of the move) is irrelevant to the outcome of the game, including the player's flag falling (5G).*

13A1. The clock after checkmate.

A player who checkmates the opponent is not obligated to then press (5H) or stop (5I) the clock, as checkmate takes priority over a subsequent flag fall. A player delivering checkmate may choose to press the clock to minimize the possibility of dispute. **See also** 9E, Checkmate or stalemate.

13A2. Flag fall before checkmate.

If a player claims a win by time forfeit (13C) before the opponent determines a move delivering checkmate, the time forfeit claim is appropriate.

13A3. Unclear if checkmate or flag fall came first.

After considering all available evidence, including testimony by the players and any witnesses, a director who is still unable to decide whether the claim of the flag fall occurred first shall deny the time claim and rule the checkmate valid.

13B. Resignation.

The player whose opponent resigns wins the game. This immediately ends the game. Saying *I resign* or tipping over the king are relatively clear ways to resign.

Stopping both clocks does not necessarily indicate a resignation. Since a player may be making a claim or seeing a director, the opponent should not assume a player who stops both clocks has resigned without further evidence.

Likewise, the offer of a handshake is not necessarily a resignation. On occasion, one player believes the handshake agrees to a draw while the other interprets it as a resignation. **See also** 15H, Reporting of Results; 16S, Priority of agreed result over time-forfeit claim and 19G2, Resignation and invalid move.

13C. Time forfeit.

a. Non-Sudden Death: The player who properly claims that the opponent has not completed the prescribed number of moves in the allotted time wins the game, provided that the claimant has mating material (14E) and a reasonably complete scoresheet (13C7) when the flag falls (5G). Move counters, on clocks equipped with them, may not be used as the only evidence in claiming that the prescribed number of moves were not completed in the allotted time.

b. Sudden Death: The player who properly claims that the opponent has not completed the game in the allotted time, and has mating material (14E), wins the game. A scoresheet is not required to win on time in a sudden death time control (15C).

See also 15H, Reporting of results and 19G3, Loss on time and invalid move.

13C1. Only players may call flag.

Only the players in a game may call attention to the fall of a flag (**See also** 5G); it is considered to have fallen only when either player points this out. A director must never initiate a time-forfeit claim.

Spectators, including players of other games, who point out the fall of a flag in any manner, may be disciplined by the tournament director to the point of expulsion from the playing room, loss of their own games, or expulsion from the tournament. The recipient of such assistance may also be penalized (20E). **See also** 16Y, Assisting players with time management prohibited; 20E1, Solicited advice; 20E2, Unsolicited advice; 20M, Spectators; and 20M5, Spectators cannot make claims.

TD TIP: The key word here is "may." Directors must exercise extreme caution in penalizing unsolicited advice. Reviewing Rule 20E, Soliciting or using advice prohibited, before making a ruling is advised. Remember in FIDE competitions the arbiter can call the flag and should do so.

13C2. Player may call own flag for protection in non-sudden death.

A player may call attention to the fall of his or her own flag. This initiates the time forfeiture procedure, the same as if the opponent had made a claim. A player will likely exercise this option in order to make it clear that any moves the opponent may subsequently fill in or correct on the scoresheet are invalid for the purpose of having an adequate score. **See also** 13C3, filling in moves with flag down.

TD TIP: This rule was designed to protect the player who is short of time, in a non-sudden death time control, from an opponent, who has plenty of time to write down moves as they are being made, who instead "blitzes" or rushes, move after move without filling in a scoresheet contrary to 15A, Manner of keeping score.

13C3. Filling in moves with flag down.

Once either player points out the fallen flag, neither is permitted to fill in or correct any previous moves missing from the scoresheet. It is especially important that a player who expects to win on time not fill in missing moves. Such additions or corrections are not considered for the purpose of determining whether the scoresheet is reasonably complete (13C7), and may obscure a valid claim.

TD TIP: Enforcement of this rule often depends on an independent witness.

13C4. Consequence of filling in moves.

A player who improperly fills in missing moves after a fallen flag has been pointed out may not win by time forfeit unless the director is certain that the player's scoresheet would have been sufficient to win on time without the improper additions. A director who is unsure on this point should give the benefit of the doubt to the opponent of the claimant.

TD TIP: Enforcement of this rule often depends on an independent witness.

13C5. How to claim.

To claim a win by time forfeit, a player should stop both clocks (5I) and state the claim. If the opponent accepts the claim, the game is over. If the opponent does not accept the claim, the claimant must present the claim to a director.

13C6. Claimant's clock.

If a player who claims a time forfeit states the claim with claimant's flag still up (5G), but then fails to stop the clock in time to avoid also exceeding the time limit, the claim will be void, unless the flag fall was observed by a director or independent witness. **See also** 5I, Stopping the clock; 13C13, Player out of time cannot claim; 16Q, Interruption of game; 21F, Player requests for rulings; 21F1, Timing of requests, and 16T, Both players exceed time control.

TD TIP: A director who is aware that a claimant has neglected to stop the clock should instruct the claimant to do so.

13C7. Definition of reasonably complete scoresheet.

Unless otherwise posted or announced in advance at the site, a reasonably complete scoresheet is one that has no more than three missing or incomplete move pairs (consecutive moves, white and black or black and white). The absence of three consecutive individual moves, e.g. white-black-white, counts as two incomplete move pairs.

The move pair is considered incomplete if either side's move is omitted or incomplete. No move pair is ever considered to be *half complete*.

Minor ambiguities in scorekeeping or errors involving no more than one symbol are of no consequence. The common error of omitting one move by one player and subsequently putting moves in the wrong columns counts as only one error. Moves that are indecipherable or recorded only with check marks are considered missing. **See also** 15, The recording of the games.

TD TIP: An example of a minor ambiguity would be for the player of the black pieces to write Nf3 on a scoresheet in place of Nf6 in the opening when Nf3 is clearly not even possible.

13C8. Use of opponent's scoresheet in non-sudden death.

The director may use the scoresheet of the claimant's opponent to determine that the requisite number of moves has been made or that the claimant's scoresheet is in error. The director may also use the opponent's scoresheet to assist in playing over the game. No player, however, may be forfeited based solely on the evidence of his or her own scoresheet.

13C9. Player may demonstrate making time control in non-sudden death.

If the opponent of the claimant demonstrates that the required number of moves must have been made in order to reach the position on the board, the director shall deny the claim.

TD TIP: If the opponent points out the correct number of moves have been made to reach the position on the board due to move repetitions but does not have an accurate score or an independent witness to verify this fact, the director should rule in favor of the claimant.

13C10. Director not obligated to play over game in non-sudden death.

If the claimant's scoresheet appears to be sufficiently complete and both scoresheets appear to be substantially identical and agree on the number of moves made, the director need not play over those moves but may instead require the player whose flag has fallen (5G) to demonstrate why the opponent's scoresheet is not sufficient to win on time.

13C11. Time forfeit claim denied in non-sudden death.

If a flag is down but a claimant's scoresheet is insufficient to win on time, two minutes shall be added to the claimant's opponent's remaining time and the game shall continue. No further time forfeit claims during that time control are allowed; a claim of time forfeit shall be allowed during subsequent time controls.

TD TIP: Example: In a 40/120 20/60 game, if a time forfeit claim for the first time control is denied on move 35, then another time forfeit claim is not available for either player (13C13) until the end of the second time control (at flag fall after three hours by one player).

13C12. Both scoresheets inadequate in non-sudden death.

If both players agree that sufficient moves have been made or that both scoresheets are inadequate for time forfeit claims, and it is impossible to establish the exact number of moves, no further claims on that time control are permitted. The subsequent time control period is in effect. The players should diagram or create a record of the position to serve as a reference point for future claims.

13C13. Player out of time cannot claim.

A player whose own flag has fallen (5G) may not win on time during that control. **See also** 16T, Both players exceed time control.

13C14. Role of director during time trouble.

It is beneficial for a director to be present in an area with games in which the players are in time trouble, to observe the players and safeguard against disturbance such as spectators or players talking or crowding too close to a game. However, it is not recommended that directors concentrate on watching clocks except to tell when they may go back to other duties. This would accomplish little, as only players may call flags down, and a fallen flag (5G) constitutes evidence equal in value to the witnessing of a falling flag. **See also** 13C6, Claimant's clock.

13C15. Variations.

Any variations on these procedures, such as use of FIDE methods that require a director or deputy to be present at each board and to claim time forfeits on behalf of the players, must be clearly announced before the start of the tournament.

13D. Late arrival for game.

The player who arrives at the chessboard more than one hour late for the beginning of the game or arrives after the expiration of the first or only time control period, whichever comes first, loses the game. The absence countdown begins at the actual starting time of the round, which is not always the scheduled starting time. A director who learns that a player is unavoidably delayed may waive the one-hour forfeit rule. **See also** 13F, Late arrival by both players; 15H, Reporting of results; 16K, Both players late; 16M, Equipment needed to start clock; 22A, Games forfeited due to nonappearance; and 28P, Unplayed games.

TD TIP: Example in a single sudden death time control: if the time control is G/30 then a player who arrives 31 minutes after the start of that game will lose. A player who arrives at any time before the flag falls may play the game with whatever amount of time is left on the player's clock.

Variation 13D1. Equipment must be set up.

To win under 13D, a player must set up a board, a set, and a clock, start the opponent's clock, and run the clock until the opponent has one hour of elapsed time or the first or only time control period has expired, whichever comes first. If both players are late, the first to arrive must split the elapsed time from the start of the game until the arrival time before starting the opponent's clock (see 16K, Both players late).

TD TIP: For example, if the first player is 30 minutes late in a non-sudden death time control period of 40/120, each player would start with 15 minutes elapsed, and the second player would not lose on time, due to non-appearance, until 45 minutes later. Another example: in a G/30 single sudden death time control, or one that is less than one hour, the first player arrives 10 minutes late. Each player would start with 5 minutes elapsed. The second player would not lose on time, due to non-appearance, until 25 minutes later.

13E. Late arrival for adjournment resumption.

The player who arrives at the chessboard more than one hour late for the resumption of an adjourned game or arrives after the expiration of the existing time period, whichever comes first, loses the game. A director who learns that a player is unavoidably delayed may waive the one-hour forfeit rule. However, if the player who sealed the move is the late player, the game is decided otherwise if either of the following conditions exists:

13E1. Checkmate.

The absent player has won the game by virtue of the fact that the sealed move produces checkmate.

13E2. Stalemate or insufficient material.

The absent player has produced a drawn game by virtue of the fact that the sealed move has caused a stalemate (14A), or if one of the positions in 14D, Insufficient material to continue, has arisen.

13F. Late arrival by both players.

If both players arrive at the chessboard more than one hour late in a non-sudden death time control period or after the flags have fallen in a single sudden-death time control, whichever comes first, the director may declare the game lost by both players. **See also** 13D, Late arrival for game; 15H, Reporting of results; 16K, Both players late; 22A, Games forfeited due to nonappearance; and 28P, Unplayed games.

13G. Players must give notice if withdrawing or skipping a round.

A player who does not notify the tournament director well in advance of the inability to play in any round and then defaults the game under 13D, Late arrival for the game, may be ejected from the tournament, and may be fined a sum up to the amount of the entry fee, payable to the organizer. The player may be barred from any of the organizer's tournaments until the fine is paid. On request, the player may be retained in or readmitted to the tournament at the director's discretion. **See also** 16K, Both players late; 22A, Games forfeited due to nonappearance; and 28P, Unplayed games.

TD TIP: It is useful to have a withdrawal signup sheet available until the pairings are made for the last round. Directors are urged to check this list before making any pairings.

13H. Sealing of invalid move.
A player who has sealed a move that the director finds has no reasonable interpretation loses the game. However, a director who finds there are two or more reasonable interpretations of an ambiguous sealed move may allow sealer's opponent to choose between the possibilities. **See also** 19G, Sealed move invalid and 19F, Sealed move ambiguous.

13I. Refusal to obey rules.
The director may declare a game lost by a player who refuses to comply with the rules. If both players refuse to comply with the rules, the director may declare the game lost by both players. **See also** 1C2, Director discretion; 21F, Player requests for rulings; and 21K, Use of director's power.

TD TIP: It is often useful, but not required, to employ the following steps before applying 13I or dealing with a rule that has no specific penalty:
Step 1: The director warns the player who does not comply with the rules.
Step 2: The director adds two minutes, or more if necessary, to the time of the opponent of the player who does not comply with the rules. Some TDs repeat this step more than once.
Step 3: The director enforces 13I after steps 1 and 2 have been unsuccessful in getting a player to comply with the rules.

14. The Drawn Game
All draw claims are also draw offers (14B). The player by making any draw claim (for example: triple occurrence of position (14C), insufficient material to continue (14D), insufficient material to win on time (14E), the 50-move rule (14F), both flags down in sudden death (14G), insufficient losing chances (Variation 14H), ...) is also making an implied offer of a draw to the opponent. If the opponent accepts the implied draw offer, the game is over.

1. The opponent may immediately accept the draw offer and end the game (14B), or instead
2. The opponent may ask the director to rule on the claim. If the director upholds the draw claim, the game is over.

3. If the director does not uphold the claim (does not declare the game a draw), the game continues. The implied draw offer is still in effect, and the opponent may accept it or reject it (14B).

TD TIP: When a draw claim is made, the director should inform the opponent of the draw offer. The opponent need not immediately accept the draw offer. Instead, the opponent may first wait and see what the director rules. The director's ruling might or might not end the game in a draw. If the claim is denied, then the director restarts the game. In restarting the game, the director assesses penalties, if appropriate according to the rules, and starts the clock. The draw claim becomes a 14B draw offer. The director should remind both players of this draw offer when starting the clock.

TD TIP: Online draw rules vary from OTB draw rules. See Rule10, The Drawn Game *(Chapter 10).*

14A. Stalemate.

The game is drawn when the king of the player to move is not in check and that player has no legal move. This type of draw is called *stalemate.* Providing that the opponent's previous move is legal, this immediately ends the game. Note that it is incorrect to refer to all drawn games as *stalemate.* The draws described in 14B through 14J are not stalemates. **See also** 9E, Checkmate or stalemate; and 15H, Reporting results.

TD TIP: This means that anything, including the fall of the flag, which happens after the stalemate move has been legally determined (see 9, Determination and Completion of the Move) is irrelevant to the outcome of the game. Also, remember a 14A stalemate draw claim is a draw offer (Rule 14, The Drawn Game).

14A1. The clock after stalemate.

Just as with a checkmate, a player who stalemates the opponent is not obligated to then press (5H) or stop (5I) the clock, as stalemate takes priority over a subsequent flag fall. A player delivering stalemate may choose to press the clock to minimize the possibility of dispute. **See also** 9E, Checkmate or stalemate.

14A2. Flag fall before stalemate.

If a player claims a win on time (13C) before the opponent releases a piece that will deliver stalemate, the time forfeit claim is appropriate.

14A3. Unclear if stalemate or flag came first.

After considering all available evidence, including testimony by the players and any witnesses, a director who is unable to determine whether the flag fall occurred first shall deny the time claim and uphold the stalemate.

14B. Agreement.

The game is drawn upon agreement between the two players. This immediately ends the game. **See also** 15H, Reporting of results; 16S, Priority of agreed result over time-forfeit claim; 19G1, Agreed draw and invalid move and 19J, Agreed result of adjourned game.

14B1. Proper timing of draw offer.

Except for a draw claim, which is an implicit draw offer (14), a player should make a proposal of a draw only after determining a move (9G) and before pressing the clock. The opponent may accept the proposal or may reject it either orally or by deliberately touching a piece (10B). In the interim, the player who made the offer cannot withdraw it. **See also** 9G3, Draw offers.

TD TIP: The first step in resolving a properly made draw claim is to notify the opponent of the claimant that all draw claims are the same as offering the opponent a draw (Rule 14, The Drawn Game); however, a rule 14 draw claim is a proper (inherent) draw offer even if a move has not been determined or completed.

14B2. Draw offer with opponent on move.

If a player offers a draw while the opponent's clock is running, the opponent may accept or reject the offer. A player who offers a draw in this manner may be warned or penalized for annoying the opponent (20G). **See also** 14, The Drawn Game.

14B3. Draw offer before moving.

A player that proposes a draw before moving must allow the offer to stand until the opponent either accepts or rejects it. Such a proposal, while unlikely to annoy the opponent, can be disadvantageous, as the player may subsequently notice a strong move and regret the inability to withdraw the offer. **See also** 14, The Drawn Game.

The opponent of a player who offered a draw in this manner has the right to require the player who offered the draw to move before deciding whether to accept the offer, and may respond, "Make your move first," or words to that effect, or remain silent. In any case, the offer may not be withdrawn.

14B4. Flag fall during pending draw offer.

A player who offers a draw may claim a win on time (13C) if the opponent oversteps the time limit while considering the proposal unless the offer is accepted before the flag fall (5G) is claimed. **See also** 14, The Drawn Game.

14B5. Repeated offers.

Repeated draw offers may be construed as annoying the opponent, and penalties are possible at the discretion of the TD (20G). If the first offer has been declined, it is improper to offer another draw unless the opponent has since offered a draw or the position has changed substantially.

TD TIP: It is a good idea for a director to issue a warning before applying any penalties for repeated draw offers.

14B6. Premature or prearranged draws.

It is unethical and unsporting to agree to a draw before a serious contest has begun. The same is true of all arrangements to prearrange game results. In case of clear violations of the moral principles of the game, penalties should be imposed at the director's discretion. **See also** 20L, Manipulating results.

TD TIP: Trying to enforce this rule is difficult. Forcing two players to continue playing when they are resolute on obtaining a result of a draw will produce a sometimes very quick game with many moves resulting in a draw anyhow. Often last-round games may not be prearranged; however, due to prize fund distribution considerations the result can be easily predicted. In cases involving prearranged draws it is wise to have clear and irrefutable evidence before imposing any penalties.

14C. Triple occurrence of position.

The game is drawn upon a correct claim by the player on the move when the same position is about to appear for at least the third time or has just appeared for at least the third time, the same player being on move each time. In both cases, the position is considered the same if pieces of the same kind and color occupy the same squares and if the possible moves of all the pieces are the same, including the right to castle (8A2, 8A3, 8A4) or to capture a pawn *en passant* (8F5). **See also** 14C8, Sudden death time pressure; 14C9, Claimant's scoresheet; and 15H, Reporting of results.

TD TIP: Remember a triple occurrence draw claim is a draw offer (Rule 14, The Drawn Game).

14C1. No repetition of moves or perpetual check draw.

There is no rule regarding a draw by *repetition of moves*. The draw is based on repetition of *position*. The three positions need not be consecutive, and the intervening moves do not matter. There is also no rule regarding *perpetual check*. It is irrelevant whether the claimant of 14C is delivering check or whether the thrice-repeated position involves check.

TD TIP: "Perpetual check" and "three consecutive positions" are often-occurring special cases of 14C, Triple occurrence of position; therefore, claimants need to make a 14C claim in order to try to secure a triple occurrence of position draw when these special cases occur; however, if a player makes a "perpetual check" or "three consecutive positions" claim it is considered first a draw offer (Rule 14, The Drawn Game).

14C2. How to claim.

If a move is required to complete the third occurrence of the position, the player claiming the draw under 14C should write this move on the scoresheet but not play the move on the board, stop both clocks (5I), and state the claim. If no move is required to complete the repetition, the player should stop both clocks without moving and state the claim.

In both cases, if the opponent agrees, the game is drawn. If the opponent does not agree, the claimant may make the claim to a director. If a director denies the claim, the claimant is still obligated to play any announced or recorded move. The director awards the opponent two extra minutes. **See also** 14C3, Player must be on move; 14C4, Claim after moving without pressing clock; and 14C7, Irrevocability of claim.

14C3. Player must be on move.

Only a player to move may claim a draw under 14C. If the opponent is on move a player may not claim, and any claim the player may have made before pressing the clock is invalid; however, the claim is then considered a draw offer (14C7). The right to claim is restored to that player if the same position appears again with the same player on move, or if any other position appears for at least the third time with the same player on move. **See also** 14B, Agreement.

14C4. Claim after moving without pressing clock.

A player who moves and then does not press the clock (5H), but allows it to run, retains the right to claim a draw under 14C. However, this procedure is not recommended. The player who moves and allows the clock to run will lose the time that elapses before a ruling if the claim is not upheld. It is preferred that the player stops both clocks (5I) in order to retain the right to claim a draw under 14C.

14C5. Claimant's clock continues to run.

If a player who claims a draw under 14C fails to stop the clocks, the director should instruct the player to stop them.

14C6. Resolution of claim.

If the claim is found to be correct, the game is drawn. If the claim is found to be incorrect, two minutes shall be added to the opponent's remaining unused time.

14C7. Irrevocability of claim.

A player who makes a draw claim under 14C cannot withdraw it; however, it is still considered a draw offer (14). If a player moves, then claims a draw and presses the clock (5H), or claims a draw, then moves and presses the clock, the move stands, and this is considered an offer of a draw (14). **See also** 14B, Agreement.

14C8. Sudden death time pressure.

In sudden death, a player with less than five minutes remaining may be awarded a draw by triple occurrence of position based on the observation of a director, deputy, or impartial witness(es). A player may stop both clocks to see a director in order to demonstrate the ability to force a triple occurrence of position. **See also** 14C, Triple occurrence of position.

14C9. Claimant's scoresheet.

Except for 14C8, the claimant must have a scoresheet adequate (13C7) to demonstrate the validity of the claim.

14D. Insufficient material to continue.

The game is drawn when one of the following endings exists as of the most recently determined legal move, in which the possibility of a win is excluded for either side (effective 1-1-19). **See also** 15H, Reporting of results:

TD TIP: Remember a 14D draw claim is first a draw offer (Rule 14, The Drawn Game).

14D1. King vs. king.

King vs. king.

14D2. King vs. king with bishop or knight.

King vs. king with bishop or knight.

14D3. King and bishop vs. king and bishop.

King and bishop vs. king and bishop, with both bishops on diagonals of the same color.

14D4. No legal moves leading to checkmate by opponent.

There are no legal moves that could lead to the player being checkmated by the opponent.

14E. Insufficient material to win on time.

The game is drawn even when a player exceeds the time limit if one of the following conditions exists as of the most recently determined legal move (effective 1-1-19) **See also** 15H, Reporting of results:

TD TIP: Remember a 14E draw claim is first a draw offer (Rule 14, The Drawn Game).

14E1. Lone king.

Opponent has only a lone king.

14E2. King and bishop or king and knight.

Opponent has only king and bishop or king and knight, and does not have a forced win.

14E3. King and two knights.

Opponent has only king and two knights, the player has no pawns, and opponent does not have a forced win.

14F. The 50-move rule.

TD TIP: Remember a 14F draw claim is first a draw offer (Rule 14, The Drawn Game).

TD TIP: a 14F draw claim would only use the standards outlined in 14F. The standards for a triple occurrence of position claim, particularly Rule 13C7, Definition of reasonably complete scoresheet, do not apply here.

14F1. Explanation.

The game is drawn when the player on move claims a draw and demonstrates that the last 50 consecutive moves have been made by each side without any capture or pawn move. If the director wishes to allow more than 50 moves for certain positions, details must be posted at the tournament before the first round. **See also** 15H, Reporting of results.

14F2. Resolution.

If the claim is found to be correct, the game is drawn. If it is found to be incorrect, two minutes shall be added to the opponent's remaining unused time.

14F3. Winning position irrelevant.

If a valid claim exists, the game is drawn regardless of the position. Even if the opponent can show an immediate checkmate, the game is drawn.

14F4. Director may count moves in sudden death.

In sudden death, a player with fewer than five minutes remaining and a simplified position in which no pawn moves or captures seem likely may stop both clocks, declare to a director an intention to invoke the 50-move rule when possible, and ask for assistance in counting moves. A director who agrees this is appropriate may count moves or use a deputy or a clock with a move counter to do so.

a.   If the director or the deputy will count moves, the count should begin by crediting moves already made and listed on the scoresheet of the player intending to claim. An opponent who believes a different number of moves have been made should present this case if and when the count reaches 50.

b.   The director or deputy may either keep score, make check marks, or combine the two.

c.   After the count by the director or deputy begins, neither player has a right to know the count until 50 moves are reached. At that point the game is declared drawn unless the opponent successfully challenges the move count.

d. The opponent may challenge either the moves on the claimant's scoresheet before the director/deputy count, the count itself, or both, but must have a scoresheet adequate (13C7) to support the challenge.

e. If the challenge is upheld, the game shall continue with the director or deputy resuming from the corrected count. If the claimant's scoresheet is responsible for the wrong count, two minutes shall be added to the remaining unused time of the claimant's opponent. If the director/deputy count was wrong, there shall be no time adjustment.

f. The director may insert a clock with a move counter that shows the remaining time of both players, set the move counter to zero, and order play to resume. When the clock indicates that both sides have completed 50 further moves, either player may claim a draw. If this method is used, the director should inform the players that if a move is erroneously not counted or double counted, the players should stop the clock and notify the director.

14G. Both flags down in sudden death.

The game is drawn if both flags are down in a sudden death time control and either player points this out. If a player whose flag is still up claims a win on time but does not stop the clock in time to prevent the flag from falling, the game is drawn, unless the flag fall was observed by a director or independent witness. **See also** 14G2, Players apparently unaware of situation; 15H, Reporting of results; 16T, Both players exceed time control; and 16Y, Assisting players with time management prohibited.

TD TIP: Remember a 14G draw claim is first a draw offer (Rule 14, The Drawn Game).

TD TIP: An increment time control of 30 seconds or more is not considered sudden death; therefore, 14G does not apply.

14G1. Checkmate and both flags down.

In a sudden death control, if a player points out that both flags are down prior to a checkmate, the game is drawn. After considering all available evidence, including testimony by the players and any witnesses, a director who is unable to determine whether the claim of both flags down occurred first shall deny the time claim and rule the checkmate valid.

14G2. Players apparently unaware of situation.

If a sudden death game continues with both flags down, the director may rule it a draw. This exception to the standard rule that only players may call

41

flags down is justified by the need to avoid delaying the tournament. **See also** 14J, Draw declared by director; 16T, Both players exceed time control; 16Y, Assisting players with time management prohibited; 18G, Adjudications; and 21D, Intervening in games.

TD TIP: An increment time control of 30 seconds or more is not considered sudden death; therefore, 14G does not apply.

14H. Claim of insufficient losing chances in sudden death.
No claim of insufficient losing chances in sudden death will be allowed.

Variation 14H. Claim of insufficient losing chances in sudden death.
This variation need not be announced in advance publicity.

14H1. Explanation.
This procedure is not available for games in which a clock is being used with either the time delay or the increment properly set, whether the game begins with such a clock or one is added during the game (14H2a). If such a clock is not being used, or such a clock is being used without the time delay or increment feature in operation, the following procedure is available.

In a sudden death time control, a player on the move with two minutes or less of remaining time may stop the clock and may make a claim of insufficient losing chances.

14H2. Resolution of Variation 14H claim.
When ruling, the director should not consider the ratings of those playing. A low-rated player who claims a draw vs. a Master should obtain the same ruling as a Master with the same position who claims a draw vs. a low-rated player. The director should also not consider the times on the clocks. **See also** 14H3, Conferring with players.

The director has four possible ways to resolve the claim.

TD TIP: Except for rule 5F5 there is no rule allowing players to ask for a properly set delay clock to be placed on their game, which would replace an analog clock or non-delay digital clock. For delay capable clocks not set with delay, see rule 16P1. Only the TD can initiate placing a clock with time delay capabilities on a game after a Variation 14H claim has been made and the steps of 14H2 have been applied. As a result, the player wishing to place a time delay clock on the game must first make a Variation 14H claim.

TD TIP: Remember a Variation 14H draw claim is first a draw offer (Rule 14, The Drawn Game).

14H2a. The claim is unclear and a delay clock is available for the game.

A director who believes the claim is neither clearly correct (14H2c) nor clearly incorrect (14H2d), but is instead uncertain as to the correctness of the claim, may place a delay clock on the game, setting it as follows: The claimant gets half of the claimant's remaining time (rounded to the nearest second); the opponent's time is unadjusted; the time delay is set for the standard delay announced at the start of the tournament. After the claimant's clock is started, the Variation 14H draw request by the claimant becomes a draw offer under 14B3, Draw offer before moving. Penalties for rule infractions remain standard. The claimant may win, lose, or draw the game.

14H2b. The claim is unclear and a delay clock is not available for the game.

A director who believes the claim is neither clearly correct (14H2c) nor clearly incorrect (14H2c), but is uncertain as to the correctness of the claim, and does not have a delay clock available, may:

1. Deny the claim while inviting a later re-claim. There is no adjustment of either player's time. After the claimant's clock is started, the Variation 14H draw request by the claimant becomes a draw offer under 14B3, Draw offer before moving. Penalties for rule infractions remain standard. The claimant may win, lose, or draw the game.

2. Watch the game while reserving judgment on the claim. The director should make every effort to resolve the claim before the flag of either player falls (5G). There is no adjustment of either player's time. After the claimant's clock is started, the Variation 14H draw request by the claimant also becomes a draw offer under under 14B3, Draw offer before moving. Penalties for rule infractions remain standard. The claimant may win, lose, or draw the game.

14H2c. The claim is clearly correct.

A director who believes the claim is clearly correct should declare the game drawn. The draw shall be awarded if the director believes that a Class C player would have little chance to lose the position against a Master with both players having ample time. The exact losing chances of any position cannot be calculated, but a director wishing a more precise standard may consider little to mean less than 10 percent. A director unsure whether a position meets the above standard should use option 14H2a or 14H2b. **See also** 14I, Advice on claims of insufficient losing chances in sudden death under rule Variation 14H.

14H2d. The claim is clearly incorrect.

A director who believes the claim is clearly incorrect should deny the claim and may subtract up to one minute from the claimant's remaining time. After the claimant's clock is started, the Variation 14H draw request by the claimant also becomes a draw offer under 14B3, Draw offer before moving. Penalties for rule infractions remain standard. The claimant may win, lose, or draw the game. **See also** 14I, Advice on claims of insufficient losing chances in sudden death under rule Variation 14H.

TD TIP: If a director chooses to resolve the claim by enforcing 14H2a, The claim is unclear, a delay clock is available for the game, or 14H2b, The claim is unclear, a delay clock is not available for the game, then the director should inform the claimant and opponent that when the claimant's clock is started that rule 14B3, Draw offer before moving, is in effect. The opponent has the right to ask the claimant to make a move before the draw offer is rejected or accepted by the opponent; however, if the claimant makes a checkmating (13A) or stalemating (14A) move, the game is over.

TD TIP: Applying rule 14H2a, The claim is unclear, a delay clock is available for the game, is the preferred method of resolving a Variation 14H claim for directors who wish to ensure the result of the game is determined by the players, rather than any outside influence.

14H3. Conferring with players.

A director who is unsure how to rule may confer privately with either player or with both players separately regarding the player's plans. The director should be careful not to say anything that might assist the player if the game is resumed.

14H4. Player with fallen flag may not claim.

A player whose flag is down (5G) may not claim insufficient losing chances.

14H5. Delay Clock, a clock with time delay capabilities, or Increment clock, a clock with increment capabilities.

If either a properly set Delay Clock (5F) or a properly set Increment Clock is used, Variation 14H and 14I are not in effect; i.e., no claim of insufficient losing chances may be made. The reaction time provided for by the delay or the added increment time for each move is likely to be sufficient for a player with insufficient losing chances to hold the position.

14I. Advice on claims of insufficient losing chances in sudden death under Rule Variation 14H.

14I1. Consulting strong players.

If the director is unsure about how to rule on a Variation 14H claim, the director may consult a Master or near-Master who has no stake in the outcome of the game in question. The director should be careful to explain the conditions of Variation 14H to such a player.

14I2. Types of positions.

In complex positions often neither side has a valid claim, while in simple positions both sides may have one. For instance, with much material on the board a Master may be down a piece without compensation but still has better than a small chance to beat a C player. But in endings such as described in 14I3, even a player behind in material should sometimes be awarded the draw.

14I3. Opposite-colored bishop endings.

In some opposite-colored bishop endings (one player having a light-squared bishop and the other player a dark-squared bishop) with most or all pawns fixed, a Master, even if a pawn or two ahead, may have little chance to outplay a C-player; these positions should be ruled draws.

14I4. Queen vs. queen, rook vs. rook.

With no pawns and queen vs. queen or rook vs. rook, the draw should be awarded unless it is one of the rare positions in which there is a quick forced win. If the claimant has additional material and the opponent does not, the ruling should still ordinarily be a draw.

14I5. Bishop or knight vs. rook, rook vs. rook and knight, queen vs. queen and bishop or knight.

With no pawns the player behind in material should not be awarded a draw, but it may be appropriate for the director to apply Variation 14H2a or Variation 14H2b.

14I6. King vs. king, rook pawn, and possibly bishop.

A player with a lone king should be awarded a draw vs. king and rook pawn, or king, rook pawn, and bishop controlling squares of the opposite color than the promotion square, if the claimant's king can stop the pawn from promoting. As in 14I4 and all other such cases, if the claimant has additional material, the ruling should still ordinarily be a draw.

14I7. Rook vs. rook and bishop.

With no pawns, unless there is an immediate win of material or an unusual problem position, a draw claim with a rook vs. opponent's rook and bishop should be denied in accordance with Variation 14H2d. The claim is clearly incorrect.

14J. Draw declared by director.

On rare occasions the director may encounter a situation in which a ruling is required and a decision in favor of either player would be unfair to the opponent (for examples see 20E2d and 20E2h). In such situations the director may rule a draw on the grounds that this is more equitable (i.e., less inequitable) than any other ruling. A draw may also be ruled in cases like 19E, Sealed move envelope missing, if the director recalls that the position was about equal but does not remember the exact position or clock times. **See also** 1C2, Director discretion; 14G2, Players apparently unaware of situation; 16T, Both players exceed time control; 16Y, Assisting players with time management prohibited; 18G, Adjudications, 21D, Intervening in games; and 21K, Use of director's power.

14K. Director declares draw for lack of progress.

If one or both of the following occur(s) then the TD may declare the game drawn:

1. The same position has appeared, as in 14C, for at least five consecutive alternate moves by each player.
2. Any consecutive series of 75 moves have been completed by each player without the movement of any pawn and without any capture. If the last move resulted in checkmate, that shall take precedence.

15. The Recording of Games

15A. Manner of keeping score.

In the course of play each player is required to record the game (both the player's and the opponent's moves), move after move, as clearly and legibly as possible, on the scoresheet prescribed for the competition. Algebraic notation is standard, but descriptive or computer notation is permitted. The player must first make the move, and then record it on the scoresheet. The scoresheet shall be visible to the arbiter (tournament directors) and the opponent throughout the game. **See also** Chapter 3, Chess Notation; 13C3, Filling in moves with flag down; 13I, Refusal to obey rules; 35F6, Scorekeeping options; and 43, Scoresheets.

TD TIP: While the rule's wording indicates making the move first and keeping the scoresheet (paper or electronic) visible at all times, it brings US Chess in alignment with FIDE procedures and sooths many of the fears surrounding electronic scoresheets—see Rule 43— it is a huge change for many players. TDs are advised to first (and possibly second and third) issue warnings to players that do not comply with this revised rule before enforcing any time penalties (1C2a. prescribes adding two minutes to the opponent's unused time).

15A. (Variation I) Paper scoresheet variation.

The player using a paper scoresheet may first make the move, and then write it on the scoresheet, or vice versa. This variation does not need to be advertised in advance. The scoresheet shall be visible to the arbiter (tournament directors) and the opponent throughout the game.

TD TIP: TDs may penalize a player that is in violation of 20C, Use of notes prohibited if the player is first writing the move and repeatedly altering that move on their scoresheet before completing a move on the board.

TD TIP: When TDs enforce the "visible scoresheet" portion of this rule they are advised to first warn players that do not make their scoresheet (or score keeping device) visible to the TD and their opponent.

15A1. Players unable to keep score.

   a. Players determined by the director to be unable to keep score due to physical handicaps may have assistance in scorekeeping as described in 35F, Rules for visually impaired and disabled players, and should be excused from scorekeeping if such assistance is unavailable.

   b. Players determined by the director to be unable to keep score for religious reasons may be excused from scorekeeping or permitted to have assistance as in 35F, Rules for visually impaired and disabled players, at the director's discretion.

   c. Beginners who have not learned to keep score may be excused from scorekeeping, at the director's discretion.

Players excused from scorekeeping are not entitled to make claims that require scoresheets; those who have assistance retain such rights.

TD TIP: Directors often deduct time from the clocks of players at the start of the game whom they excuse from keeping score (the most common example would be that of a player excused from keeping score for genuine religious reasons). Their opponents will need to give up thinking time in order to keep score, which the excused player need not do. A good rule of thumb is to deduct 5% of the total game time allotted for each individual player, up to 10 minutes, from the player's clock that is excused from keeping score. Unless a clock is being used that can be set with seconds as well as minutes and hours (usually a digital clock), partial minutes should be rounded to the nearest minute. For example, in a 20/60 SD/30 contest the player excused from keeping score would lose 5 minutes (5%×90 minutes = 4.5 minutes, rounded to 5 minutes) on an analog clock and 4.5 minutes on a digital clock with that capability. In a 30/60 SD/60 game that same player would lose 6 minutes (5%×120 minutes = 6 minutes) on both an analog and digital clock. In a G/45 contest that same player would lose 2 minutes (5%×45 minutes = 2.25 minutes, rounded to 2 minutes) on an analog clock and 2.25 minutes on a digital clock with that capability. A 40/120 20/60 game can exceed 200 minutes of playing time, as long as 20 moves are made every hour after the first time control; therefore, that same player would lose no more than 10 minutes (5%×200 minutes = 10 minutes or 5%×300 minutes = 15 minutes, which is rounded to 10 minutes because it exceeds the 10 minute maximum limit).

15B. Scorekeeping in time pressure, non-sudden death time control.

If either player has less than five minutes remaining in a non-sudden death time control and does not have additional time (increment) of 30 seconds or more added with each move, both players are excused from the obligation to keep score until the end of the time control period. Doing so, however, may make it impossible to claim a draw by triple occurrence of position (14C) or the 50-move rule (14F) or a win on time forfeit (13C). Scorekeeping by both players must resume with the start of the next time control period, and missing moves should be filled in (15F).

TD TIP: Only players in games with increment time controls of 30 seconds or more and using properly set increment capable clocks are required to keep score at all times, even in the last five minutes of any time control period. Players using improperly set increment clocks or non-increment capable clocks, even those clocks adjusted for an increment time control, are regulated by Rule 15B

15C. Scorekeeping in time pressure, sudden death time control.

If either player has less than five minutes remaining in a sudden death time control and does not have additional time (increment) of 30 seconds or more added with each move, both players are excused from the obligation to keep score. A scoresheet is not required to win on time in a sudden death control (13C).

TD TIP: Only players in games with increment time controls of 30 seconds or more and using properly set increment capable clocks are required to keep score at all times, even in the last five minutes of any time control period. Players using improperly set increment clocks or non-increment capable clocks, even those clocks adjusted for an increment time control, are regulated by Rule 15C.

15D. Use of opponent's scoresheet for assistance.

A player who has an incomplete scoresheet (13C7) and wishes to consult the opponent's scoresheet for assistance may ask to borrow it from the opponent under the following conditions:

15D1. Clock times.

Both players have at least five minutes remaining in the current time control.

15D2. Borrower's clock runs.

The clock of the player making such a request is running and shall continue to run until the scoresheet has been returned.

15D3. Compliance.

The opponent is urged to comply with such a request, but this is not mandatory. If the opponent denies the request, the player may stop both clocks and see a director. A director who agrees that the request is appropriate shall instruct the opponent to lend the player the scoresheet. The opponent may not refuse as all scoresheets belong to the organizers. **See also** 15G, Ownership of scoresheets.

15D4. Excessive requests.

Repeated requests of this type may be deemed by the director to be inappropriate, and the offender may be penalized under 20G, Annoying behavior prohibited.

15E. Borrowing not needed.

A player who is able to read the opponent's scoresheet without borrowing it is free to use the information gained for assistance in keeping score.

15F. Reconstruction after time control.

After the end of a time control, if the next control is not sudden-death, each player must make all efforts to fill in any missing moves on that player's scoresheet.

15F1. Reconstruction of scoresheet by one player.

After the completion of a time control, a player who alone has to complete the scoresheet must do so before making another move, and with that player's clock running if the opponent has made a move. An additional set and board may be used.

15F2. Reconstruction of scoresheets by both players.

After the completion of a time control, if both players need to complete their scoresheets, the clocks should be stopped until they are completed. Additional chess sets and boards may be used. This does not apply if the director rules that it is unnecessary. **See also** 15F4, Reconstruction when the next time control is sudden death.

15F3. Reconstruction impossible or unnecessary.

If it is impossible or unnecessary to reconstruct the moves as prescribed above, the game shall continue. The players should make a clear diagram of the position reached, and the next move played will be considered the first one of the following time control unless the players agree that a later move number has been reached.

TD TIP: For example: in a 40/90 20/30 game both players were in time trouble in the first time control and blitzed off many moves. Both players agree that they made time control but cannot reconstruct the game to reach the current board position. The position is diagrammed and the players continue from that position with the next move by White being move number 41 (or another move number greater than 40 if both players agree). The scoresheet from that point forward is considered complete (13C7) in order to make any claim including a draw by triple occurrence of position (14C) or the 50-move rule (14F) or a win on time forfeit (13C).

15F4. Reconstruction when the next time control is sudden death.

Upon making the time control, if the next control is sudden death, it is less important to fill in the missing moves. The director has the option of waiving the requirement of reconstructing.

15G. Ownership of scoresheets.

The scoresheets of all games in a tournament are the property of the sponsoring organization(s). If the organizer requires that a copy of each game score be submitted by the players, duplicate scoresheets must be provided, and players who fail to submit scoresheets may be penalized.

15H. Reporting of results.

When a game is completed, the result must be immediately reported in the manner required by the director. Both players, not just the winner, are responsible for registering the result. If they do not do so, they may each be penalized. **See also** 29H, Unreported results.

15I. Results reported incorrectly.

If the director learns of the correct result for any just-completed round either before or just after pairings have been made for the next round, the director should correct the pairings if this can be done without disturbing too many games already in progress. The correction may either be based on the correct result or on treating the incorrectly reported result as an unreported result (29H), at the director's discretion. Whichever of these is chosen, the result must be corrected before pairing subsequent rounds, if any, and the corrected result shall be used for prize purposes.

If the error occurred in an earlier round, other than the round described above, the director shall still proceed as above, but has discretion as to whether to use the correct result or the incorrect result for prize purposes. This decision should be based on how much earlier in the tournament the error occurred and how many pairings were affected.

TD TIP: Sometimes errors occur in the reporting of game results. Those errors need to be corrected immediately. Fortunately the same methods used to correct unreported game results also work very well for incorrectly reported game results. The difficulty arises when incorrectly reported results do not come to the director's attention until after several rounds, or even the end of the tournament. As long as there is no chance of a prize being involved, correcting the results is easy. When prizes or a chance to win a prize are involved the director should take care. Correcting incorrectly reported results that cause a player, paired in easier score groups for many rounds, to suddenly qualify for a prize seems unfair. It is the player's responsibility to check the wall charts for errors. While there is no question that such an incorrect result should be rated, the director needs to decide on a case-by-case basis whether or not to allow the new correct results to affect the awarding of prizes.

16. The Use of the Chess Clock

16A. Allowable time controls.

The US Chess office maintains a list, available on request, directly from the US Chess office or at www.uschess.org, of the currently allowable time limits for different types of tournaments. **See also** 5C, Ratable time controls.

16B. How to set clocks.

16B1. Analog clocks.

Clocks should be set so that each unit will register six o'clock when the first time-control period expires. If there is a second time control of any length of one hour or less it should expire at seven o'clock (even if that requires that the clocks be reset), a third such control at eight o'clock, etc. **See also** 5F1a, Increment capable clock not available; 5F2a, Delay capable clock not available; 35F5, Special Clock.

16B2. Digital clocks.

Time delay or increment clocks should be set according to the manufacturer's directions so that any visual device used to indicate that a player's time has been exhausted for all time control periods is activated. Such mechanisms may include one or more of a light, a display of all zeros, or a display of a flag. Players should explain the flag fall mechanism and the clock's operation to their opponents. The time delay or increment should be set according to the director's instructions, with the time delay or increment in force starting at move one (5E1) unless the time control specifies otherwise. Clocks equipped to do so should be set for a Bronstein or a delay mode for delay controls or for Fischer, added time, or increment mode for increment time controls.

TD TIP: Not all digital clocks correctly give the increment for move one when you set increment on the clock. For clocks that don't, the increment time in seconds should be added manually to the base time, if possible, so each player gets the increment for move one. For example, for G/3;inc2, each player gets 3.02 (three minutes and two seconds) to complete move one. If the clock only gives 3.00 for each player's first move when the clock is set—with a base time of three minutes and increment of two seconds—then, if possible, two seconds should be added to each player's base time when setting the clock. If a game is started without the increment applied for move one, it is recommended that the TD not allow the clock to be subsequently adjusted to add the increment for move one. This failure to adjust the clock initially should not be allowed as grounds to contest a later time forfeit claim.

16B2a. Sound.

Digital clocks must be set to produce no sound. This includes, but is not limited to: beeping when a player has run out of time in the final time control; beeping when a player reaches the end of any time control; warning beeps to indicate a player is approaching the end of a time control; and beeping when a player presses the clock. A digital clock that can be set to produce no sound is preferable to a clock that cannot.

16B2b.

Clock of player not out of time continues to run. If possible, digital clocks must be set so that when one player runs out of time in a time control, the opponent's clock continues to run normally. This capability is variously called "halt on end," "claim mode," or "freeze." A digital clock that can be set to satisfy the requirement of this rule is preferable to a clock that cannot.

TD TIP: Not all digital clocks correctly give the increment for move one when you set increment on the clock. For clocks that don't, the increment time in seconds should be added manually to the base time, if possible, so each player gets the increment for move one. For example, for G/3;inc2, each player gets 3.02 (three minutes and two seconds) to complete move one. If the clock only gives 3.00 for each player's first move when the clock is set—with a base time of three minutes and increment of two seconds—then, if possible, two seconds should be added to each player's base time when setting the clock. If a game is started without the increment applied for move one, it is recommended that the TD not allow the clock to be subsequently adjusted to add the increment for move one. This failure to adjust the clock initially should not be allowed as grounds to contest a later time forfeit claim.

16B2c.

Players are responsible for setting clock correctly. Players are responsible for knowing how to set their own clocks to conform to rule 16B2. Players should be prepared to explain the clock's operation to the opponent before the start of the game. This includes how the clock indicates a player has run out of time and how to pause both clocks if necessary to summon a director. **See also** 5F7, Players responsible for knowing how to set the clock.

For more information on delay or increment clocks see Chapter 4, Equipment Standards; 5F, Standard Timer; 35F5, Special clock;42B, Digital clocks; 42D, Delay clock preferable in sudden death; and 42E, Increment clock preferable in increment time controls.

TD TIP: Directors are not expected to know how to set all digital clocks (5F).

TD TIP: Some players due to incapacity or due to religious reasons cannot use some types of clocks such as electric, electronic or with digital displays. After a director determines that such conditions are genuine, an analog clock is permissible. Some players for the same reasons cannot use a clock at all. In such cases, the opponent may be asked, but not required, to press the clock on behalf of both players, a method that some TDs report has worked well. The TD may also require such a player to provide an assistant, or may help such a player find an assistant among spectators or players with byes. Directors often deduct time from the clocks of players excused from setting and pressing the clock. See also the TD TIP after 15A1, Players unable to keep score.

16C. Removing a player's hand from clock.
Players must remove their hands from the clock button after depressing the button and must keep their hands off and away from the clock until it is time to press it again. **See also** 5H, Pressing the clock.

16C1. Using the clock.
Each player must operate the clock with the same hand that moves the pieces.

16C2. Picking up clock.
Each player is forbidden to pick up the clock.

16D. Special rules for time pressure.
See 11D1, Illegal move in time pressure;15B, Scorekeeping in time pressure, non-sudden death time control and 15C, Scorekeeping in time pressure, sudden death.

16E. When flag is considered down.
The flag is considered to have fallen when either player points this out. **See also** 5G, The flag and 13C1, Only players may call flag.

16F. Evidence provided by flag.
In the absence of an evident defect in the clock or flag mechanism, the fallen flag (5G) is considered as proof that the time-control period has ended or that time has run out for that time period. **See also** 16G, Premature flag fall and 16H, Apparent flag fall can cause forfeit.

16G. Premature flag fall.
a. With an analog clock, if a clear white space shows between the right side of the minute hand of the clock and the left side of the 12 marker on the clock's face, the flag is considered to have fallen prematurely.

b. With a delay clock, if the device used to indicate that a player's time is exhausted is activated, due to an incorrect or defective move counter, an incorrect setting, or a defect (16O) of any kind, the flag is considered to have fallen prematurely. Since the move counters, on clocks equipped with them, may not be used as the only evidence in claiming that the prescribed number of moves were not completed in the allotted time (13C), both players' scoresheets may be used as evidence of an incorrect or defective delay clock.

If either 16Ga or 16Gb occurs, the director should deny the claim of a time forfeit (13C) and the game is continued, with a different clock, if possible. A later time-forfeit claim (13C) in that control by either player is still allowed.

16H. Apparent flag fall can cause forfeit.
a.   Analog clock: even though it may seem that the flag (5G) fell early, if the clear white space described in 16Ga is not apparent, the player's time has expired.

TD TIP: For instance, if the right side of the minute hand is touching the left side of the hour marker, even though it may not reach to the center of that marker, the time has been used up. Players should realize that this possibility exists and should refrain from using all their apparent time if not essential.

b.   Delay clock: because each delay clock manufacturer applies the delay and flag fall procedures in slightly different ways, it may then appear that the flag fell early as described in 16Gb; however, the player's time has expired.

16I. Starting the clock.
At the time determined for the start of the game, after the board and pieces are set up, the clock of the player with the white pieces is started. During the game, each of the players, having moved, stops the player's clock and starts that of the opponent. **See also** 5H, Pressing the clock and 16N, Beginning the round.

16J. Black not present.
If Black is not present for the start of the game, White shall start his own clock, make his move on the board, and start Black's clock.

TD TIP: If a director observes that White has started Black's clock without moving, the director should remind White to make a move immediately. If, upon arriving, Black observes that White has started Black's clock without moving, Black may immediately start White's clock or stop the clock and make a claim. Either way, if the clock has a move counter, it may be necessary to adjust it before the game commences. The director may assess the standard penalty (1C2A), or other penalties if appropriate, against the player who improperly started Black's clock without moving.

If White makes a move before the clock is started, the move counter may be off by a half-move. If White starts Black's clock without moving, the counter may be off by a half-move or a full move. The director should, at an early stage in the game, verify the setting of the move counter, and ask the players to correct it if necessary.

16K. Both players late.

If both players arrive late, the first to arrive must split the elapsed time before starting the opponent's clock. For example, if the first player to arrive is 40 minutes late, the clocks should be set to reflect 20 minutes of elapsed time on each side. **See also** 13F, Late arrival by both players; and 13D, Late arrival for game.

16K1. Elapsed time not reflected.

If the first late player to arrive fails to do this and instead sets the clocks to reflect no elapsed time on either side, this setting stands unless corrected by a director or changed by agreement between the two players.

16K2. Elapsed time incorrectly reflected.

If the first late player to arrive sets the clocks to give the opponent a disadvantage, such as charging the opponent with all the elapsed time, and this is noticed by or pointed out to the director, the improper times shall be corrected and the player responsible for them penalized at the director's discretion.

16L. Possible stipulations.

The director may require that clocks face a certain direction or that Black or White sit on a particular side of the table. In the absence of such a requirement, unless Black is late arriving for the start of the game (39A1), Black determines which side of the board the clock is on, and the player arriving at the chessboard first may choose either side of the table to sit on. **See also** 39A1, Black player late.

16M. Equipment needed to start clock.

Except for splitting the elapsed time if both players are late or lack equipment, no player may subtract time from a late opponent except by starting a clock. A late opponent's clock may not be started until the board and pieces are in place. If equipment becomes available only after the round has started, the elapsed time from the beginning shall be divided equally between the two players. **See also** 13F, Late arrival by both players and 13D, Late arrival for game.

16N. Beginning the round.

With the exception of games rescheduled by the director, all clocks should start promptly at the time specified for the round. If feasible, the director should give a warning and then announce that play must begin. In a tournament where it is impractical for the director to announce that play should start, players should be urged in advance to begin games promptly and informed that no permission is needed to start clocks at the specified time if the pairings are posted. **See also** 5H, Pressing the clock; 6A, The first move; and 16I, Starting the clock.

16O. Defective clocks.

Every indication given by a clock is considered to be conclusive in the absence of evident defects. A player who wishes to claim any such defect must do so as soon as aware of it. A clock with an obvious defect should be replaced, and the time used by each player up to that time should be indicated on the new clock as accurately as possible.

The director should use judgment in determining what times shall be shown on the new clock. A director who decides to subtract time from one or both players shall leave that player(s) with the greater of either five minutes to the time control or at least one minute for each move the player still needs to meet the time control.

16P. Erroneously set clocks.

An erroneously set clock should be handled in the same fashion as a defective clock. As in 16O, the director should use judgment in deciding whether to make time adjustments. The most common situation of this type involves an analog clock set to expire at 7:00 rather than the correct 6:00. This is best handled by pointing out to both players that the time control expires at 7:00. Clocks can also be reset for the correct time controls and the correct elapsed time for each player.

Sometimes this hour difference is not pointed out and there is an eventual time claim. Even though the clock may show 6:00 with a flag down, or the signaling device on a delay or digital clock indicates a flag fall, if the total elapsed time shown for both players is about an hour more than possible, considering when the game started, the player should not be forfeited, and should be given the hour in question.

TD TIP: Often digital and delay clocks are a challenge to set properly. The director should use judgment in deciding if a digital or delay clock was set improperly deliberately, or inadvertently. Adding two minutes to the injured player's unused time should penalize deliberate incorrect settings. In either case the error(s) should be corrected. If the players cannot adjust the digital or delay clock properly then an analog clock with the proper settings may be used instead. A few common errors in setting digital and delay clocks: (1) using the "Fischer" instead of the proper "Bronstein" setting, (2) secondary sudden death time controls that are set improperly or not at all, and (3) inaccurate move counters.

TD TIP: *Directors are encouraged to intervene in the game to correct an incorrectly set clock without requiring a player to make a claim first. Incorrectly set clocks can cause multiple problems for the entire tournament. This intervention is best done early in the game.*

16P1. Delay or increment not set.

If a delay- or increment-capable clock is used at an event with a delay or increment time control and the delay or increment is not set, this is handled in the same fashion as an erroneously set clock. The delay or increment should be set for the remainder of the game. The director should use his or her best judgement when determining the clock settings.

16Q. Interruption of game.

If the game is to be interrupted for some reason beyond the control of the players, such as a defective clock, disruption of the pieces, re-establishing the position after an illegal move, making the claim of a draw or win or a rules violation, or for any other reason that assistance by the tournament director may be required both clocks should be stopped by one of the players. When doing so, the player must state the reason for stopping the clocks, and see the director if necessary to resolve the situation. **See also** 5I, Stopping the clock; 13C6, Claimant's clock; 21F, Player requests for rulings; and 21F1, Timing of requests.

16R. Illegal Moves

See 11A, Illegal move during last 10 moves;11D, Illegal move; and 16Q, Interruption of game.

16S. Priority of agreed result over time-forfeit claim.

A resignation or an agreement to draw remains valid even when it is found later that the flag of one side had fallen. **See also** 13B, Resignation; 14B, Agreement; and 19G1, Agreed draw and invalid move.

16T. Both players exceed time control.

If both players exceed the time control, no claim of time forfeit is possible. In a non-sudden death control, the game continues. In a sudden death control, the game is drawn. **See also** 13C6, Claimants clock; 13C13, Player out of time cannot claim; 14G, Both flags down in sudden death; 14G2, Players apparently unaware of situation; and 16Y, Assisting players with time management prohibited.

TD TIP: *An increment time control of 30 seconds or more is not considered sudden death, therefore if both players should exceed time control, the clocks should be reset to the "next" time control of the time increment (e.g. 30 seconds) per move.*

16U. Avoiding the need to reset clocks.

It is recommended for analog clocks that secondary and subsequent time controls allow one hour per player so that the minute hand will be at twelve (12:00) and the flag will fall when the player's time expires. This avoids the need to reset clocks and the problems sometimes caused by resetting. The latter include questions or disputes about player resetting, directors being diverted from other duties to reset, time shortage situations with no flags when players forget to reset, and players whose flags have just fallen resetting the clock before the opponent claims a forfeit win. Check the manufacture's manual for instructions on properly setting a delay clock to reset automatically after the end of the first time control. **See also** 16B, How to set clocks and 16W, resetting clocks when necessary.

16V. One vs. two controls when time is limited.

If there is not enough time for a second control of an hour per player, it is recommended the tournament have only one control unless the organizer believes the players would prefer otherwise. For instance, if games must end in two hours, G/60 should be preferred to 30/30 followed by SD/30 unless players have indicated a preference for the latter.

16W. Resetting clocks when necessary.

When using an analog clock, if a period of less than one hour is used for a second or later control period, when both players complete the number of moves required of the previous time-control period, the players should reset both clocks by moving them forward one hour minus the length of the next time-control period. The director may specify alternate procedures. With a few exceptions, properly set digital clocks usually reset automatically. **See also** 16B, How to set clocks and 16U, Avoiding the need to reset clocks.

16X. Extra minute not added.

The old rule permitting an extra minute on each side of a mechanical (analog) clock to compensate for possible inaccuracies is no longer in effect.

16Y. Assisting players with time management prohibited.

No one, except a player's opponent, may call that player's attention to the fact that a flag is down, the opponent has moved, or the player has forgotten to press the clock after moving. These prohibitions also apply to the director. For a rare exception regarding calling flags in sudden death, see 14G2, Players apparently unaware of situation. **See also** 1C2, Director discretion; 11I,

Spectators; 13CI, Only players may call flag; 14J, Draw declared by director; 18G2, Director declares game over; 20E2, Unsolicited advice; 20M5, Spectators cannot make claims; 21D, Intervening in games; and 21K, Use of director's power.

17. Scheduling

17A. Determination of game times.
All games must be played in the tournament rooms at the times designated by the organizers unless the director specifies otherwise. For example, a player whose game ends late or is adjourned may be granted additional time to eat or rest (a half hour is common), or a first-round game may be scheduled for play before the start of the tournament. **See also** 23B, Determination of game times.

17B. Delayed games.
If the director grants a player a late start, the opponent may not start the player's clock until the time specified by the director.

17B1. Informing opponent of new time.
The director should inform the opponent of a player allowed a delayed start of the revised starting time, either by writing the new time on the pairing sheet or by telling the player involved.

17B2. Opponent not informed of new time.
If the director fails to provide the notice described in 17B1, the opponent presumably will start the player's clock at the originally scheduled time. In such cases, the opponent will eventually be required to reset the clocks to reflect the revised starting time and grant the player the time promised by the director.

17C. Changes in round times.
Changes in starting times of rounds should be made only in the event of an emergency. It is especially undesirable to make rounds earlier than previously scheduled, as players may forfeit or lose time as a result. **See also** TD TIP to <u>Rule 5</u> (Chapter 10).

18. The Adjournment of the Game

18A. Description.
If a game is not finished at the end of the time prescribed for play, the director may indicate that it is time for adjournment or accept the request of either player to adjourn. At that point the player on move, after deciding which move to make, does not play that move on the board but instead writes it in unambiguous notation on the scoresheet, puts the scoresheet and that of the opponent in the sealed move envelope (18D), seals the envelope, stops both clocks, and then records the remaining time on the outside of the envelope.

Until stopping both clocks the player retains the right to change the sealed move. If the player who is told to adjourn makes a move on the chessboard, for whatever reason, that move becomes the sealed move and cannot be changed. **See also** 9A, Transfer to a vacant square.

If either player is recording the game in a scorebook, the director may take possession of the entire score book or allow the sealed move to be written on a separate piece of paper and sealed in the envelope.

18B. Sealing a move early.
In tournaments in which the adjournment time is fixed beforehand, normally after the full period of the first time control, a player who has completed the number of moves required may ask the director for permission to seal early. Such a player absorbs the time remaining before the scheduled adjournment by having his or her remaining time decreased by the amount of time remaining in the session. Such requests are ordinarily granted during the last hour of the session.

18C. When to adjourn.
Unless announcing in advance that all games will adjourn at a specific time, the director has discretion as to when to adjourn any game after the first time control. The wall clock shall control the duration of all playing sessions, but the director should refrain from adjourning a game in which one or both players are in serious time trouble. This situation could arise, for example, if the game was started late and half the elapsed time before the start was not deducted from each clock.

18C1. Adjournment despite time pressure.
If it is necessary for the start of the next round, a game may be adjourned in a secondary time-control period in which one player is short of time but the other has a large amount. The director should be aware that despite the time pressure of one player, the game might not end soon, delaying the start of the next round.

18C2. Allowing breaks.
In tournaments with more than one round per day, it is customary to allow a player whose game has just been adjourned a standard amount of time to eat or rest (a half hour is common) before beginning the next game. On occasion, this may require the next round opponent to start that game after the regularly scheduled starting time. **See also** 17A, Determination of game times.

18D. The sealed move envelope.
The following should be indicated on the sealed move envelope: names and colors of the players, position immediately before the sealed move, time used by each player, name or color of the player who sealed the move and number

of that move, date and time for resumption, and the signatures of both players, indicating they verify and understand the information written on the envelope.

18E. Custody of sealed move envelope.
The director is responsible for custody of the envelope.

18F. Problems of the next-to-last round.
Substantial effort should be made to complete all unfinished games, especially those involving prize contenders, from previous rounds before the last round begins. This must, however, be balanced by the need to start the final round as close to the scheduled time as possible.

18F1. Considerations.
When deciding whether to adjourn games in such cases, the director must weigh the harm to other contenders that might ensue if one of the players loses the final game and then decides to resign the adjourned game, either because a long delay in resumption seems likely or for unethical reasons. On the other hand, delaying the last round for many hours can cause immense player dissatisfaction; some in contention may even withdraw rather than wait.

18F2. Pairing players unaffected by result.
A director who does not wish to adjourn a long game may seek private assurances from both players that they will not withdraw and will play the last round regardless of the result of the long game. This would allow all players to be paired except those whose pairings would be affected by the result of that game.

18F3. Sudden-death.
Widespread use of sudden-death time controls has minimized the problems associated with last-round pairings. **See also** 28Q, Pairing unfinished games and 29F, Last-round pairings with unfinished games.

18G. Adjudications.
Only under emergency circumstances may a director permanently adjudicate a game; that is, declare a result based upon best play by both sides. When used in other than emergency situations, this fact must be clearly specified in all tournament publicity and posted and announced at the site. **See also** 14G2, Players apparently unaware of situation; 14J, Draw declared by director; 16Y, Assisting players with time management prohibited; and 21D, Intervening in games.

18G1. Example of emergency.
An *emergency* situation could arise, for example, if a player with substantial time remaining and a poor position disappears for more than 15 minutes or is present but shows little interest in considering the position. Such behavior is unsportsmanlike and the director is encouraged to adjudicate, possibly after a

warning. **See also** 1C2, Director discretion; 20H, Long absence during play; 21F, Player requests for rulings; and 21K, Use of director's power.

18G2. Director declares game over.

18G does not prevent a director from declaring the result of a game that has ended without the players noticing this. For example, if the game has been decided by checkmate (13A), late arrival for game (13D), late arrival for adjournment resumption (13E), stalemate (14A), or insufficient material to continue (14D), the director may declare the game over. **See also** 1C2, Director discretion; 13C1, Only players may call flag; 14G2, Players apparently unaware of situation; 14J, Draw declared by director; 16Y, Assisting players with time management prohibited; 21D, Intervening in games; 21F, Player requests for rulings; and 21K, Use of director's power.

19. Resumption of the Adjourned Game

19A. Setup.

When the game is resumed, the position immediately before the sealed move shall be set up on the chessboard, and the times at adjournment shall be indicated on the clocks.

19B. Opening the envelope.

The envelope (18D) shall be opened only when the player who must reply to the sealed move is present. The director then opens the envelope, makes the sealed move on the chessboard, and starts the player's clock.

19C. Opponent of sealing player absent.

The clock of an absent player who must respond to the sealed move shall be started at the beginning of the adjournment session, but the envelope containing the sealed move shall be opened only when the player arrives.

19D. Sealing player absent.

If the player who has sealed the move is absent, the player responding to the sealed move is not obliged to play a move on the chessboard. Such a player has the right to record the move in reply on the scoresheet, seal it in an envelope, and press the clock (5H). The envelope should then be given to the director and opened on the opponent's arrival.

19E. Sealed move envelope missing.

If the envelope (18D) containing the move recorded in accordance with 18A has disappeared, the game shall be resumed from the position at the time of adjournment with the clock times as they were at the time of adjournment.

If it is impossible to reestablish the position, the game is annulled, and a new game must be played unless the director determines either that it is impractical to do so or another solution offers greater equity. If the time used cannot be reestablished, the director must decide how to reset the clocks. **See also** 1C2, Director Discretion; 14J, Draw declared by director; and 21K, Use of director's power.

19F. Sealed move ambiguous.

A director who feels an ambiguous sealed move has two or more reasonable interpretations may allow the sealer's opponent to choose among the possibilities. The sealer's opponent's clock will run while considering which to choose. **See also** 13H, Sealing of invalid move.

19G. Sealed move invalid.

If the envelope contains no sealed move or the sealed move is illegal and the director finds there is no reasonable interpretation of it, the player who sealed the move loses the game. **See also** 13H, Sealing of invalid move.

19G1. Agreed draw and invalid move.

If the players agree to draw and then find that an invalid move was sealed, the draw stands. **See** 14B, Agreement.

TD TIP: In the cases of an agreed draw or resignation, both players should notify the director. The director should be alert to the possibility that players may have reached agreement without notifying the director.

19G2. Resignation and invalid move.

If a player resigns (see 19J) and then finds that the opponent sealed an invalid move, the resignation stands. **See also** 13B, Resignation.

19G3. Loss on time and invalid move.

If the opponent of the player who sealed loses the game due to failure to appear in time for its resumption and then finds that the sealed move was invalid, the loss on time stands. **See** 13C, Time forfeit.

19H. Game resumed with wrong times on clock.

If, upon resumption, the times have been incorrectly indicated on either clock, the error must be corrected if either player points this out before making a move. If the error is not so established, the game continues without any correction, unless the director determines that another solution offers greater equity.

19I. Game resumed with incorrect position.

If, upon resumption, the position is set up incorrectly, this is considered an illegal move. If discovered within ten moves of resumption, the position must be corrected. The clock times are not adjusted. **See also** 11E, Incorrect adjourned position.

19J. Agreed result of adjourned game.
If both players agree on the result of an adjourned game before resumption, both players must notify the director. **See also** 14B, Agreement.

TD TIP: Sometimes the sealed move is mate or stalemate, so the sealed move ends the game; however, this is considered unsportsmanlike behavior on the part of the player that knowingly sealed such a move. This kind of behavior may be fined or punished.

20. Conduct of Players and Spectators

20A. Conduct of players.
Players shall participate in the spirit of fair play and good sportsmanship, and must observe the US Chess Code of Ethics. **See also** Chapter 6: US Chess Code of Ethics.

20B. Use of recorded matter prohibited.
During play, players are forbidden to make use of handwritten, printed, or otherwise recorded matter. While the penalty is at the discretion of the director, a forfeit loss is usually ruled if the material is relevant to the game, while a lesser penalty or warning is common otherwise. For example, a player on move five of a King's Indian Defense would usually be forfeited for reading a book on the King's Indian but given a warning or time penalty for reading one on rook endings. **See also** 1C2, Director discretion and 21K, Use of director's power.

TD TIP: Often players will use headphones to listen to material unrelated to the game. This is not a violation of Rule 20B; however, a director may inspect the listening device(s) used to make sure that the material is indeed unrelated to the game.

20C. Use of notes prohibited.
The use of notes made during the game as an aid to memory is forbidden, aside from the actual recording of the moves, draw offers, and clock times, and the header information normally found on a scoresheet. This is a much less serious offense than 20B; a warning or minor time penalty is common, with more severe punishment if the offense is repeated. **See also** 1C2, Director discretion; 15, The Recording of Games; and 21K, Use of director's power.

20D. Use of additional chessboard or computer prohibited.
A player who analyzes a game in progress on another chessboard or consults a computer about the position is guilty of a serious violation of the rules. Though the director still has discretion, the usual penalty is loss of the game.

See also 1C2, Director discretion; 21K, Use of director's power; and 36H, Consultation.

20E. Soliciting or using advice prohibited.

During play the players are forbidden to make use of any notes, sources of information or advice (solicited or not), or analyze on another chessboard. **See also** 1C2, Director discretion; 20N, Electronic communication devices; and 21K, Use of director's power.

20E1. Solicited advice.

This is a serious violation and a forfeit loss is often ruled. **See also** 1C2, Director discretion and 21K, Use of director's power.

TD TIP: The director has the right to require that cell phones and other communication devices be turned off in the tournament room.

20E2. Unsolicited advice.

Ruling on unsolicited advice can be difficult. The giver deserves a penalty, but what of the recipient? The director's task is to prevent a player from benefiting from advice but also not unduly penalize the player for another's offense. There is sometimes no good solution to this problem, but here are a few examples of possible rulings.

a. A Class D player suggests a winning move to a Master. If, as is likely, the director feels the Master would probably find the move without recourse to the advice, no penalty should be imposed.

b. A Master suggests a winning move to a Class D player. If the director feels the D player would probably not find the move without help, the ruling may be that the D player is prohibited from making the move.

c. A move is suggested, and the director is not sure if it is a good one. The recipient seems to have other acceptable moves. The ruling might be that the player must play a different move, as this seems least likely to cause injustice.

d. A winning move is suggested. All other moves seem to lose and the director believes it unclear whether the player would have likely found the move without help. This situation is especially difficult. If the move is allowed, the opponent will feel cheated by the spectator. If it is not permitted, the player will feel cheated, claiming he or she would have found it without help.

Neither ruling is incorrect, but perhaps fairer would be to rule the game a draw (see 14J) or to show the position to several players of similar rating to the one involved, who are unaware of and have no stake in the dispute, to help determine whether a player of that strength is likely to find the move.

e. A weak move is suggested. No need to penalize the recipient.

f. A player with five moves to make in ten minutes and an unclear position forgets to press the clock and this is pointed out by a spectator 30 seconds later. The director may only guess whether the player would have noticed the clock before the flag fell, and if so, how much time would have elapsed. A time penalty of a few minutes might be appropriate.

g. The situation is identical to f above except that nine of the ten minutes have elapsed before the spectator's intervention. The director must consider that having not noticed for nine minutes, the player may well not have pressed the clock in the last minute either. A forfeit is unfair as the player might have noticed in the final minute, but not taking strong action may be even more unfair to the opponent.

Imposing a time penalty on a player already surprised to have only a minute left may be reasonable. It is unclear whether the player would be helped or hurt by the spectator's intervention and a subsequent decision by the director to take away most of the last minute.

h. The situation is the same as g above except that the player who forgot to press the clock has an easy win and will have no problem making the last five moves in a few seconds if necessary. To give the player even a few seconds would mean defeat for an opponent who had good chances to win on time before the spectator interfered.

Leaving any time for the negligent player would be unfair to the opponent, but ruling a time forfeit would be unfair to the negligent player. The *lesser of evils* solution might be to declare the game a draw in accordance with 14J.

i. In all such situations, if the unsolicited advice comes from a relative, close friend, teammate, or coach, the director may impose a more severe penalty than otherwise and may consider the advice solicited.

j. In a team or individual/team event, if unsolicited advice is given by a teammate or coach, the director has the option of forfeiting the game for team purposes but allowing it to continue for individual purposes and US Chess rating, possibly with a further penalty.

See also 1C2, Director discretion; 11I, Spectators; 13CI, Only players may call flag; 14G2, Players apparently unaware of situation; 16Y, Assisting players with time management prohibited; 20M5, Spectators cannot make claims; 21D, Intervening in games; and 21K, Use of director's power.

20F. Analysis in the playing room prohibited.
No analysis is permitted in the playing room during play or during adjourned sessions. **See also** 1C2, Director discretion; 21F, Player requests for rulings; and 21K, Use of director's power.

20F1. Adjournment help outside playing room allowed.

While a game is adjourned, a player may receive help outside the playing room from any source, including other players, books, or computers. A prohibition on such help would be unenforceable and would penalize only those honest enough to observe it.

20G. Annoying behavior prohibited.

It is forbidden to distract or annoy the opponent in any manner whatsoever. A director, upon a complaint by the opponent, has discretion to determine whether any particular behavior is in violation of this rule and to impose penalties. **See also** 1C2, Director discretion; 21F, Player requests for rulings; and 21K, Use of director's power.

20G1. Inadvertent annoying behavior.

Sometimes a player's actions, though annoying to the opponent and possibly others, are clearly unintentional. For instance, a player may occasionally cough. While the director has the right to invoke rule 20G, this is quite harsh if the player's actions are involuntary. A partial solution is to assign such a player to a board in another room or far away from other games.

TD TIP: What is annoying to one person is perfectly acceptable to another. That is why the director decides what is and is not annoying. Uncommon and obtrusive activity is more likely to also be annoying activity. Often if a director just makes players aware that their activity is annoying, the activity stops; however, if that and a warning do not prevent the annoying activity, then stronger penalties can be imposed at the discretion of the director.

20H. Long absence during play.

Players with games in progress should not leave the playing room for more than 15 minutes without permission from the director. A first offense usually does not warrant a forfeit unless there is additional evidence suggesting a further rules violation during the absence. **For further information** see 18G1, Example of emergency.

20H1. Quitting without resigning.

It is rude and unsportsmanlike to abandon a lost position without resigning. Any player with a bad position who is absent without permission for over 15 minutes risks having the game adjudicated. **See also** 18G1, Example of emergency and 20H, Long absence during play.

20I. Discussion of games.

Players should not discuss their games in progress with anyone; this may lead to penalties under 20E, Soliciting or using advice prohibited. The director has the option of banning all talking in the tournament room, even if not loud enough to be disturbing. **See also** 1C2, Director discretion; 20K, Penalties; 21F2, Facts are agreed upon; and 21K, Use of director's power.

20J. Last round discussion.

Especially in the last round, it is improper for contenders paired against each other to engage in discussions about the game or its outcome before or during the game. **See also** 1C2, Director discretion; 20K, Penalties; 21F, Player requests for rulings; and 21K, Use of director's power.

20K. Penalties.

Infractions of these rules may incur penalties, including time penalties, loss of the game, expulsion from the tournament, or other penalties or combinations of penalties. **See also** 1C2, Director discretion; 13I, Refusal to obey rules; 21F, Player requests for rulings; and 21K, Use of director's power.

20L. Manipulating results.

Collusion to fix or throw games, whether before or during the game, in order to manipulate prize money, title norms, ratings, or for any other purpose is illegal and may result in severe sanctions, including revocation of US Chess membership. Such agreements include arrangements to split prize money no matter what the result of the game. **See also** US Chess Code of Ethics.

20M. Behavior of spectators.

20M1. Spectators have no special privileges.

Spectators not playing in the tournament have no special privileges. For instance, if a player complains that a particular spectator's presence near his or her game is disturbing, rather than investigate the complaint to determine its validity, it may be correct for the director to simply require the spectator to move away from that game. If more complaints are received about the same person, the director may ask that spectator to leave the premises. If the spectator has paid an admission fee, it may be appropriate to refund this fee.

If a player repeatedly complains about various spectators for no apparent reason, the director may choose to disregard such complaints, informing the player that spectators are allowed at the tournament.

20M2. Spectator is player with game in progress.

If the offending spectator is a player in the tournament, especially one with a game in progress close to the complaining player, the situation is less clear. More consideration should now be given to the merits of the complaint, as it is reasonable for an entrant to expect to be able to watch nearby games while playing his or her own game, and this may be impossible without provoking the complaint. But if in doubt, the director should still consider the rights of players to be preeminent over those of spectators.

20M3. Ongoing problems.

Occasionally there may be an ongoing situation in which a player complains that another player's presence is disturbing, or each complains that the other is disturbing. One way to deal with this problem in future rounds is to assign the players to special boards far away from each other or in different rooms. **See also** 1C2, Director discretion; 21F, Player requests for rulings; and 21K, Use of director's power.

20M4. Prohibitions.

It is highly improper, and warrants ejection from the premises, for any spectator to discuss a player's position or time management with that player, to point out that it is the player's move, or to talk in a loud enough voice to be heard by a player with a game in progress. **See also** 1C2, Director discretion; 21F, Player requests for rulings; and 21K, Use of director's power.

20M5. Spectators cannot make claims.

Spectators, including parents and coaches, may point out irregularities to the director in a manner neither heard nor noticed by the players, but have no right to make claims of any kind on behalf of players. If a problem arises during play, a player of any age should understand that he or she should promptly stop both clocks and see a director. A spectator who makes a claim may be ejected. **See also** 1C2, Director discretion; 11I, Spectators; 13C1, Only players may call flag; 14G2, Players apparently unaware of situation; 16Y, Assisting players with time management prohibited; 20E2, Unsolicited advice; and 21K, Use of director's power.

20M6. Spectator visibility.

To minimize claims of illegal assistance, if a relative, close friend, or coach of a player is permitted to stand near that player during play, that spectator should stand behind that player rather than in front, so the spectator is not visible to the player. **See also** 1C2, Director discretion; 21F, Player requests for rulings; and 21K, Use of director's power.

20N. Electronic communication devices.

Players are not allowed to leave the playing venue without permission from the arbiter. The playing venue is defined as the playing area, rest rooms, refreshment and smoking area, adjacent hallways and other places as designated by the arbiter/TD.

Without the permission of the arbiter/TD a player is forbidden to have a mobile phone or other electronic means of communication in the playing venue, unless they are completely switched off.

TD TIP: "Permission of the director" allows for maximum flexibility. No specific penalty is prescribed. In the absence of announced rules for a specific event, the standard penalties apply (see 20N1). Organizers are free to announce whatever penalty is appropriate for their event. This rule addresses possession of a communications device. In practice, the device ringing or making some other sound may be the only practical way to detect a cell phone— but this rule is not aimed at penalizing the noise; it is aimed at penalizing the possession of a communications device.

20N1. Disturbing noise or disruption of games.

Audible disruptive noises such as a cell phone ring tone, pager beep, alarms and other noises cause a disruption in the playing hall. These noises are often very loud and disturb the entire room. The following are guidelines for penalizing such disturbances:

a. First offense standard penalty is to subtract 10 minutes or half the remaining time from a player's clock, whichever is less. *Variant: Depending on the importance of the event the standard penalty may be up to immediate loss of the game in progress. If a variant is used, it must be announced at the opening remarks for the event and posted prominently in the playing hall and at all entrances.*

b. Second (and subsequent) offense for the same player during the same event is loss of the game currently in progress.

c. If the incident occurs in the playing hall, but after the offender's game for the round is completed while other games are still in progress, then the above penalties apply to the subsequent round. In the case of a loss (e.g. second offense), that player is not paired for the next round.

d. If the incident occurs after the game for the last round is complete while other games are still in progress, the offender is treated like a non-participating spectator and is ejected from the playing hall. *Variant: Depending on the importance of the event and the disturbance created, the player may receive a ½ point total score penalty for prize distribution.*

21. The Tournament Director

21A. The chief tournament director.

Responsible for all play, the tournament director must see that the rules are observed. The director is bound by the official rules of chess, by US Chess tournament rules and code of ethics, and by all US Chess procedures and policies.

21B. Duties and powers.

The chief tournament director's duties and powers normally include the following: to appoint assistants as required to help in the performance of his or her duties; to accept and list entries; to provide suitable conditions of play; to familiarize players with the playing facility and other tournament conditions; to prepare pairings; to display wall charts; to rule on disputes and enforce such rulings; and to collect scores, report results, and forward US Chess and membership applications, tournament results and fees to the sponsoring organization and for the official record. **See also** 1C2, Director discretion; 21F, Player requests for rulings; and 21K, Use of director's power.

21C. Delegation of duties.

The chief director may delegate any duties to assistants, but is not thereby relieved of responsibility for performance of these duties.

21D. Intervening in games.

The director's intervention in a chess game shall generally be limited to the following:

21D1. Answering rules questions.

Answering rules and procedural questions.

21D2. Correcting illegal moves observed.

Correcting any illegal moves observed, unless time pressure exists (11D1) or Variation 11H1 is used (the director does not correct illegal moves unless asked by a player).

21D3. Warning players.

Warning players about or penalizing players for disruptive, unethical, or unsportsmanlike behavior. **See also** 1C2, Director discretion; 13I, Refusal to obey rules; 21F, Player requests for rulings; and 21K, Use of director's power.

21D4. Settling disputes.

Settling disputes, including those regarding time forfeits and claims of draws.

21D5. Informing players.

Informing players about opponents' late arrivals or about opponents' leaving the room for an extended period.

21D6. Fees.

Collecting fees.

See also 1C2, Director discretion; 11I, Spectators; 11J, Deliberate illegal moves; 13C1, Only players may call flag; 14G2, Players apparently unaware of situation; 14J, Draw declared by director; 16Y, Assisting players with time management prohibited; 18G, Adjudications; 18G1, Example of emergency; 18G2, Director declares game over; 20E2, Unsolicited advice; 20M5, Spectators cannot make claims; 21F, Player requests for rulings; and 21K, Use of director's power.

21E. The playing director.

A tournament director must not only be absolutely objective, but must also be able to devote full attention to directing duties; for this reason, a director, on principle, should not direct and play in the same tournament. In US Chess National Events, the director cannot be a playing director.

However, in club events and others that do not involve substantial prizes, it is common practice for the director to play. A director may also serve as a house player (28M1). Those who choose this double role should be especially careful to maintain objectivity. If possible, a playing director should appoint another director to make rulings involving his or her own games.

A playing director who must devote time to a dispute in another game may stop his or her own clock during this period. While the clock is stopped, the director should not look at the position of his or her own game, but the director's opponent is permitted to do so. **See also** Rule 4, The Chief TD and Assistant TDs (Chapter 10).

21F. Player requests for rulings.

A player has the right to stop both clocks to ask the director to rule upon a point of law, procedure, or conduct. The director must first establish the facts without disturbing other games. Extended discussions between director and player(s) is inappropriate in the tournament room; a hallway or headquarters room is more desirable. **See also** 5I, Stopping the clock; 13C6, Claimant's clock; and 16Q, Interruption of game.

21F1. Timing of requests.

A player with a valid claim or complaint of any type should immediately stop both clocks (5I) and see a director. In most cases, the player who defers such a claim waives the right to make the claim. However, a delayed claim may still be in order if it is based on evidence not previously available, such as the testimony of a witness, or if the situation causing the claim remains in existence. **See also** 13C6, Claimant's clock and 16Q, Interruption of game.

21F2. Facts are agreed upon.

If the facts are agreed upon, the director should rule as follows:

a. If no penalty is prescribed by the rules and there is no occasion to exercise the director's discretionary power to penalize, the players should be directed to proceed with play.

b. If a case is clearly covered by a rule that specifies a penalty, the director should enforce that penalty. **See also** 1C2, Director discretion; 13I, Refusal to obey rules; and 21K, Use of director's power.

c. If an infraction has occurred for which no penalty is prescribed, the director's discretionary power to penalize may be exercised. **See also** 1C2, Director discretion; 1C2a, Standard penalty;13I, Refusal to obey rules; and 21K, Use of director's power.

21F3. Facts are not agreed upon.

If the facts are not agreed upon, the director should proceed as follows:

a. A director who is satisfied that the facts have been ascertained should rule accordingly.

b. A director who is unable to satisfactorily determine the facts must make a ruling that will permit play to continue.

See also 1C2, Director discretion; 11I, Spectators; 11J, Deliberate illegal moves; 13C1, Only players may call flag; 13I, Refusal to obey rules; 14G2, Players apparently unaware of situation; 14J, Draw declared by director; 16Y, Assisting players with time management prohibited; 18G2, Director declares game over; 20, Conduct of players and spectators; 20E2, Unsolicited advice; 20M5, Spectators cannot make claims; 21D, Intervening in games; 21F2, Facts are agreed upon; and 21K, Use of director's power

21G. Evidence.

Unbiased evidence is required to support any claim by a player that the opponent violated a rule.

21H. Appeals.

A director who believes that an appeal of a ruling on a point of fact or the exercise of a discretionary power to penalize might be in order should advise the player of the right to appeal.

21H1. How to appeal.

A player may appeal any ruling made by the chief director or an assistant director, provided that the appeal is made within one-half hour and before the player resumes play, unless additional time is granted by the director. The director may require that the appeal be made in writing. The appeals committee may penalize frivolous appeals. **See also** 21I7, Groundless appeals.

21H2. Director may reserve decision.

The director may reserve a decision temporarily and direct that play continues before the appeal is heard. In this case, the appellant must continue play *under protest*, that is, without prejudice to the appeal, regardless of the outcome of further play. If the appellant wins that game, the appeal will be considered moot.

21H3. Response of chief director.

A chief tournament director who believes that the appeal is justified may reverse or modify any decision made by the chief tournament director or another director. A chief director, who believes that the appeal has some merit, but not enough to be upheld, should advise the appellant of the right to pursue the appeal further.

21H4. Appointment of committee or referee.

If a player notifies the director of intent to pursue the appeal further, the director shall appoint a committee (21I) or a special referee (21J) to hear the appeal, unless the orderly progress of the tournament would be disturbed by such action. If the director determines that either appointment would be disruptive, the player may reserve the right to share in the prize fund by requesting to be paired for future rounds as if the appeal were upheld. The player has the same right in the case of intending to appeal a local decision to US Chess.

21I. Appeals committee.

21I1. Composition.

An appeals committee should consist of at least three persons, preferably US Chess-certified tournament directors. A committee of two is sufficient if both are certified at the senior director level or higher. Every attempt should be made to appoint individuals to the appeals committee who have tournament director's certification level equal to or higher than that of the chief tournament director of the tournament. To ensure impartiality a special referee (21J) is preferred over an appeals committee.

21I2. Procedure.

When a committee hears an appeal, all persons except committee members, the director, and both players shall be excluded from the hearing. Witnesses may be called, but only to answer questions from the parties concerned, after which they will be dismissed. The director shall furnish the committee with the current edition of the *Official Rules of Chess* and shall call attention to the rules applicable to the dispute.

21I3. Witnesses.

The committee shall elicit the testimony of witnesses as it sees fit. In hearing the appeal, the committee must give preeminent weight to the director's testimony as to anything said or done in his or her presence.

21I4. Consultation.

The committee may consult a special referee (21J) by phone for advice, or may vote to refer the dispute to a special referee.

21I5. Function of committee (standard of review).

The function of an appeals committee is not to substitute its judgment for that of the director, but rather to overrule the director only if it is clear the latter's ruling is incorrect. The committee should not overrule a proper decision simply because it prefers an alternate proper decision.

21I6. Decision.

After hearing the testimony, the committee members shall deliberate among themselves to reach a decision, which shall be put in writing, signed by all the members (even if one or more members voted against the decision), and given to the chief director. In the event of a tie vote, the director's decision shall stand.

21I7. Groundless appeals.

If the committee finds that the appeal is clearly groundless, it may penalize the player for that reason, or leave the penalty to the director's discretion. In ruling on an appeal, the committee may exercise all powers accorded to the chief director by the rules and other US Chess procedures.

21J The Special Referee

A special referee is a director with substantial experience who is available to provide advice or make a ruling by telephone. Phone numbers of special referees can be found currently on the US Chess web page using the TD/Affiliate page and are also occasionally printed in *Chess Life*. To ensure impartiality a special referee is preferred over an appeals committee (21I).

21J1. Usage.

The director may refer any appeal to a special referee, but should keep in mind that unless the facts are agreed upon, or the players' differences easily summarized, substantial delay and phone cost may result. Use of a special referee is most appropriate when the tournament director is certified at a lower level than the referee, and when a director of comparable certification to the referee is not immediately available to serve on an appeals committee.

21J2. Selection.

When selecting the referee to call, and the alternates to call if the original selection cannot be promptly reached, the director should be sensitive to any reasonable objection by either player against the use of a particular referee.

21J3. The phone call.

When placing any call to the referee, the director should invite both players to be present. The director should not inform the referee of the players' names, but refer to them as *White* and *Black*.

21J4. Player contact with referee.

Neither player has an automatic right to speak to the referee. A director who finds such discussion unnecessary may choose not to allow it. It is desirable that both players know in advance what the director will say and agree that it will correctly reflect their viewpoints.

21J5. Validity of referee's decision.

The decision of a special referee carries weight equal to that of an appeals committee. No decision of a special referee may be appealed to an appeals committee, nor may any decision of an appeals committee be appealed to a special referee. However, a special referee who believes the dispute can best be settled on-site may refer it to an appeals committee, which then should be appointed.

21K. Use of director's power.

21K1. Conciliation.

The director should make every effort to resolve a dispute by informal, conciliatory means before resorting to the exercise of the director's formal discretionary power to penalize. **See also** 1C2, Director discretion and 13I, Refusal to obey rules.

21K2. Beware abuse of power.

Tournament directors should realize that the powers given to them under these rules should be used sparingly, to restore equity or to penalize a serious infraction so as to discourage its recurrence. No one's interests are served by what appears to be the arbitrary or high-handed exercise of authority. **See also** 1C2, Director discretion and 13I, Refusal to obey rules.

21L. Appeal to US Chess.

Any decision of an appeals committee or special referee, or of the director when an appeals committee or special referee is not appointed, may be appealed to US Chess. **See also** 24B, Appeals to US Chess.

21L1. Procedure.

Appeals in writing must be postmarked within seven days of the end of the tournament to the US Chess office. Appeals submitted after the seven-day deadline may be considered at the discretion of the committee hearing the appeal. Appeals may be submitted via e-mail, but the business office or the committee(s) hearing the appeal may require a signed statement. The office will refer an appeal to the appropriate committee(s) but may immediately reject obviously groundless appeals. Most appeals will be referred to the Rules Committee, but some appeals may be more appropriate for the Tournament Director Certification Committee or the Ethics Committee. A good-faith deposit must be included with the appeal. The executive director shall from time to time review and set the required deposit amount in consultation with those committees that handle appeals. The deposit will be returned unless the ruling authority finds the appeal to be groundless and rules that the deposit is to be forfeited. US Chess reserves the right to make final decisions concerning the rules and procedures that govern its competitions. **See also** 24A, Rules Committee; and 24B, Appeals to US Chess.

TD TIP: In rare cases a committee(s) ruling is appealed to the US Chess Executive Board. Even more rare would be an appeal of any US Chess Executive Board decision directly to the US Chess Delegates at the annual delegates convention. In order for an appeal to be considered by the delegates many exact rules and regulations must be followed. Contacting an experienced delegate would be advisable if an appeal to the delegates at the convention is to be pursued.

22. Unplayed Games

22A. Games forfeited due to nonappearance.
A player who does not appear for the game, or appears too late, is given zero points and the opponent is given one point. On pairing sheets (28J) and wall charts (28O), the forfeit is circled or indicated by an *F*. Computer wall charts may use the symbol *X* for the winner and *F* for the loser of an unplayed game. **See also** 13D, Late arrival for game; 13F, Late arrival by both players; and 28P, Unplayed games.

22B. Full-point byes.
If there is an odd number of players for a round, and a suitable house player (28M1) not in the event cannot be found to fill in, one player will receive a full-point (1) bye. **See also** 27A3, Upper half vs. lower half; 28A, Pairing cards or program; 28J, The first round; 28K, Late entrants; 28L, Full-point byes; 28L4, Full-point byes after half-point byes; 28L5, New players in four-round event; 28M, Alternative to byes; 28S, Reentries; and 29C1, Upper half vs. lower half.

22C. Half-point byes.
For the convenience of players, the director may allow half-point (0.5 or ½) byes for missed rounds. **See also** 27A3, Upper half vs. lower half; 28A, Pairing cards or program; 28J, The first round; 28K, Late entrants; 28L, Full-point byes; 28L4, Full-point byes after half-point byes; 28L5, New players in four-round event; 28L, Full point byes; 28M, Alternative to byes; 28S, Reentries; and 29C1, Upper half vs. lower half.

TD TIP: It is useful to have a bye signup sheet available until the announced cut off time for requesting byes ends. Directors are urged to check this list before making any pairings.

22C1. Availability.
Half-point byes may be offered during the first half of a tournament or the middle round of a tournament with an odd number of rounds, with or without advance notice. If pre-tournament publicity does not address this subject, players may contact the organizer to inquire about availability.

If half-point byes are allowed for any rounds during the second half of a tournament, they should be mentioned in pre-tournament publicity. An exception may be made in the event of emergency.

22C2. Deadline for bye requests.

All requests for half-point byes should be made at least an hour before the bye round unless the director requires otherwise.

22C3. Byes and class prizes.

It is recommended that if class prizes are likely to be won with even or minus scores, half-point byes should be unavailable or limited to one per player in such classes.

22C4. Irrevocable byes.

If half-point byes are allowed for the final round, players must give irrevocable notice of such byes before beginning their first game, or if the organizer so announces, their second game. The deadline for claiming such byes should appear in pre-tournament publicity. It is recommended that other byes in the second half of the tournament be treated similarly and that notice of all scheduled irrevocable byes be posted on or near the wall charts (28O).

TD TIP: It is useful for directors to note on bye signup sheets the latest time players can request last round byes. Directors concerned about awarding unearned prize money need to be very careful in allowing players to sign up for half-point byes in the last half of the tournament, especially the last round; therefore, it is common that those bye requests be made well in advance of the start of the second half of the event, especially for the last round.

22C5. Cancellation of irrevocable byes.

If the director agrees, a player may cancel an irrevocable half-point bye under the condition that if the player wins, the result will be treated as a draw for prize purposes.

22C6. Full-point byes after half-point byes.

A full-point bye should not be assigned to a player who has previously taken or committed to a half-point bye unless all others in the score group have already had a bye or a no-show forfeit win. **See also** 28L, Full-point byes.

TD TIP: If a director is using a pairings program then it is wise to check the pairings after they have been made to ensure that Rule 22C6 has been applied properly, especially in the case where a player has requested a bye in a future round.

23. Organization and Membership

23A. Responsibilities of organizer.
Tournaments rated by US Chess must be organized by a US Chess affiliate or by US Chess itself. This organizer is responsible for all financial matters related to the tournament and may select an individual or a committee to handle the physical and financial arrangements. These include finding a playing site, setting a date and the times of the rounds, determining the entry fees and prizes, hiring tournament directors, and advertising the event.

The organizing affiliate must select a chief tournament director (also referred to as *director*, *TD*, or *arbiter*) whose US Chess certification level is appropriate for the type of tournament anticipated. The tournament director is responsible for all decisions in the tournament regarding rules.

23A1. Obligation to pay guaranteed prizes.
An affiliate that guarantees prize money but fails to pay it in full may have its US Chess affiliation revoked, and the individual(s) responsible for that affiliate may be denied the right to affiliate under a different name. **See also** 32, Prizes.

If extraordinary circumstances such as extreme weather conditions or civil unrest prevent most potential entrants from playing in a tournament, the organizer may appeal to the US Chess executive director for permission to limit the prizes to 100 percent of entry fees collected.

23A2. Tournament cancellations.
Tournaments announced in *Chess Life* may be canceled only if one of the following conditions exists:

a.   A timely cancellation notice appears in an appropriate issue of *Chess Life*.

b.   Physical conditions, such as closure of site or extremely inclement weather, render the site unusable.

A disappointing number of advance entries is never a valid reason for cancellation. Organizers who cancel a tournament in a non-emergency situation without proper notice will be prohibited from announcing tournaments in *Tournament Life* or elsewhere in *Chess Life* for three years. (Additional penalties are also possible.)

23A3. Advance entry refunds.
Unless otherwise stated in all advance publicity, advance entry fees are refundable to players who give notice of withdrawal before the close of registration for round one.

23A4. No refunds once event starts.

A player who begins play in the first round is not entitled to a refund of the entry fee or any portion of it, even if forced to miss most games due to a medical or other emergency. Variations of this policy are at the discretion of the organizer.

23B. Determination of game times.

The organizer determines game times unless the director makes or accepts other arrangements. **See also** Rule 17, Scheduling.

23C. US Chess membership requirement.

For the inclusive dates of the tournament, each player must be a member in good standing of US Chess, unless US Chess regulations waive this requirement.

TD TIP: This is a tricky task. Often players at registration say they have joined US Chess via various methods that do not produce a receipt such as paying recently by check or credit card (on the phone or web). Sometimes they have a receipt from an organizer or another TD that is unfamiliar to the person processing the registration. Some directors decide on a case-by-case basis whether or not they are convinced of the validity of the renewal.

TD TIP: Some directors strictly enforce Rule 23C by making all players pay a US Chess membership fee if the player's membership cannot be verified with a membership card, in a hard copy or disk rating supplement, or online at the US Chess website. This last approach may upset some players who have recently renewed but cannot verify the renewal; however, the funds collected at registration for those US Chess memberships extend those memberships for an extra year.

TD TIP: Another approach would be for the director to collect a membership fee from players whose memberships are not verifiable and hold onto those funds in escrow until US Chess rates the tournament. If at that point the director is notified by US Chess that those players are not members, then the director can pass along the membership fees being held in escrow directly on to US Chess. A copy of the US Chess non-member notice can be passed along to the players with their membership receipts. All other escrow US Chess membership fees should then be returned to the players that US Chess did not identify to the director as non-members.

24. Interpretation of the Rules

24A. Rules Committee.
US Chess maintains a standing Rules Committee to review questions pertaining to the rules of play. In case of doubt as to the application or interpretation of these rules, the US Chess Rules Committee will examine the case in point and render an official decision.

24B. Appeals to US Chess.
All proper appeals made to the US Chess National Office shall be referred to the appropriate committee(s), which in most cases is the Rules Committee. Occasionally appeals are more appropriate for other committees. A copy of any appeal considered by the committee shall first be furnished to the chief tournament director plus any other appropriate director(s) of the tournament involved, who should respond with a written statement of his or her own position and any other pertinent documentation. Failure to respond may result in disciplinary action. A copy of the decision(s) of the committee(s) shall be sent to all interested parties. **See also** 21L, Appeal to US Chess; 21L1, Procedure; and Certification Restrictions (48, Restrictions; 49, Due Process; 50, Penalties; 51, Appeals; and 54, Professional Misconduct).

CHAPTER TWO

The
OFFICIAL RULES
OF CHESS
TOURNAMENT
SECTION

25. Introduction

A player entering a competition has a right and an obligation to know the rules and conditions. What follows, therefore, is an exposition of U.S. tournament procedures as they are now practiced. The most significant features of a tournament should be noted in the advance publicity and posted prominently at the tournament site. These include round times, speed of play, major pairing variations, prizes, and tiebreak procedures. Players should understand, however, that last-minute circumstances can sometimes force revisions of earlier plans, though conscientious organizers and directors do all they can to avoid changes in announced conditions for competition.

The most common types of US Chess-rated tournaments are the Swiss system and the round robin. Rules for their conduct are discussed below.

26. Variations and Exceptions

26A. Notification.
Any variations from these published standards, including variations discussed in this rulebook, should be posted and/or announced at the tournament prior to their use, preferably before the first round.

26B. Major variations.
A variation sufficiently major that it might reasonably be expected to deter some players from entering should be mentioned in any *Chess Life* announcement and all other detailed pre-tournament publicity and posted and/or announced at the tournament.

27. The Swiss System tournament

The Swiss system can accommodate a large number of players in a relatively short time and has therefore become widespread. Although not as accurate as the completed round robin in determining a winner, the ratings-controlled Swiss is more precise than earlier versions. Since its methods are complex, novice directors should learn them by working with an experienced director.

A Swiss tournament should ideally have a number of rounds adequate to reduce the number of players with perfect scores to one. This result can be guaranteed by limiting entries to a number no greater than two raised to the power of the number of rounds ($2^{number\ of\ rounds}$ = ideal number of players that produce a single winner). For example, a three-round Swiss will produce no more than one perfect score for up to eight players ($2^3=2\times2\times2=8$), a four-round Swiss can handle up to sixteen players ($2^4=2\times2\times2\times2=16$), a five-round up to thirty-two players ($2^5=2\times2\times2\times2\times2=32$). **See also** 28R, Accelerated pairings in the first two rounds.

In practice, however, these numbers are only guides due to the unpredictable number of draws. A properly paired Swiss system usually produces no more than one perfect score from at least double the theoretical number of players. It cannot, however, guarantee a clear winner, nor can it assure that competitors for the same awards will face opposition of similar strength.

It is both a weakness and strength of the Swiss system that slow starters will tend to have faced weaker fields than players who do well in the early rounds but finish with the same end result. While this situation has an element of inequity, it tends to keep more players in the running for a longer time, making Swiss tournaments competitive and exciting.

27A. Basic Swiss system rules.

The following rules are listed in order of priority from 27A1 for the highest priority to 27A5 for the lowest. If it is not possible to adhere to all rules in making pairings, the director should generally follow the rule with the higher priority. However, there are cases in which 27A4, Equalizing colors, or 27A5, Alternating colors, have priority over 27A3, Upper half vs. lower half, (see 29E5, Colors vs. ratings) and even a variation in which 27A4, Equalizing colors, can have priority over 27A2, Equal scores (see 29E5f, Colors in a series; 29E5f1, Last round exception; and 29E5h, Priority of equalization over ratings).

27A1. Avoid players meeting twice (highest priority).

A player may not play the same opponent more than once in a tournament. Even this most basic of all pairing rules must be violated when the number of rounds is greater than or equal to the number of players. If it is necessary for players to play each other twice, then top priority should subsequently be given to having them face each other no more than twice. If two players were paired against each other earlier in the tournament, but the game was forfeited due to the nonappearance of one, they may be paired against each other again.

27A2. Equal scores.

Players with equal scores are paired whenever possible. Note that if accelerated pairings (28R) are used, pairings for round two disregard this rule. For exceptions to the priority of this rule see 29E5f, Colors in a series; 29E5f1, Last round exception; 29E5h, Priority of equalization over ratings; and 28S1, Reentry playing opponent twice.

27A3. Upper half vs. lower half.

Within a score group, i.e., all players who have the same score, the upper half by ranking (28A) is paired against the lower half. **See also** 28J, The first round; 29C1, Upper half vs. lower half; and 29E2, First-round colors. For exceptions to the priority of this rule see 29E5, Colors vs. ratings.

27A4. Equalizing colors.

Players receive each color the same number of times, whenever practical, and are not assigned the same color more than twice in a row. In odd-numbered rounds, the objective is to limit the excess of one color over the other to one. **See also** 29E, Color allocation; 29G, First round colors; 29E3, Due colors in succeeding rounds; 29E4, Equalization, alternation, and priority of color. For exceptions to the priority of this rule see 29E5, Colors vs. ratings; 29E5f, Colors in a series; 29E5f1, Last round exception; and 29E5h, Priority of equalization over ratings.

27A5. Alternating colors.

Players receive alternating colors whenever practical. **See also** 29E, Color allocation; 29E3, Due colors in succeeding rounds; 29E4, Equalization, alternation, and priority of color. For exceptions to the priority of this rule see 29E5, Colors vs. ratings; 29E5f, Colors in a series; 29E5f1, Last round exception; and 29E5h, Priority of equalization over ratings.

28. Swiss System Pairings, Procedures

28A. Pairing cards or program.

Before the first round, the tournament director prepares a pairing card (Figure 2) for each player, or uses a computer program to enter each player. The player's name, rating, and US Chess ID number are written on the card or entered into the program. For scholastic tournaments, the school or team is also included. Directors who want states or cities on their wall charts add this information as well. **See also** 28C, Ratings of players.

TD TIP: To verify a player's ID number and rating you can check the US Chess rating list (imported to the hard drive) and the Internet at www.uschess.org. To save a lot of time at registration, check the manuals for the pairings programs to see if they can directly import player information from the data downloaded to a hard drive from the US Chess rating list or the US Chess web site. Contact US Chess for more information.

TD TIP: At scholastic events, pairing by hand or with a pairing program, it is useful to give each school team and each of the team members the same school code. This will prove helpful in both preventing team members from being accidentally paired against each other (28N2) and producing team reports. Team codes can be recorded on the pairing cards or in a manner indicated by the pairing software.

If cards are used, they are placed in order of rank, from the highest rated to the lowest. Unrated players and players with the same rating are ranked in random order, with the unrated players being placed at the bottom of the group. The director then numbers the cards, giving the highest-rated player number 1, the second highest number 2, and so on until all the cards are numbered. That number is the player's *pairing number*, which will be used throughout the tournament.

Some directors prefer to assign an arbitrary rating of 1200 or 1300, for pairing purposes only, to all unrated players. Such assignments usually place them at or near the bottom, causing pairings similar to those that would result if they were paired as unrated. One major difference is that in a score group with an odd number of players the lowest rated player drops, but not an unrated player. An unrated player who is scoring well in the tournament would often be the highest-rated player in the score group if all games played up to that point had already been rated.

TD TIP: When assigning a rating to any player (including unrateds) for pairing purposes, directors should make sure they use the pairing numbers, and not the ratings of players, when prioritizing the basic Swiss System rules. Most pairings programs have a separate entry field to perform this task. Consult your pairings program manual to find out more information on how to handle director-assigned player ratings.

The pairing cards are used to prepare the wall chart (28O) and to pair each round. Computer programs also do both, as well as the sorting and numbering described above, all automatically. (See **Figure 5** on the next page)

PAIRING NO. _____ RATING _____

Round No.	COLOR		Opponent No.	Circle if unplayed SCORE		TIE BREAK	
	W	B		GAME	TOTAL	A	B
1							
2							
3							
4							
5							
6							
7							
8							

NAME _____

ADDRESS _____

_____

USCF ID No. _____ EXP. DATE _____

OTHER _____

ENTRY FEES $_____ OTHER FEES $ _____

USCF DUES $ _____ OTHER DUES $ _____ TOTAL $ _____

PRIZE: Place _____ AMOUNT $ _____

Figure 5

88

28B. Numbering late entrants.

Players who enter after pairing numbers have been assigned are issued the next available unassigned pairing numbers. These numbers should be accompanied by a symbol such as an asterisk to serve as a reminder that rating and not pairing number should be considered when ordering them in their score groups.

Some directors assign an intermediary pairing number such as 12A for a player rated below player 12 but above player 13. Directors need to take care to ensure that this will not cause problems or confusion with the wall chart. The intermediary numbers may not be used in the ratings report sent to US Chess; therefore, directors must renumber each of the players assigned an intermediary pairing number on the wall chart, remembering to also cross reference this new pairing number with all their opponents' pairings information (see illustration). **See also** 28K, Late entrants.

A director using a computer program is able to automatically insert the late entrants in their proper places with other player numbers being appropriately and automatically revised.

Other useful information such as address, fees paid, membership expiration date, etc., may also be recorded on the pairing card or in data fields in pairing programs. US Chess sells standardized pairing cards as well as pairing programs for Swiss system tournaments.

28C. Ratings of players.

The rating entered on a player's card is the last-published US Chess rating in the rating list specified in the *Tournament Life* section of *Chess Life*, unless use of a different rating list was specified in the advance publicity for the tournament, or the director has assigned a player a rating. Note that an assigned rating (28E) used for a tournament may or may not be used for future tournaments. **See also** the first *TD TIP* for 28A.

TD TIP: Players sometimes show the director a US Chess crosstable, or their rating from the US Chess web page. It is common practice to allow players to use those ratings if those ratings are higher than their last published rating (28E1).

28C1. Multiple US Chess ratings.

If a player is mistakenly assigned more than one US Chess rating, the director should try to combine these ratings. Two examples:

    a. If the ratings are 1900/5 (1900 based on 5 games) and 1700/4 (1700 based on 4 games), the rating used should be 1811, calculated as follows: $1900 \times 5 = 9500$, $1700 \times 4 = 6800$, $9500 + 6800 = 16300$, $16300/9 = 1811$.

b. If a player with an old established rating of 1900 is erroneously started over as 1700/5 (1700 based on 5 games), the rating used should be that of a 1900 player who draws 5 games vs. 1700 player, or 1860. See the chapter on The US Chess Rating System.

28C2. Foreign or FIDE ratings.

A foreign or formerly foreign player with a foreign or FIDE rating or category is required to disclose such a rating or category when entering a tournament, if any of the following circumstances exist:

a. The player lacks an established US Chess rating.

b. The player's US Chess rating has not been published during the past two years.

c. The director requests this information.

If a player fails to disclose such a rating as required and plays in the tournament, the director may withhold any rating-based prize or unrated prize the player may win. Directors have the right not to accept entries from players who fail to disclose rating information.

TD TIP: Often a director can find a player's FIDE rating by checking a recent or old Informant *or the official FIDE web site.*

28D. Players without US Chess ratings.

Players without official US Chess ratings are eligible only for place (or top non-class) prizes and prizes for unrated players unless alternate procedures are used to assign ratings (28E), such as the following recommendations:

28D1. Non-US Chess ratings verified.

Players who are known to have ratings or categories of other types, such as foreign, FIDE, regional, or US Chess Quick (or if a Quick tournament, US Chess regular), which can be verified.

It is recommended that such players not be considered unrated and that their ratings be used, adjusted if necessary to be consistent with the US Chess rating scale. If a player has more than one non-US Chess rating, the highest should be used.

Currently, the following adjustments are believed to be roughly appropriate. Changes are likely in the future and will be announced in US Chess rating supplements.

a. Bermuda, Jamaica, Canada, and US Chess Quick (or US Chess regular at Quick tournament): No adjustment needed.

b. Quebec (FQE): Add 100 points.

c. FIDE: The following three formulas are provided for guidance:

(1) US Chess = FIDE + 50
(2) US Chess = 0.895 (FIDE) + 367
(3) US Chess = FIDE + 100

Formula (1) represents an average conversion. This means that 50 percent of the time the FIDE-rated player will be stronger than his or her converted US Chess rating would indicate. This becomes important for prize considerations when the FIDE rating is in the low 2100s; i.e., FIDE players between 2100 and 2149 will remain in the US Chess Expert class after their ratings are converted with this formula. By using formula (2), the FIDE-rated player will be stronger than his or her converted US Chess rating only 10 percent of the time, thus providing a degree of protection for the players with established US Chess ratings. Formula (3) provides a great degree of protection for players with established US Chess ratings without compromising the integrity of the FIDE player's strength compared to their new converted US Chess estimate rating. The above is for players with FIDE ratings but no US Chess ratings.

d. England: Multiply the 3-digit rating by 8 and add 700.
e. Germany (Ingo System): Multiply by 8, and subtract answer from 2940. Lower Ingo numbers reflect greater strength.
f. Most nations not named: Add 200 points.
g. Ratings or categories of the former Soviet Union or of the Philippines: Add 250 points. If a category, use the midpoint—for instance, a Russian Candidate Master should be 2100 + 250 or 2350.
h. Brazil, Peru, Colombia, or possibly other nations' ratings: These have proved highly unreliable. Players from these countries should not be considered eligible for prizes for classes below 2200 based on such ratings.

28D2. Non-US Chess ratings claimed without verification.
Players who state they have a rating, as listed in 28D1, which cannot be verified.

Directors may assign ratings (28E), but they should not be under 2200 if this would make the player eligible for a class prize.

28D3. US Chess label or printout ratings.
Players who have unofficial initial US Chess ratings on labels or printouts that have not yet appeared in a rating supplement, and who are believed to have no foreign ratings or categories.

Directors are encouraged to use such ratings without adjustment. Players with fewer than four career games, though, are unrated.

28D4. Director-calculated ratings.
Players who have played in one or more US Chess-rated events from which their approximate strength may be calculated but do not yet have even unofficial ratings, and who are believed to have no foreign ratings or categories.

Directors may calculate and use such ratings, but if their calculation puts the player within 100 points of a higher prize category, the assignment (28E) should be raised to put the player in the higher category. Players with fewer than four career games are unrated.

28D5. Assignments based on nonrated activity.
Players lacking known results in US Chess-rated tournaments and believed to have no foreign ratings or categories, but whose strength may reasonably be approximated from other play, such as nonrated club activity, tournaments, or speed games.

Directors may assign ratings (28E), but they should not be under 2200 if this would make the player eligible for a class prize.

28D6. No information on player available.
There are players with no known results, ratings, or categories of any kind.

These players are unrated and should be indicated by *NEW* on the pairing and wall chart. They should not be assigned ratings for prize purposes. If assignments are used for pairing purposes, these should not appear on the wall chart.

28D7. Improperly assigned ratings.
If a director assigns a player rating (28E) that is in violation of any part of 28D, and this is pointed out before prizes are awarded, that player shall not be eligible for prizes based on the assigned rating.

28E. Assigned ratings for rated players.
The director may assign a rating to any rated player.

28E1. Rating level.
The assigned rating shall not be lower than the player's last published US Chess rating, or its foreign or FIDE equivalent, adjusted if necessary, if the player lacks a US Chess rating.

28E2. Cause for assignment.
A rating may be assigned only for reasonable cause, including, but not limited to, the following:

a. The player has shown significant superiority to those in a particular class.

b. The player has demonstrated a tendency to achieve much better results when significant prizes are at stake than when they are not.

c. The player's rating has recently dropped into a lower class due to results that are statistically highly unlikely.

d. The player's moves, time management, statements, or other actions during play in a previous tournament have caused the director to conclude that the player did not make a reasonable effort to avoid losing games.

28E3. Notification.
The director should notify a player assigned a rating, in advance of the tournament if possible, so the player will have this information when deciding whether or not to enter. However, such notification is not always possible, since the cause for assignment may not be evident to the director until the late-registration period, or even during the tournament.

28F. Validity of wall-chart ratings.
A properly assigned rating that appears on the wall chart without disclaimer is valid for both prizes and pairing purposes unless it is erroneous and a correction appears on a subsequent wall chart.

Directors who wish to use an assigned rating (28E) for pairing purposes but not prize eligibility should include a disclaimer on or near the wall chart next to the player's rating to explain that the rating is not valid for prize purposes.

28G. Old ratings.
Old ratings of inactive players are still valid. If an old rating cannot be located or confirmed from memory by a reliable person, the director should allow the player to receive a class prize only after confirmation of the old rating.

28H. Revising ratings after tournament begins.
The director for reasonable cause may revise the rating of any player at any time. If this results in a player being ineligible for the section he or she is playing in, the following procedures, 28H1-28H3, shall apply:

28H1. Removal.
The player shall be removed from that section.

28H2. Reassignment.
The director may offer the player the opportunity to continue in the tournament in an appropriate section, with half-point byes for games missed.

28H3. Entry fee refund.

a. If the erroneous rating assignment is due to false, misleading or incomplete information provided by the player, including failure of the player to disclose a rating, the director is not required to refund the entry fee.

b. If the erroneous rating assignment is primarily a mistake by the director or tournament staff, the entry fee should be refunded. If the player is given the option of continuing in a higher section, it is still appropriate to refund all or part of the fee if the player has missed sufficient rounds to substantially reduce prize chances.

28I. Opponents of expelled players.

If a player is removed from an event or section because of being made ineligible by a corrected rating (28H), the following adjustments shall be made to that player's opponents:

28I1. Expulsion before last round of tournament is paired.

Use the same procedure outlined in Rule 28I2.

28I2. Expulsion after last round of tournament is paired.

Earlier opponents of the expelled player shall have their results adjusted for tournament scoring purposes (**See also** 28I3) as follows:

a. A player who lost to the expelled player shall instead receive a half-point bye.

b. A player who drew the expelled player shall instead receive a win by forfeit.

28I3. Extra rated games

The actual results of each opponent vs. the expelled player shall be transferred to an "extra rated games" chart for US Chess rating purposes (28M4).

28J. The first round.

The director (or computer) flips a coin to decide who will play white on the first board, the higher- or lower-rated player. After ordering all the players by rating, the director divides the cards into two equal sized groups, pairing the highest player in the upper half against the highest player in the lower half, the second-highest in the upper half against the second-highest in the lower half, etc. Pairing programs do this automatically. **See also** 22B, Full-point byes; 22C, Half-point byes; 27A3, Upper half vs. lower half; 28A, Pairing cards or program; 28K, Late entrants; 28L, Full-point byes; 28M, Alternative to byes; 28S, Reentries; 29C1, Upper half vs. lower half; 29D, The odd player; 29E2, First round colors..

TD TIP: *Directors often number the cards once they are in rating order. They then proceed to remove all requested byes; if there is, at that point, an odd number of players, the card for the lowest rated player, who will be assigned a bye, is removed. The cards are then divided into halves as described above.*

Colors are alternated down through each half. If the coin toss determined that the higher-rated player on board one would receive white, the higher-rated on board two receives black, and so on. If there is an odd number of players, the lowest-rated player, but not an unrated player, receives a one-point bye. **See also** 22B, Full-point byes; 28L, Full-point byes; and 28M, Alternative to byes.

TD TIP: *When using a pairing program make sure that it is set up not to give a bye to an unrated player or to players that have requested a bye in a future round.*

The boards are numbered in the playing hall and the individual or team pairings are posted on pairings sheets (See **Figure 6**, below), which indicate each player's or team's opponent, board number, and color. It is customary to assign the highest-rated player or team in the top score group to board one, the second-highest in that group to board two, etc. The director may modify the pairings somewhat, especially in the early rounds, in order to avoid pairing family members, close friends, or members of the same club against one another.

TD TIP: *Consult the pairing software manual for information on how to set up the program to avoid unwanted pairings and for information on producing an alphabetical list of players, their opponents, their board numbers, and their colors. Many players find an alphabetical list more convenient than a board-by-board pairing list.*

TD TIP: *It is useful to post more than one set of pairings in large events; however, to prevent confusion regarding where game results are to be posted, remove all sets of extra pairings about 15 minutes into the round.*

Pairings for Round 5				
Bd	Result	White	Result	Black
1		Enpassant, Edwin		Attack, Allen
2		Bishop Barbara		Files, Fred
3		Goodplayer, Gordon		Chesser, Curtis
4	.5	Defender, Donald	.5	Helpmate, Harry

Figure 6

28K. Late entrants.

The director may accept and pair entrants after the announced closing time for registration, but late entrants shall forfeit any round missed if it is inconvenient or too late to pair the players for play, or may take a half-point bye (22C) if the tournament offers them for that round. **See also** 28B, Numbering late entrants and 28S, Reentries.

28L. Full-point byes.

28L1. Explanation and display.

In any round in which the total number of players in a tournament or section of a tournament is uneven, one player is given a full-point bye. The player's score is posted as a win on the wall chart but circled to indicate that the game was not played. Wall charts generated by computer may print *bye*, or circle the score. **See also** 22B, Full-point byes and 28M, Alternatives to byes.

28L2. Determination.

In the first round, the bye is given to the player with the lowest US Chess rating but not to an unrated player or a late entrant. In subsequent rounds, it is given to the lowest-rated player in the lowest score group but not to an unrated player. If there are no rated players eligible for the bye in the lowest score group, it is given to an unrated player who has played in a US Chess-rated tournament too recently to obtain a published rating. If this, too, is impossible, a new player may be assigned the bye. New players should be indicated by *NEW* on the pairing card and wall chart. **See also** 28J, The first round; 28S, Reentries; and 28L4, Full-point byes after half-point byes.

Variation (unannounced) 28L2a. Giving the bye to a higher rated player.

Give the bye to a higher rated player if doing so improves the overall color allocation for the lowest score group, subject to the limits specified in rules 29E5a and 29E5b. **See also 29E5a, The 80-point rule**; and **29E5b, The 200-point rule.**

28L3. Players ineligible for full-point byes.

A player must not be given a full-point bye more than once, nor should one be awarded to a player who has won an unplayed game due to the opponent's failure to appear.

TD TIP: Not all pairing software takes care of this task automatically; therefore, directors should check the software manual to determine the correct setting(s) to ensure that 28L3 is in force. Directors may also check software pairings each round to ensure that 28L3, as well as all other pairing rules, are being enforced.

28L4. Full-point byes after half-point byes.

A full-point bye should not be awarded to a player who has previously taken or committed to a half-point bye unless all others in the score group have already had a bye or a no-show forfeit win. **See also** 22C, Half-point byes.

TD TIP: Not all pairing software takes care of this task automatically; therefore, directors should check the software manual to determine the correct setting(s) to ensure that 28L3 and 28L4 are enforced. Directors may also check computer pairings each round to ensure that 28L3 and 28L4, as well as all other pairing rules, are being enforced.

28L5. New players in four-round events.

Directors should try to ensure that new players play at least four games in their first tournament in order to obtain official ratings. In a four-round event, if only new players are available for byes in the bottom score group, the bye may be given to a player one score group above. This should not be done if the player receiving the bye has a substantial chance for a prize. It is preferable to use 28M, Alternatives to byes, than to assign a bye to a new player. **See also** 22C, Half-point byes.

28M. Alternatives to byes.

Awarding byes may be necessary for the smooth progress of a tournament, but they deprive a player of an expected game. To avoid this, several methods have been used successfully. Directors are encouraged to provide games for players who do not want byes. These methods may be combined. **See also** 22B, Full-point byes; 22C, Half-point byes; 27A3, Upper half vs. lower half; 28A, Pairing cards or program; 28J, The first round; 28K, Late entrants; 28L, Full-point byes; 28S, Reentries; and 29C1, Upper half vs. lower half.

28M1. The house player.

Sometimes a spectator will agree to play a game against a player who would otherwise expect a bye. It is desirable that this spectator has a rating approximately within the range of the lowest score group, but this is not required. The player is voluntarily giving up a free point to play, so no one can legitimately claim the opponent is too weak.

Sometimes the player would rather play an unusually strong opponent than receive a bye. This also is acceptable, but if the strong opponent is rated too high for the section, the director may consider retaining the original bye and listing both players for a rated game in a higher section or an *extra rated games* section. **See also** 28M4, Extra rated games.

TD TIP: Directors have found it useful to first ask the player receiving the bye if they would like to keep the bye or play a house player. Some players prefer to take the bye to rest for the next round or ensure that they will not be assigned a bye in future rounds. Directors and organizers who require the odd player to essay a game against a house player, rather than give the player the choice, would be wise to announce this policy in pre-tournament publicity and at the site. A popular alternative, described below, is to use a permanent house player, not eligible for prizes, who is paired normally, not necessarily against the odd player who would have received the bye.

If a permanent house player is available, this is the best solution. Such a player is paired normally whenever there is an odd number, not paired when there is an even number, and may even receive half-point byes if the tournament allows them.

TD TIP: Directors using pairing software find it best to award the permanent house player byes for all rounds and then remove those byes if the house player is needed. This technique prevents the pairing program from automatically pairing the house player, leaving the decision in the hands of the director round by round.

It is not required that a house player be paired against the player who would otherwise receive the bye. Sometimes it is more appropriate to insert a relatively strong house player into a higher score group. In this case, neither the player paired against the house player nor the one who otherwise would have received the bye has the right to refuse to play.

A US Chess-rated commercially available computer may be used as a house player only if computer participation for the tournament was advertised in advance (36C).

Usually, a player whose full-point bye is replaced by a temporary house player should be assigned no additional full-point byes in the tournament. An exception may be appropriate if the house player was strong and the player is competing for a class prize against others who have received full-point byes.

28M2. Cross-round pairings.
The player who expects the bye is asked to wait until one of the games in the lowest score groups has finished. The loser of that game is then asked to play the next-round game early, after a brief rest. The director then pairs the two players and marks the pairing and the result in the appropriate round boxes for each player: for the player who would have received the bye, in the current round; for the opponent, in the next round. This sometimes has the advantage of eliminating the need for a bye in the following round.

Cross-round pairings work best in scholastics and events for low-rated players (e.g., under 1400), because the bottom boards in such events usually play very quickly. If a cross-round pairing is planned and there is a significant delay before the game starts, the director may offer the option of such a pairing only if both sides start with time elapsed from their clocks. Either player may refuse, which may lead to the cross-round pairing being abandoned and the original bye reinstated.

The use of cross-round pairings should be specially indicated on the US Chess rating report. When using a pairing program see the manual for information on how to set the software to perform this task

28M3. Cross-section pairings.

In a tournament with multiple sections, there may be more than one section with a bye for a particular round. In this case, a cross-section pairing may be more desirable than a cross-round pairing, as the game can begin immediately. The player in the lower of the two sections involved retains the bye, but is added to the pairings and wall chart of the higher section for a rated game. The player in the higher section has a game that counts for both score and rating purposes, rather than a bye. Such a player should not subsequently be assigned a full-point bye or a bye alternative.

28M4. Extra rated games.

Directors may accommodate players who wish to play a rated game without giving up a full-point bye by placing both players in an *extra rated games* section with its own wall chart. This section is also used by directors to report correct results of games to US Chess that remain uncorrected (for pairing and prize purposes) in other sections. **See also** 15H, Reporting of results; 15I, Results reported incorrectly; 28I3, Extra rated games; and 29H3, Double forfeit of unreported game.

28N. Combined individual-team tournaments.

Scholastic events are often held as individual Swiss systems, with both individual and team awards. Players are paired individually and team standings are determined by adding the scores of each school's top scorers, usually the top four. The director should try to avoid pairing teammates against each other, but an absolute prohibition of such pairings can give an unfair advantage in the individual standings to players on strong teams, who may be "paired down" against players with a lower score rather than facing each other. **See also** 28A, Pairing cards or program and 31A, Combined individual-team tournaments.

28N1. Plus-two method.

a.   If a score group can be paired among itself without players from the same team facing each other, this should always be done.

b.   For score groups of less than plus two (*plus two* means at least two more wins than losses), if there is no way to pair the score group without players from the same team facing each other, these players should be raised or lowered into the nearest appropriate score group to avoid pairing teammates.

c. For score groups of plus two or greater (at least two more wins than losses), players should not be removed from their score group in order to avoid playing those from the same team.

Variation 28N2.

Players from the same team should never be paired against each other unless it is the last round, one is in first place, and if this leader is not paired against a teammate he or she will have to play someone with a lower score.

Variation 28N3.

Rule 28N1 may be modified to use a score other than plus two as the point at which teammates will not be paired out of their score group to avoid facing each other.

Variation 28N4.

The director may decide when it is appropriate to pair players from the same team against each other to maximize fairness in individual or team standings.

28O. Scoring.

The tournament director records the results of the games on the pairing cards or enters them into the computer. These results should also be posted, as quickly as convenient, to wall charts that are prominently displayed (See **Figure 7**, next page.)

#	Name/Rtng/ID	Rd 1	Rd 2	Rd 3
1	Allen Attack	B 5	W 4	B 2
	2000 11111111	1	2	2
2	Barbara Bishop	W 6	B 3	W 1
	1950 22222222	1	2	3
3	Curtis Chesser	B 7	W 2	B 5
	1900 33333333	1	1	1.5
4	Donald Defender	W 8	B 1	W 7
	1850 44444444	1	1	2
5	Edwin Enpassant	W 1	B 8	W 3
	1800 55555555	0	1	1.5
6	Fred Files	B 2	W 7	B 8
	1750 66666666	0	0	0
7	Gordon Goodplayer	W 3	B 6	B 4
	1700 77777777	0	1	1
8	Harry Helpmate	B 4	W 5	W 6
	1650 88888888	0	0	1

Figure 7

TD TIP: Directors may want to prepare a handout to explain to new tournament players how to interpret the information that appears on wall charts. For example: In this illustration Allen Attack is rated 2000 and is first on the list because he is the highest rated player in the tournament. Information about what color he played against which opponent is indicated in round one as Black against player number 5, Edwin Enpassant (B 5). He won the game (each win = 1 point, each draw = 0.5 points (or ½), and each loss = 0 points). In round two he played white against player 4 (W 4) and won again (indicated by a 2: round one score of 1 + the win in round two = 2). In round three Allen played Black against player number 2 (B\2); he lost that game (2 = round two cumulative score of 2 + round three score of 0 for losing).

28O1. Computer wall charts.

An advantage of using a computer is that it can print updated wall charts each round. In a large event, avoiding the need to enter the color and opponent of each player on the wall chart saves considerable time.

However, it is still recommended that the scores of each player be manually updated as soon as possible. It may be tempting to wait so that the computer can print out all or many scores, but making the players wait for hours to learn results may make the tournament less enjoyable.

28P. Unplayed games.

If a player fails to appear within one hour of the start of the round or by the end of the first time control, whichever comes first, the game is scored as a forfeit loss for the player and a forfeit win for the opponent. That player is then dropped from the tournament unless he or she presents an acceptable excuse to the director. The player's subsequent games are also scored as zero. A player may also withdraw from the tournament by notifying the director, in which case the remaining games are scored as zero.

The scores of unplayed games, including byes, are marked with an *F* or circled on the pairing cards, on the wall chart, and on the rating report. Unplayed games are not US Chess rated. Note that a game in which both sides make moves is always rated, even if a player forfeits on time or for an infraction of the rules; this type of forfeit is never marked with an *F* or circled. **See also** 13D, Late arrival for game; 13F, Late arrival by both players; 22, Unplayed Games; Rule 8D1, Games Not Played (Chapter 10).

TD TIP: Directors using pairing software should consult the software manual for details on how the program handles this procedure.

28Q. Pairing unfinished games.

If at all possible without imposing unreasonable delay in the start of the next round upon the other players, all games from one round should be finished before the next round is paired. If this is not possible, the director has several options (**See also** 18F3, Sudden death):

28Q1. Modified Kashdan system.

The director may approach a game in progress, instruct the player on move to seal (18A), and inform both players that either player who offers a draw and so informs the director before pairings for the next round begin will be paired as having drawn, and that either player who does not do so will be paired as having won. The director should stop both clocks before this intervention and restart the clock of the player who is to seal at its conclusion.

This modified method, probably the best way to handle adjournments, has several advantages over the original Kashdan system, in which the director privately asked each player what result he or she was seeking. It is much quicker, does not pressure players to respond immediately, and makes it clearer to the players that the draw offer may be accepted at any time during adjournment.

TD TIP: If both players indicate they are playing for a draw, the director can declare the game over with a result of a draw for both players.

28Q2. Temporary adjudications.

The director can adjourn the unfinished game(s) and either pair the players as having drawn, having won and lost, or having won and drawn. The latter might be appropriate if one player has winning chances and the opponent has drawing chances. If necessary, the director may consult strong players whose own pairings are not affected for help. **See also** 18F, Problems of the next-to-last round and 29F, Last round pairings with unfinished games.

28R. Accelerated pairings in the first two rounds.

In a tournament where the number of players far exceeds the number two raised to the power of the number of rounds (see 27, The Swiss System Tournament), more than one perfect score is possible, and top contenders may not play each other. The director has pairing options that have the effect of adding an extra round or two to the tournament without any additional games being played.

Accelerated pairings are most effective in a one-section tournament, an Open Section, or a section in which no more than about half the players are in the same 200-point rating class. Accelerated pairings may fare poorly in a primarily one-class section, as an accelerated pairing for round two will pit the lower-rated 1-0 against the higher-rated 0-1; thus, decreasing the odds (instead of the intended increasing of the odds) that the higher rated player will win.

28R2, Adjusted rating method, is more effective but more complicated than 28R1, Added score method, while the little-tested Variation 28R3, Sixths, is intended for events with an especially small ratio of rounds to players and large rating differences.

28R1. Added score method.

Before the first round, the players are numbered, ordered by rank, byes removed, the odd player assigned a bye, if any, removed, and the remaining players are divided into two equal sized groups. The director notes the top number in the lower half and, for the first two rounds, mentally adds one point to the scores of all players ranked above that number, for pairing purposes only. The director divides the players accordingly and pairs normally.

TD TIP: Pairing software usually has an option to do accelerated pairings.

The effect, in the first round, is to have the top quarter play the second quarter and the third quarter play the fourth quarter. For the most part, the effect in the second round will be to have the top eighth play the second eighth, the second quarter play the third quarter, and the seventh eighth play the last eighth. This method decreases the number of perfect scores.

28R2. Adjusted rating method.

Before the first round, after the bye, if any, is issued, the players are arranged in the normal order, top rated to lowest rated. Then the field is divided from top to bottom into four groups (A1, B1, C1, and D1) as close to the same size as possible, and paired as follows:

A1 vs. B1 and C1 vs. D1. These first-round pairings are the same as in Variation 1.

For the second-round pairings, the players are regrouped as follows:

1. A2: Winners from A1 vs. B1. If there is an odd number of players, the lowest-rated drops to the top of C2.

2. B2: Non-winners from A1 vs. B1, with players who drew having a temporary 100 points added to their ratings. If there are more players in B2 than C2, the lowest-rated losers from B2 are dropped to the top of D2, until B2 has the same number of players as C2. If there are fewer players in B2 than C2, the highest-rated players from D2 are raised to the bottom of B2 until B2 has the same number of players as C2.

3. C2: Non-losers from C1 vs. D1, with players who drew having a temporary 100 points subtracted from their ratings.

4. D2: Losers from C1 vs. D1.

Each of these groups is arranged in rating order, including the temporary adjustments for first-round performances. Then each group is paired as follows:

1. A2: This group is divided into halves. The upper half plays the lower half according to basic pairing methods.

2. B2 and C2: These groups play each other, with the top player in B2 facing the top in C2, etc., according to basic pairing methods. This will result mostly in players with different scores playing—1 vs. 0, 1 vs. 0.5, or 0.5 vs. 0—though an occasional 0.5 vs. 0.5 is also possible. Whenever the players have different scores, the one with the lower score will be higher-rated.

3. D2: This group is divided in half. The upper half plays the lower half according to basic pairing methods.

For the third and subsequent rounds, the temporary rating adjustments are ignored and the pairings are made according to the basic system.

This variation of accelerated pairings produces only about half the number of perfect scores achieved with the basic system. It therefore decreases the likelihood of multiple perfect scores, and causes the final standings to be more dependent on games between the top-rated players.

Variation 28R3. Sixths.

Apply the same principles as 28R2, but divide the field into sixths in the first round and pair the first sixth vs. the second, third vs. fourth, and fifth vs. sixth. In round two, pair the winners of 1 vs. 2 against each other, the non-winners of 1 vs. 2 against the winners of 3 vs. 4, the non-winners of 3 vs. 4 against the winners of 5 vs. 6, and the non-winners of 5 vs. 6 against each other.

28S. Reentries.

Tournaments with alternate schedules allowing players a choice of starting times for the early rounds often permit reentry, in which the player abandons or takes byes in the earlier-starting schedule in order to enter the later-starting schedule. For example, there may be a three-day schedule with round one at 8:00 p.m. Friday and a two-day schedule with round one at 10:00 a.m. Saturday, with the two schedules merging for round two starting Saturday afternoon. A player who loses or draws on Friday night may choose to *start fresh* by reentering the two-day schedule, in which case the Friday game, while still rated, would not damage the player's chances for prizes. **See also** 22B, Full-point byes; 22C, Half-point byes; 27A3, Upper half vs. lower half; 28A, Pairing cards or program; 28J, The first round; 28K, Late entrants; 28L, Full-point byes; 28M, Alternative to byes; and 29C1, Upper half vs. lower half.

TD TIP: Whether the director is pairing a tournament by hand or using pairing software, it is wise to note reentered players by adding a RE (for reentered) at the end of their name to distinguish the reentries from their original entries.

28S1. Reentry playing opponent twice.

If one player has reentered and the other has not, they should not be paired against each other for a second time (27A1). Even though the reentry is considered a new entry, from the standpoint of the opponent who did not reenter it is the same player.

28S2. Reentries playing each other twice.

If two reentries have already faced each other while each was playing his or her original entry, they are both considered a new entry and may be paired against each other for a second time, since neither new entry has faced the other new entry.

28S3. Reentry colors.

Reentries are treated as having no color history; the colors from their original entries are disregarded. **See also** 29E, Color allocation.

28S4. Reentry with half-point byes.

Players sometimes reenter the same schedule with half-point byes replacing games missed. 28S1, 28S2, and 28S3 all apply to such reentries as well.

28S5. Reentry scores.

Unless the organizer states otherwise prior to the beginning of the first round, a player who reenters carries the better score, or the best score in the case of multiple reentries, into the later rounds. In the case of equal scores, the latest score must be used. The color and opponent history of the entry carried forward accompanies it in all cases. The organizer, however, has the option of declaring in advance that a reentry must abandon all recourse to the earlier entry(ies), in which case the latest score and color history are carried forward, regardless of comparison to all earlier results. **See also** 32C5, Reentry prizes.

28T Variation. Players may request a non-pairing against each other.

Individual players may request that they not be paired against each other in any tournament. Due to the pairing problems involved, the director may not be able to honor this request.

TD TIP: Honoring requests of players to not be paired against each other can present serious pairing difficulties for the director, especially in small events and in the later rounds in any tournament; however, sometimes players who often play against each other outside of the tournament do not enjoy traveling to a tournament to simply play against each other again. Some directors honor the player's request for the first half of the tournament only. Directors may automatically "not pair" players from the same family, club, team, area, etc. without a request from the players; however, if at all possible those directors might want to consider consulting with those players first. After all, those players may not mind being paired against each other.

29. Swiss System Pairings, Subsequent Rounds

29A. Score groups and rank.

The words *score group* and *group* refer to players having the same score, even if there is only one player within a group. The players in each such score group are paired against each other (27A2) unless they have already faced each other (27A1) or are odd players (29D) or must play odd players paired from another score group (29D). In a combined individual and team tournament, players are sometimes paired out of their score groups to avoid facing teammates (28N). Individual rank is determined first by score (the greater the number of points, the higher the rank within the tournament) and then by rating within a score group (the higher the rating, the higher the rank).

TD TIP: Score group determines rank when players are paired outside of their score group. Rating determines rank within a score group. For example:

the lowest-rated player in the 4 point score group is rated 1991. The highest-rated player in the 3.5 score group is rated 2105. The 1991 player is ranked higher (the 4-point score group) than the 2105 player (the 3.5 score group). This ranking may be important when determining colors.

29B. Order of pairing score groups.

In general, the director pairs the groups according to rank, starting with the highest and working down. If games within some score groups are still unfinished shortly before the scheduled start of the next round, the director may wish to modify this order and pair around the groups with games still going on, taking care to provide for any *odd players*. It may be worthwhile to ask the players involved in a long game to confirm that they are playing the next round, as notice to the contrary after the game would be too late and would affect the odd player situation.

It may be helpful to make a quick table beforehand, listing the different score groups in descending order and the number of players in each group, and drawing arrows to show where players must be dropped (in the case of the odd player) to play someone from the group below.

TD TIP: Instead of a chart, some directors have been successful placing little sticky notes, drawing arrows and/or noting the number of players in each score group, on the top of a pile of pairing cards for that score group. Pairing programs take care of this task automatically.

29C. Method of pairing score groups.

In the second and subsequent rounds, the players are paired as follows:

29C1. Upper half vs. lower half.

If there is an even number of players within a group, they are placed in order of rank (rating), divided in half, and the upper half is paired against the lower half, in as close to consecutive order as possible (e.g., in a group with 20 players, the first ranked would play the eleventh ranked, the second the twelfth, and so on). **See also** 22B, Full-point byes; 22C, Half-point byes; 27A3, Upper half vs. lower half; 28A, Pairing cards or program; 28J, The first round; 28K, Late entrants; 28L, Full-point byes; 28M, Alternative to byes; 28S, Reentries; 29D, The odd player; 29E2, First round colors; 29E3, due colors in succeeding rounds; 29E4, Equalization, alternation, and priority of color; and 29E5, Colors vs. ratings.

29C2. Other adjustments.

Transpositions are made in order to avoid pairing players who have already played each other and to give as many players as possible their equalizing or due colors. To this end it is also permissible to make an interchange between the bottom of the upper half and the top of the lower half. **See also** 27A1, Avoid players meeting twice; 29E, Color allocation; 29E3, Due colors in succeeding rounds; 29E4, Equalization, alternation, and priority of color; and 29E5, Colors vs. ratings.

29D. The odd player.

Pairing players out of score group.

There will often be situations where some players cannot be paired within their score group. This will always be true if there is an odd number of players with a given score, and can also happen when players within a score group have already played each other, or are otherwise restricted (family members, same scholastic team, requested non-pairs, etc.) from playing. At least one, and possibly more, players will have to be dropped to play in a lower score group. In such situations, the first priority (other than avoiding restricted pairings) is to have players play as close to their score group as possible.

29D1. Determination.
a. In the case of an odd number of players, the lowest-rated player, but not an unrated player, is ordinarily treated as the odd player and is paired with the highest-rated player he or she can play in the next lower group. Care must be taken in doing this that the odd player can be paired in the next score group, that the remaining members of both affected score groups can be paired with each other, that the odd player has not played all the members of the next lower group, and that the color consequences are acceptable (29E, 29E3). **See also** 28S3, Reentry colors; 29E4, Equalization, alternation, and priority of color; and 29E5, Colors vs. Ratings.

b. If the conditions in (a) cannot be met, then try treating the next lowest rated player as the odd player, or pairing the odd player with a lower ranking player in the next score group. In deciding whether to make a switch of either the odd player or the opponent, you should look only at the rating difference of the players being switched. There is no rating limit on the permitted switch if it is needed to keep the score groups intact. However, switches to correct colors should stay within the appropriate limits (29E5). **See also** 28S3, Reentry colors; 29E, Color allocation; 29E3, Due colors in succeeding rounds; 29E4, Equalization, alternation, and priority of color

c. If the entire score group is unrated, then an unrated player must be designated as the odd player and dropped.

29D2. Multiple drop downs.

It is sometimes necessary to jump over an entire score group to find an appropriate opponent for an odd player.

A pairing which drops a player down for one or more score groups should be chosen over a pairing which drops two or more players down for one or more score groups (This can be relaxed in low score groups if necessary to allow the bottom score groups to be paired legally). It is acceptable to pair the player against a somewhat lower-rated player to equalize or alternate colors, but only within the rules for transposition as explained in 29E5, Colors vs. ratings.

The odd player is normally paired with the highest-rated player he or she has not met from the next lower group. It is acceptable to pair the player against a somewhat lower-rated player to equalize or alternate colors, but only within the rules for transposition as explained below.

Examples:

1. **One odd player:** If Group 1 has only one player with a perfect score, who has already played the only two members of Group 2, then the player from Group 1 must play the highest-rated player in Group 3 that he or she has not yet played in the tournament, provided that this allows the remaining members of Groups 2 and 3 to be paired.

2. **Two odd players:** If the only two players in Group 1 have already met, they would both be odd players. It is desirable for them to be paired with the highest-rated players in Group 2 whom they have not played before. The higher-rated player from Group 1 should be paired with the highest-rated player in Group 2, and the lower-rated player from Group 1 should be paired with the next-highest rated player in Group 2, provided that this allows the remaining members of Group 2 to be paired.

3. **Two odd players from two different score groups:** There is only one player in Group 1. There is only one player in Group 2. These players have already played each other. In this example we have a player dropping down more than one score group. The player being dropped from the higher score group is considered to be the higher-ranked and is paired first.

TD TIP: Dropping an odd player over multiple score groups just to improve color allocation is an unacceptable practice. Applying 28S3, Reentry colors, 29E, Color allocations, 29E3, Due colors in succeeding rounds, 29E4, Equalization, alternation, and priority of color; and 29E5, Colors vs. Ratings is more proper. If applications of those rules do not solve the color allocation problems, then the possibility of selecting a different odd player may be more equitable.

29E. Color allocation.

The director assigns colors to all players. The objective in a tournament with an even number of rounds is to give white and black the same number of times to as many players as possible; in an event with an odd number of rounds, each player should receive no more than one extra white or black above an even allocation.

In addition to the task of equalizing colors, the director, after the first round, tries to alternate colors, by giving as many players as possible their due (*correct* or expected) color, round by round. The due color is usually the color a player did not have in the previous round, but not always. For example, a player who had white in rounds one and two and black in round three has a due color of black in round four, as equalization has priority over alternation. **See also** 27A4, Equalizing colors; 27A5, Alternating colors; 28J, The first round; 29E2, First round colors; 29E3, Due colors in succeeding rounds; 29E4, Equalization, alternation, and priority of color; 29E5, Colors vs. ratings; and 29M, Recommendations.

29E1. Unplayed games.

Unplayed games, including byes and forfeits, do not count for color.

29E2. First-round colors.

22B, Full-point byes; 22C, Half-point byes; 27A3, Upper half vs. lower half; 28A, Pairing cards or program; 28J, The first round; 28K, Late entrants; 28L, Full-point byes; 28M, Alternative to byes; 28S, Reentries; 29D, The odd player; 29E3, due colors in succeeding rounds; 29E4, Equalization, alternation, and priority of color; 29E5, Colors vs. ratings; and 29M, Recommendations.

TD TIP: *Example: After the coin toss, the number one player in the top section of a class tournament was assigned to play white. All other top boards in all other sections are assigned white based on this one coin toss. In each of the sections the other players are assigned colors according to 29E2. Pairing programs do this automatically.*

29E3. Due Colors in succeeding rounds.

As many players as possible are given their due colors in each succeeding round, so long as the pairings conform to the basic Swiss system rules. **See also** 27A, Basic Swiss system rules; 27A4, Equalizing colors; 27A5, Alternating colors; 29C2, Other adjustments; and 29M, Recommendations.

29E3a. Due colors defined.

A player who has had an unequal number of whites and blacks is due the color that tends to equalize the number of whites and blacks. A player who has had an equal number of whites and blacks is due the opposite color to that he received in the most recent round. Colors assigned in games won or lost by forfeit do not count in deciding due color. A player who has played no games is due neither white nor black.

29E4. Equalization, alternation, and priority of color.

Equalization of colors takes priority over alternation of colors. First, as many players as possible are given the color that tends to equalize the number of times they have played white and black. After that is accomplished, as many players as possible should be given the color opposite to that which they played in the previous round. **See also** 27A, Basic Swiss system rules; 27A4, Equalizing colors; 27A5, Alternating colors; 29A, Score groups and rank; 29C2, Other adjustments; and 29M, Recommendations.

TD TIP:
Example 1. A player who has had BWB is due white (equalization of
colors).
Example 2. A player who has had BW is due black (alternation of colors).
Example 3. A player who has had WWB is due black (equalization takes
priority over alternation).
Example 4. A player who had white in round one, then won by forfeit in
round two, is due black in round three regardless of which
color he had been assigned in the unplayed round two game.

Pairing players due the same color. Whenever it is necessary to pair two players who are due the same color the following rules apply:

1. If one player has had an unequal number of whites and blacks, while the other has had equal colors, the player who has had unequal colors gets due color. Example: WBW gets black over BxW, where x denotes any unplayed game—full-point bye, half-point bye, forfeit win, forfeit loss, etc.

2. If both players have had an unequal number of whites and blacks, the player with the greater total color imbalance gets due color. Example: WWBW gets black over xWBW.

3. If both players have had an equal number of whites and blacks, or both are equally out of balance, and if they had opposite colors in the previous round, the players should be given colors opposite to that which they played in the previous round. Example: WWB gets white over WBW.

4. If both players have had an equal number of whites and blacks, or both are equally out of balance, and if they had different colors in one or more prior rounds, priority for assigning color should be based on the latest

111

round in which their colors differed. One or both players should be assigned the color opposite to that which they played in that round. Example 1: WBWB gets white over BWWB, because the first player had black in round two, the latest round in which colors differed. Example 2: BWxBW gets white over BWBxW, because the first player had black and the second had no color in round 4, the latest round in which colors differed.

5. If both players have had the same color sequence, the higher-ranked player gets due color. The higher-ranked player is the player with the higher score. If the players have the same score, the higher-ranked player is the higher-rated (*rank* is defined in 29A).

TD TIP: Rule 5 takes effect only if rules 1-4 do not decide the issue. Unless the players have had identical color sequences, rules 1-4 should be used.

Variation 29E4a. Priority based on plus, even, and minus score groups.

When applying rule 5 above, the higher-ranked player in plus and even score groups receives priority for color allocation, while the lower-ranked player in minus score groups receives priority. This variation minimizes color problems in the very low score groups, as well as the very high, which are more likely to have color problems in later rounds because these are statistically the smallest groups.

Variation 29E4b. Alternating priority.

When applying rule 5 above, if two players within a score group are both due the same color, the higher-rated player receives due color. But if several such situations exist within the group, the first higher-rated player receives due color, the second does not, the third does, and so on, alternating entitlement from higher- to lower-rated player. This applies both to equalizing and alternating colors.

Variation 29E4c. Priority based on lot.

When applying rule 5 above, in the last round of a tournament, the director may choose to let opponents with equal entitlement to colors choose their own colors by lot, but only after making all the pairings necessary to come closer to equalized and alternate allocations. For example, if after four rounds both players had received WBWB, for the fifth and final round the director might choose to let the players choose for colors rather than assign them automatically by using one of the procedures outlined above. If this system is adopted, it must be used for all such cases without exception. **See also** 29E5f1, Last-round exception and 29I, Class pairings.

Variation 29E4d. Priority based on rank.

Rule 4 above does not apply. If both players have had an equal number of whites and blacks (or both are equally out of balance), and if they have had the same colors in each of the preceding two rounds, then the higher-ranked player gets due color.

TD TIP: Variation 29E4d was the old main rule in the 4th edition of this rulebook; therefore, it is possible that it is still used by some directors and pairing programs. It is recommended that, when this variation is used, written notice be posted before the start of the tournament.

29E5. Colors vs. ratings.

Correct Swiss pairings should consider both colors and ratings, so a tournament director should exercise care not to distort either unduly. To improve colors a director may use either a transposition or an interchange of players. **See also** 27A, Basic Swiss System Rules; 27A3, Upper half vs. lower half; 27A4, Equalizing colors; 27A5, Alternating colors; and 29C2, Other adjustments.

A transposition is the practice of changing the order of players within the upper half or lower half of a group. An interchange involves switching a player from the bottom of the upper half with a player from the top of the lower half. **For more information** and examples see 29E5e, Comparing transpositions to interchanges and 29E7, Examples of transpositions and interchanges.

TD TIP: Sometimes pairings get switched more than once. Directors switch players if they have faced each other before, are teammates, or are family members. Excluding those reasons, sometimes transpositions and interchanges occur more than once with the same player for any particular round. The arithmetic for interchanges and transpositions applies only to the first natural pairing (or the pairing after the aforementioned switches are made by the director) before any transpositions or interchanges are made compared to the final pairing after all transpositions and interchanges have been made.

Transpositions and interchanges should be limited as follows:

29E5a. The 80-point rule.

Transpositions and interchanges for the purpose of maximizing the number of players who receive their due color should be limited to players with a pre-tournament rating difference of 80 points or less.

Example: WB vs. WB. To give one of these players a second straight black in round three is only moderately undesirable and does not justify a switch of over 80 points. **See also also** 29E5b, The 200-point rule; 29E5c, Evaluating transpositions; 29E5d, Evaluating interchanges; 29E5e, Comparing transpositions to interchanges; 29E5h, Priority of equalization over ratings; and 29E7, Examples of transpositions and interchanges.

29E5b. The 200-point rule.

Transpositions and interchanges for the purpose of minimizing the number of players who receive one color two or more times more than the other color should be limited to players with a pre-tournament rating difference of 200 points or less. **See also** 29E5a, The 80-point rule; 29E5c, Evaluating transpositions; 29E5d, Evaluating interchanges; 29E5e, Comparing transpositions to interchanges; 29E5h, Priority of equalization over ratings; and 29E7, Examples of transpositions and interchanges.

TD TIP: *It has been observed by experienced directors that there are fewer concerns from players paired to play the white pieces in violation of 29E5b then when the situation is reversed and they are paired to play the black pieces in violation of this same rule*

Variation 29E5b1.

Transpositions and interchanges for the purpose of minimizing the number of players who receive black two or more times more than white should be limited to 200 points.

Example: BWB vs. BWB. To give one of these players black for the third time in round four is highly undesirable, justifying a switch limit of 200 points.

29E5c. Evaluating transpositions.

All transpositions should be evaluated based on the smaller of the two rating differences involved. For example:

2000 WB vs. 1800 WB

1980 BW vs. 1500 BW

These would be correct third-round pairings were it not for the color problems. Unless a switch is made, there will be a color conflict on each board.

To trade the 1800 for the 1500 is apparently a 300-point switch, which would violate 29E5a, The 80-point rule. But this is not really the case. The same pairings may be achieved by trading the 2000 for the 1980, only a 20-point switch. However, when manipulating pairing cards the actual interchange takes place by switching the cards in the lower half of the score group.

The resulting pairings, 2000 white vs. 1500 and 1800 white vs. 1980, are considered to require only a 20-point switch and thus satisfy the 80-point rule.

In larger groups, the situation is sometimes more complicated, as a permissible transposition may generate numerous additional transpositions, not all of which satisfy the limits for allowable transpositions. This is especially common when some of the otherwise-desirable pairings are impossible because the players have already faced each other.

In such situations, the director may strictly observe the limits for transpositions or may be flexible. If colors in the group are substantially improved, it is acceptable for the limits to be exceeded somewhat. **See also** 29E5a, The 80-point rule; 29E5b, The 200-point rule; 29E5d, Evaluating interchanges; 29E5e, Comparing transpositions to interchanges; and 29E7, Examples of transpositions and interchanges.

29E5d. Evaluating interchanges.

For an interchange, the director need only consider one rating difference rather than the smaller of two. The difference between the two players switched is the relevant difference; there is no need to look at the other switch that would produce the same pairings.

While interchanges are theoretically acceptable if the rating difference of the switch is within the limits set forth in by 29E5a, The 80-point rule, and 29E5b, The 200-point rule, interchanges do violate basic principle 27A3, Upper half vs. lower half, and so tend to catch players by surprise, causing them to express their concerns. While interchanges are sometimes necessary, they should not be used if adequate transpositions are possible. **See also** 29E5d, Evaluating interchanges; 29E5e, Comparing transpositions to interchanges; and 29E7, Examples of transpositions and interchanges.

TD TIP: Experienced directors have observed that players in contention for prizes tend to express their concern about interchanges more often than players not in contention for prizes.

29E5e. Comparing transpositions to interchanges.

A transposition that satisfies 29E5a, The 80-point rule, should be preferred to any interchange, provided it is at least as effective in minimizing color conflicts.

If pairing a round in which 29E5b, The 200-point rule, is used because, for instance, many players have had more blacks than whites, an interchange involving a smaller rating switch than a transposition should be preferred to the latter unless the transposition satisfies the 80-point rule.

Example 1:

2050 WBW vs. 1850 WBW

1870 BWB vs. 1780 BWB

These fourth-round *natural pairings* should be switched to improve color allocation. The interchange of trading the 1870 with the 1850 is only a 20-point switch, while the transposition of switching the 1850 with the 1780 is a 70-point change, the smaller number of 70 (1850–1780=70) and 180 (2050–1870=180). However, since the interchange is only a 20-point switch while the transposition, which meets the requirement of 29E5a, The 80-point rule, is a 70-point change, use of the interchange is not necessary, and the pairings should be 1780-2050 and 1870-1850.

Example 2:

2050 WBW vs. 1850 WBW

1870 BWB vs. 1750 BWB

This is almost the same situation as in Example 1, except the bottom player of the group (1750) is now rated 30 points lower. In this case, transposing the 1850 with the 1750 would be a 100-point switch. This is allowed, as we are trying to avoid assigning two more blacks than whites to someone on board two, so 29E5b, The 200-point rule, applies. But even though it is permitted, it does not meet the requirement of 29E5a, The 80-point rule, and thus does not have priority over an interchange.

The interchange of switching 1870 and 1850, a 20-point switch, is preferred, and the pairings should be 1870-2050 and 1750-1850.

29E5f. Colors in a series.

No player shall be assigned the same color three times in a row, unless there is no other reasonable way to pair the score group or unless necessary to equalize colors.

Variation 29E5f1. Last-round exception.

Except for the last round, when it may be necessary to pair the tournament or class leaders, players shall not be assigned the same color in three successive rounds. **See also** 27A, Basic Swiss system rules; 27A3, Upper half vs. lower half; 27A4, Equalizing colors; 27A5, Alternating colors; 29E, Color allocation; 29E3, Due colors in succeeding rounds; 29E4, Equalization, alternation, and priority of color; 29E4c, Priority based on lot; 29I, Class pairings; and 29M, Recommendations.

29E5g. Unrateds and color switches.

If a player is switched to or from an unrated opponent to improve color allocation, this is not in violation of the 80 or 200-point rules for transpositions and interchanges.

Variation 29E5h. Priority of equalization over ratings.

Equalization of colors has priority over rating differences; 29E5a, The 80-point rule, and 29E5b, The 200-point rule, do not apply.

TD TIP: This variation has been more successful at club and local events than at large state or national tournaments.

29E6. Color adjustment technique.

The order in which pairings are switched to improve colors can make a difference, both in the final pairings and in the time it takes to arrive at them. Two methods that have been commonly used are the *Look Ahead* method and the *Top Down* method. The *Look Ahead* method is more accurate and easier to use.

TD TIP: Directors using pairing programs should consult the software manuals on choosing how to implement the desired method.

29E6a. The *Look Ahead* method.

The director counts to see if more than half the group is due for the same color (29E3). If not, he or she starts with the top pairing and works down, correcting as many color conflicts (games in which both players are due for the same color) as possible. Unless there is a problem with 29E5a, The 80-point rule, or 29E5b, The 200-point rule, or too many players have already faced each other (27A1), all colors will balance. **See also** 29E4, Equalization, alternation, and priority of color.

If more than half the group is due for the same color, the objective is to *avoid pairings in which neither player is due for that color*. This will maximize the number of pairings in which both sides receive their due color.

Note that *neither due for that color* could mean *both players due for the other color, both players due no color* (for instance, both players in round two having played no game in round one), or *either player due for the other color while the opponent is due for no color*.

TD TIP: In a score group that has color assignment problems such as those described here, it is best to avoid pairings where neither player is due for the color that is causing a color-assignment problem in a score group. The best use for each of those players would be to pair them using 29E5a, The 80-point rule, and 29E5b, The 200-point rule, against players that must play a particular color based on rules like 29E, Color allocation, and 29E4, Equalization, alternation, and priority of color.

A player may be due based only on alternation while most in the group are due based on equalization. For example, if pairing round four and most in the score group have had two blacks, a player with one of each color and an unplayed game is due for neither color based on equalization. Alternation is not an issue, as equalization has priority (29E4), so the player is due for neither color.

Assume most players in a group are due for white. The director examines the *natural pairings*. Any pair of players who have already faced each other are changed (27A1) by the switch involving the minimum rating change described in 29E5a, The 80-point rule, and 29E5b, The 200-point rule, while also avoiding pairings in which neither player is due for white.

The tentative pairings are checked for games in which neither player is due for white (or could be assigned either color). If there are none, the pairings are final. If such pairings exist, as many of such pairings as possible are changed by making switches to higher or lower boards, involving the minimum possible rating differences.

Color conflicts are now minimized and pairings stand. While no direct attempt was made to avoid pairings of both players due for white, these were held to a minimum. **See also** 29E7, Examples of transpositions and interchanges.

Variation 29E6b. The *Top Down* method.

Using this method, the director, after adjusting to avoid pairing players who have already played (27A1), first considers the color situation on board one of the score group, the board involving the top-rated player in the group. If both players are due for the same color, the pairing is changed by moving up the highest-rated player in the lower half whose color fits, and exchanging that player with the one in the pairing on board one from the lower half, providing the pairing does not violate 29E5a (80-point rule) or 29E5b (200-point rule).

The director then moves down to board two, then board three, etc., correcting any color conflicts encountered in the same manner.

Eventually, the number of color conflicts should be the same as in the *Look Ahead* method. But the pairings are often inferior, and time may be wasted making adjustments that do not reduce the number of color conflicts. **See also** 29E7, Examples of transpositions and interchanges.

29E7. Examples of transpositions and interchanges.

For definitions of the terms *transposition*s and *interchanges* see 29E5, Colors vs. ratings. In each case, we start by looking at what the pairings would be were there no color problems.

Example 1:

2300 BWB vs. 2040 BWB

2220 BWB vs. 1990 WBW

2180 BBW vs. 1980 WBW

2050 BWB vs. 1950 WBW

Using the *Look Ahead* method, the director finds five players due for white, three due for black. Thus, pairings in which neither player is due for white should be avoided. But there are no such pairings, so the above pairings stand. Note that the 2180 is due for white because equalization has priority over alternation (29E3).

The *Top Down* method runs into real problems here. First, the director *corrects* the colors on board one and pairs 2300 vs. 1990. Then, he or she does likewise on boards two and three, resulting in 2220 vs. 1980 and 2180 vs. 1950. This leaves a bizarre pairing on board four: 2050 vs. 2040. When the director is asked why two players with ratings so close are playing each other in a group of eight, the response might be *to improve colors*. Let's hope no one will notice that the colors for this strange pairing are wrong, too!

The remaining examples will show only the *Look Ahead* method.

Example 2:

     2320 WBWB vs. 1980 WBWB

     2278 BWBW vs. 1951 WBWB

     2212 BWBW vs. 1910 BWBW

     2199 WBWB vs. 1896 BWBW

     2178 WBWB vs. 1800 WBWB

The director's count shows six players out of ten overall due for white. This means pairings in which neither player is due for white should be avoided.

The only pairing in which neither is due for white is 2212 vs. 1910 (both are due black). There are two options for correcting this.

a.   The first possibility is 2320 vs. 1910. This would require a 70-point transposition in the lower half (1980–1910=70) or a 108-point transposition in the upper half (2320–2212=108), so we count the switch as 70, the smaller number.

b.   The second option for correcting the colors is 1800 vs. 2212. This is a 110-point transposition in the lower half (1910–1800=110) but only a 34-point transposition in the upper half (2212–2178=34), and so is preferable to option a.

The resulting pairings:

White	Black
2320	1980
1951	2278
1800	2212
2199	1896
2178	1910

Example 3 shows a different way to pair this same score group on the last three boards. This method is not better or worse, just different. It has both advantages and disadvantages, which are explained below. The director should pick either the method in Example 2 or the one in Example 3 and use it consistently throughout the tournament.

Example 3:

2320 WBWB vs. 1980 WBWB

2278 BWBW vs. 1951 WBWB

2212 BWBW vs. 1910 BWBW

2199 WBWB vs. 1896 BWBW

2178 WBWB vs. 1800 WBWB

The director's count shows six players out of ten overall due for white. This means pairings in which neither player is due for white should be avoided.

The only pairing in which neither is due for white is 2212 vs. 1910 (both are due black). There are two options for correcting this.

c.   The first possibility is 2320 vs. 1910. This would require a 70-point transposition in the lower half (1980–1910=70) or a 108-point transposition in the upper half (2320–2212=108), so we count the switch as 70, the smaller number.

d.   The second option for correcting the colors is 1800 vs. 2212. This is a 110-point transposition in the lower half (1910–1800=110) but only a 34-point transposition in the upper half (2212–2178=34), and is preferable to option c.

When transposing the 1910 and the 1800, though, there is an intermediate player, 1896. While it is not incorrect to simply swap the 1910 and the 1800 and leave the 1896 undisturbed, it is considered more correct to do a three-way swap, as follows: the 1800 moves up two boards, the 1910 shifts down one, and the 1896 shifts down one. In this way, an additional player moves down a board, but the ratings change of each of the downward moves is not as large.

The resulting pairings:

White	Black
2320	1980
1951	2278
1800	2212
2199	1910
2178	1896

Example 4:

2210 B vs. 1900 B
2200 B vs. 1830 B
2150 W vs. 1820 W
2120 B vs. 1790 B
2080 B vs. 1500 B
1920 W vs. 1350 bye

Eight players are due for white, three for black, and one for neither, so pairings in which neither player is due for white should be corrected. We can quickly see that 2150 vs. 1820 and 1920 vs. 1350 are the problems. The 1350 player who received a bye in the first round is considered not due for white.

Switching (transposing) 1820 up a board is a 10-point change (1830-1820=10) on one side, 50 points (2200-2150=50) on the other. The lower number is used, so it is a 10-point transposition. Moving 1820 down a board is a 30-point transposition on both sides (2150–2120 or 1820–1790=30). The 10-point change is selected and board two and three pairings are switched.

The two bottom boards may be paired as 2080 vs. 1350 and 1500 vs. 1920. The smaller of the two switches is 150 points (1500–1350=150), permissible under the 200-point rule to avoid two extra blacks for a player on the fifth board (29E5b).

However, there is a better way. An interchange between 1920 and 1900 also corrects the colors, and is a switch of just 20 points (1920–1900=20). An interchange has priority if it involves a smaller switch than a transposition, and the transposition requires a switch of over 80 points (29E5a).

The resulting pairings:

White	Black
2210	1920
2200	1820
1830	2150
2120	1790
2080	1500
1900	1350

Example 5:

2100 BWB (3 points) vs. 2080 BWB (3 points)

1990 WBW (3 points) vs. 2050 WBW (2.5 points)

1980 BWB (2.5 points) vs. 1800 BWB (2.5 points)

Here, an odd player must drop from the 3 point group to the 2.5 point group. The two groups combined will have three pairings, and giving someone three blacks out of four games unfortunately cannot be avoided.

The natural pairings shown above, dropping the low 3 (1990) to face the high 2.5 (2050), are highly undesirable, leaving the colors wrong in all three games.

One way to improve colors would be to switch the 2050 with the second highest 2.5, the 1980. This would be a switch of 70 (2050–1980=70) or 190 (1990–1800=190), which counts as 70.

The alternative would be to switch the 2080 and the 1990 in the 3-point group. This would be 90 (2080–1990=90) or 50 (2100–2050=50), counting as 50, and thus slightly preferable.

The resulting pairings:

White	Black
2100	1990
2080	2050
1980	1800

TD TIP: *All of this is done automatically when the director uses a computer pairing program that is set up properly; however, the director is still ultimately responsible for the pairings and should make it a practice to review the final pairings made by any program.*

29E8. Variation (unannounced) team pairings take precedence over color equalization.

In a combined swiss individual and team tournament, the need to avoid pairing players from the same team shall take precedence over the need to equalize colors.

29F. Last-round pairings with unfinished games.

Every reasonable effort should be made to have all games finished before pairing the last round. If this would unduly delay the start of the last round and inconvenience a large number of people, then last-round pairings can be made and the round begun. In this case, the director must be very watchful of the unfinished games to prevent the results from being arranged to affect the prizes. **See also** 18F, Problems of the next-to-last round and 28Q, Pairing unfinished games.

TD TIP: Unless there is an extraordinary problem, games with sudden-death time controls have no problems with unfinished games by the time the last round needs to be paired.

29G. Re-pairing a round.

29G1. Round about to start.

If a player withdraws without proper notice as the pairings are nearing completion, the director must decide whether time permits a complete revision of the pairings, the most desirable solution.

If time does not allow this, one solution is to *ladder down* the pairings. For example, if a player with 2 points withdraws, the opponent faces a player with 1.5 points, that player's opponent faces a player with 1 point, and so on down until a bye is assigned or the original bye is paired.

In doing this, the director should attempt to find opponents within the same rating range and due for the same color. If the original pairings included any odd players, their pairings may be useful to change. For instance, if a player with 2 points withdraws and another 2 was paired against a 1.5, the opponent of the withdrawn player may be paired against the odd player with 2, leaving a 1.5 to be *laddered down* rather than a 2.

The use of an appropriately-rated house player should be considered as an alternative to re-pairing.

If a computer pairing program is used, the round can usually be properly re-paired without significant delay, avoiding need for *laddering* or a house player.

29G2. Round already started.

The director has the right to make changes in the pairings, if necessary, to correct errors or to handle sudden withdrawals, but it is recommended that no game be canceled in which Black's fourth move has been determined.

29G3. Selective re-pairing.

If some games have started and others have not, it is often possible to correct the problem satisfactorily by telling those who have started to continue and the others to wait and re-pairing those waiting as a separate group, using normal methods.

29H. Unreported results.

Occasionally, both players fail to report the result of their game. The result once learned by the director, counts for rating purposes. The result (except for 29H3) may also be counted for prize purposes at the director's discretion if it is reported in a timely manner. The director's decision should be based on how much earlier in the tournament the unreported result occurred and how many pairings were affected. **See also** 15H, Reporting of results; and 15I, Results reported incorrectly.

*TD TIP: **See also** the TD TIP for rule 15I for further guidance in dealing with unreported and incorrectly reported results.*

In a Swiss tournament, if it is time to pair the next round and a result is still unreported, the director has several options and should choose the one that offers the greatest equity:

29H1. Ejection.

One or both players may be ejected from the tournament. This is appropriate only if there have been prior non-reporting problems with the player(s) involved.

29H2. Double forfeit of next round.

Both players may be removed from the following round pairings, and forfeited for that round.

29H3. Double forfeit of unreported game.

Both players may be scored and paired as losses. The real result, when learned, may be recorded as an *extra rated game* (28M4).

29H4. Half-point byes next round.

Both players may be removed from the following round pairings and given half-point byes for that round, assuming that half-point byes are available in the event for that round.

29H5. Guess the winner.

If there is a great rating difference in the unreported game, the director may pair the higher-rated player as a win and the lower-rated as a loss. Such a *guess* is usually right, as not only is an upset statistically unlikely, but players scoring upsets rarely neglect to report results, while those defeating opponents rated well below them tend to have a higher *non-reporting rate* than average. The TD may have seen the game in progress, and therefore have an idea of who was winning. **See also** 29H9, Results reported after pairings done.

29H6. Pair as a win and a draw.

A variation of 29H5 is to pair the higher player as a win and the lower as a draw. This has the advantage of penalizing someone for non-reporting but also guarantees a wrong pairing (the penalty is being paired in a higher score group). If the director is not sure whether 29H5 or 29H7 is the better option, this may be an appropriate compromise. **See also** 29H9, Results reported after pairings done.

29H7. Pair as a double win.

The director may pair both players as having won. This has the advantage of generally penalizing the loser, or both players if the game was drawn, with a harder pairing. The disadvantage is that when the loser is paired a full point up in the next round, this may reward the opponent in that round with an inappropriately easy pairing. **See also** 29H9, Results reported after pairings done.

This option is more appropriate in a class tournament than one involving mixed classes in the same section; it also works better with even or minus scores than plus scores, and in early rounds rather than late rounds.

29H8. Multiple missing results.

If more than one game is unreported, all players who failed to report may be omitted from the next round pairings, and paired against each other once the results are known. If this method is used, care must be taken not to allow a player with a chance for prizes an unusually easy pairing—in effect a reward for failing to report the result. This method may also be used in combination with other methods.

29H9. Results reported after pairings done.

If the unreported result is reported or discovered after the pairings are posted for the next round, but shortly before the start of that round, and the director used options 29H5, 29H6, or 29H7, it is not generally recommended that the round be delayed by doing all pairings over. However, the director may consider changing some pairings. **See also** 29H10, Computer pairings.

a. If Option 29H5, Guess the winner, was used, and the higher player actually lost, the pairings can usually be quickly improved by switching the opponents of the two players who failed to report. Another option, if

125

the director does not fear significant delay, is to re-pair either or both of the two score groups involved.

b.   If Option 29H5, Guess the winner, was used, and the game was actually a draw, there may be no simple way to improve the pairings. However, they are probably not that bad (involving just half-point, not full-point, errors), and the director may allow them to stand.

c.   If Option 29H6, Pair as a win and a draw, was used, and the higher player actually won or drew, the pairings are even better than in **b**. But if the higher player lost, the situation is similar to **a**, and the director should consider at least transposing the pairings of the two non-reporters.

d.   If Option 29H7, Pair as a double win, was used, the pairings generally should not be changed. If this option has caused a serious problem, then it was incorrect to use it. The director facing this dilemma must choose between letting the pairings stand or doing many pairings over and delaying the round.

29H10. Computer pairings.

If a computer makes pairings, delaying the start of the round to correct all the pairings becomes a more viable option, since the computer may be able to do this in a few minutes.

The director of a large tournament should remember that in addition to the time required to re-pair, there may be significant delay if players must leave their boards, find new pairings, go to new boards, and set up again.

29I. Class pairings.

In tournaments with significant class prizes, class pairings may be used in the last round, if announced in advance. This allows prizes to be decided by direct encounters between those competing for them. A major benefit is to avoid games in which a player in contention for a large prize faces a higher-rated opponent who is not, a situation that invites collusion to produce a win for the player in contention.

Class pairings should be used only when it is mathematically impossible for any player in that class to win a place prize that is greater than first in the class. If even one player can win more than first in the class, the system should not be used at all. **See also** 29E5f1, Last round exceptions and 29E4c, Priority based on lot.

Class pairings may unfairly affect special prizes, such as top junior or senior, a factor a director may wish to consider.

TD TIP: *This method is not used if a class player is also in contention for a place prize. For example, a 1495 player is in contention for a top prize as* *well as the "C" prize. If class pairings are used, the 1495 player could be paired against a weaker class "C" opponent instead of the stronger "natural" higher rated opponent, also in contention for a place prize. The "natural" opponent will most likely then be paired against an opponent rated higher than 1495. This unusual pairing may allow the 1495 rated player to win the place prize.*

29I1. Full-class pairings.

The first common method of class pairings simply treats the class as a separate Swiss system tournament, and pairs accordingly. If there is an odd number of players in the class, the bottom player should be paired as normally as possible outside the class. **See also** 28M1, The house player; 29D, The odd player; and 29J, Unrateds in class tournaments.

29I2. Partial class pairings.

Another system pairs players within a rating class who have a chance for class prizes with each other, and then treats the rest of the field normally. This method can be useful when using a computer program that does not do class pairings, since it can greatly reduce the number of pairings that must be made by hand and entered into the computer.

29J. Unrateds in class tournaments.

In sections or events restricted to players under a specified rating with unrated players also allowed, if there are two or more unrated players with plus scores in the same score group, the director may pair them against each other. This system is most appropriate in events with meaningful cash prizes; it tends to make it more difficult for players to win undeserved prizes. **See also** 28C, Ratings of players; 28D, Players without US Chess ratings; and 33F, Unrateds.

TD TIP: Organizers sometimes limit unrated players in class tournaments to their own section with their own prizes. Occasionally unrated players are also given the opportunity to play in the highest section or class with the understanding that they only qualify for the top prizes or a special unrated prize.

29K. Converting small Swiss to round robin.

A 5-round Swiss with six entries or 3-round Swiss with four entries may be converted to a round robin format. This may be acceptable for a quick one-day tournament, but often works poorly for a two-day or three-day six-player round robin.

Withdrawals are likely to cause many more unplayed games in a round robin than in a Swiss and to distort the results more. The round robin format is also not compatible with late entries or half-point byes. It is true that the Swiss may pair players against each other twice, usually the two leaders in the last round, but most players prefer such a rematch to not playing at all.

29L. Using round robin table in small Swiss.

A better option than 29K, Converting small Swiss to round robin, is to maintain an event as a Swiss when there is a small turnout, but to use a round robin pairing table to minimize the possibility of players' facing the same opponents twice.

For instance, if a 5-round Swiss has six players, pair round one as in a normal Swiss. Then assign round robin pairing numbers, which cause the first-round pairings to have been correct for round one of a six-player round robin, using the pairing table in *Chapter 12*. Do not announce that the tournament will be a round robin; it may not be.

As long as there are no dropouts or additions, pair each subsequent round using the round robin table by selecting the round from the table in which the top player in the top score group receives the proper Swiss opponent. Do not use the colors from the table, but assign them according to Swiss rules. If three in a row of the same color is inevitable using a pairing line from the table, there is the option of using the next best line.

TD TIP: Here is an example list of six players in a five round Swiss, in Swiss rating order (highest rated through lowest rated), with round robin pairing numbers (generated by the round 1 pairings from table B in Chapter 12: Round Robin Pairing Tables): 1. (2205), 6. (2050), 5. (1803), 2. (1650), 3. (1493), 4. (1402). The pairings for round one: 1. (2205) vs. 2. (1650), 3. (1493) vs. 6. (2050), 5. (1803) vs. 4. (1402). Notice that the pairings are Swiss pairings using the pairings numbers from round 1 located in the round robin pairings table B in Chapter 12.

If everyone completes the tournament, it will in effect be a round robin, but if there are dropouts or late entries it is possible to switch to Swiss methods at any time. For instance, in the last round if only four players are still in the tournament, use Swiss methods and pair them against each other even if one or both encounters are rematches. This is far better than sticking to round robin pairings and awarding two byes.

The above method may also be used with slightly more players to avoid rematches. For instance, it may be appropriate in a four-round Swiss with five or six players, a five-round Swiss with six to eight players, a six-round Swiss with seven to ten players, a seven-round Swiss with eight to twelve players, or an eight-round Swiss with nine to fourteen players.

Note that in such small Swisses it is especially important to recruit an appropriately rated permanent house player (28M1) if possible, since otherwise byes will have a more harmful effect than in a larger Swiss. Repeated announcements among spectators offering free entry to such a house player are warranted, with the condition that such a player will be paired only when there would otherwise be an odd number. It is even possible to allow such a house player to be eligible for prizes in the event he or she plays sufficient games to be in contention.

TD TIP: *Some directors may find 29L1, Variation: 1 vs. 2 pairings, easier to administer than using this combination of round robin and Swiss systems when faced with a small number of players that almost matches the number of rounds in a tournament, especially if the event is longer than one day.*

Variation 29L1. 1 vs. 2 pairings.

This pairing system is exactly the same as the Swiss pairing system except that the players in the upper half do not play the players in the lower half in the first or any other round. Instead, in round 1 after the players have been ranked, each odd ranked player is paired with the even ranked player following them on the ordered ranking list; i.e.; 1 vs. 2, 3 vs. 4, 5 vs. 6, etc. In all other rounds the players are ranked in rating order within their respective score groups and paired in groups of two starting with the two top-rated players in the top score group. Odd players should be paired to the player in the next lower score group who closest matches with them in rating, using normal color priorities. Color allocation, transposition, avoiding players meeting twice, byes, late entries, and withdrawals are applied exactly the same way as in a Swiss event.

TD TIP: *Because it handles withdrawals and late entries as easily as the Swiss system, this 1 vs. 2 pairing system is easier, for some directors, to administer than 29L, Using round robin table in small Swiss, in events with the number of players almost equal to the number of rounds; however, the 1 vs. 2 pairings system can accommodate many players in any size tournament. This system has seen some popularity at the club and local level. It is a hybrid of the traditional club "ladder" system (where one player challenges another player for their spot on the ladder) and the Swiss System.*

29M. Recommendations.

Some disparity in color allocation is inevitable in the Swiss system, as score has priority over color. Tournaments with an even number of rounds cause the most problems, because when a disparity exists, it is larger. Tournaments with an odd number of rounds are therefore apt to keep more players happy, and are easier to pair because it is easier to maintain the expected 3-2 or 4-3 color allocations. **See also** 27A4, Equalizing colors; 27A5, Alternating colors; 28J, The first round; 29E, Color allocation; 29E2, First round colors; 29E3, Due colors in succeeding rounds; 29E4, Equalization, alternation, and priority of color; and 29E5, Colors vs. ratings.

30. The Round Robin Tournament

30A. Description.
This tournament format is also known as *all-play-all*. Formerly the almost-exclusive format for chess competitions, the round robin is most often used now for important events where time is not a factor, club events with one game per week, and one-day four-player events known as *quads*.

Although it is the fairest-known tournament format when there are no withdrawals, it cannot accommodate many players, and so is used much less than the Swiss system. A round robin tournament is easy to pair. Players are assigned numbers by lot, and the pairings are read from Crenshaw tables, Chapter 12.

30B. Scoring.
Scoring is the usual one/one-half/zero, except that players who withdraw before playing half their scheduled games shall be scored as not having competed at all. Their completed games must still be rated, but they are not considered part of their opponents' records for prize purposes.

30C. Withdrawals.
Dropouts cause major problems in round robins. In special invitationals they may be held to a tolerable level, but in open weekend tournaments and weekly club events serious problems are common. Unlike the Swiss, in which a forfeit affects at most one game, a dropout may generate numerous inequities in a round robin, whether notice is given or not.

30D. Penalties for withdrawals.
Players who withdraw without sufficient reason or who repeatedly withdraw from round robins may be denied entry in future such events, or may be charged a special deposit, which will be refunded upon completion of all games. The latter is in addition to any deposit the organizer may choose to require of all players in an effort to minimize withdrawals.

30E. Effect of withdrawals on colors.
If there is a withdrawal, the Crenshaw-Berger system provides tables for adjustments to equalize colors. **See also** Round Robin Pairing Tables.

30F. Double round robins.

In double round robins, each player or team plays each of the others twice, the second time reversing the original color assignment.

30G. Quads.

Quadrangular tournaments divide the entrants into groups of four in rating order. The four highest-rated players form the first group, etc. These players then play three-game round robins following the Crenshaw tables. **See also Chapter 12** Round Robin Pairing Tables.

When the total number of entries is not divisible by four, the director may create a 3-round Swiss among the lowest five to seven players. This works well with a field of six, but not with five or seven since a large percentage of the field will receive a bye. The simplest method of evening the field is to seek another player. If more than one player appears, the late players should be informed that only an odd number prepared to enter immediately will be accepted.

A five-player section may be held as a round robin if all players agree. Players should be warned that this may take much longer since each player will have four opponents and a sit-out. This format is most appropriate with lower-rated players.

The preferred pairing table for quads is as follows: (Players' numbers are assigned in order of rating, not randomly as in larger round robins.)

Round one: 1–4, 2–3; round two: 3–1, 4–2; round three: 1–2, 3–4 (colors by toss in this round)

TD TIP: Some TDs prefer to randomly assign pairing numbers by lot for Quads.

30H. Holland system.

The Holland system uses round robin preliminaries to qualify players for finals, which are usually also round robins. There is no standard format, but a typical one might be to divide players into groups of similar strength of about eight to twelve players each, with the winner or top two in each prelim qualifying for the championship finals and others possibly for lower finals.

The Holland system, once the standard U.S. tournament format, was surpassed by the more flexible Swiss system in the 1940s and is used today largely for Blitz (G/5) tournaments, in which the lack of delay for pairings is especially advantageous.

30I. Unbalanced Holland.

A Holland variant used successfully in Blitz events places the top-rated players in the first preliminary section, the next highest rated in the second, etc., rather than balancing the strength of the sections. Prizes are awarded for each prelim, and all plus scores in the first prelim qualify for the finals, along with the top two players from the second prelim and the winners of each other prelim.

31. Team Chess

Many varieties of team chess exist in the U.S. Different leagues, inter-club events, and tournaments have somewhat different rules. The concern here is principally for team tournaments, but the points made may have wider applicability. Except for 31A, Combined individual-team tournaments, all comments apply to events with team vs. team pairings.

TD TIP: Directors are advised to have a team captains meeting before the first round to make sure the special variations on the particular style of team chess for any one event are well understood by the teams involved.

31A. Combined individual-team tournaments.

As the name suggests, these are not true team tournaments. They are particularly popular as scholastic events because they allow schools to enter any number of players instead of a team with a fixed roster. The tournament is played as a normal Swiss, except that efforts are made to avoid pairing teammates (i.e., players from the same school) with each other. **See also** 28A, Pairing cards or program and 28N, Combined individual-team tournaments.

TD TIP: No large combined individual-team tournament is paired by hand any longer. The amount of detailed paperwork plus keeping track of team members for reports and pairings along with calculating team and individual tiebreaks makes this style of tournament an ideal candidate for pairing by computer.

31A1 The Rollins (Military) Scoring system for combined events.

This system offers a means to determine team and individual champions from a single event (usually a Swiss). The individual champion is determined using the normal rules and announced tie-breaks for the event. The number of eligible team members (for example, 4, 5 or 6) is determined as announced in the event promotion. Eligible teams are then selected by identifying the respective highest scoring players for each team. Based on the total number of players, each player receives a score that is the inverse of his overall placing. Example: The top player in a 100 player event receives 99 points, second place receives 98 points, etc. Individual scores for eligible team members are then combined to derive the team score. The highest team score is declared the Team Champion.

TD TIP: This method is especially useful for Swiss tournaments where the number of teams is small and the total number of participants is large. See rule 28N, and the Scholastic regulations, for the typical scoring method used at individual/team tournaments.

A WORKING MODEL The following scoring happens in a fictional tournament that is a 6 round Swiss event consisting of 100 players and four teams. In this example, the Top Individual player (determined from the 6 round Swiss tournament) was from the Army and the Army won the Team Championship as well (determined from the standings from the individual tournament). (See Table 31 A.1)

Table 31A.1 Rollins System for Combined Events

	Army Team	Pts.	Navy Team	Pts.	Air Force Team	Pts.	Marine Team	Pts.
Player 1	1st	99	3rd	97	2nd	98	4th	96
Player 2	5th	95	7th	93	8 th	92	10th	90
Player 3	6th	94	9th	91	11 th	89	12th	88
Player 4	13th	87	14th	86	16 th	84	15th	85
Player 5	17th	83	18th	82	22nd	78	23rd	77
Player 6	19th	81	20th	80	21st	79	24th	76
Place/Total		539		529		520		512

* This is the official scoring system of the US Armed Forces Open Chess Tournament.

31B. Player rankings.

Players on a team are ranked according to rating; the higher-rated players play on lower board numbers. Alternates must be lower-rated than regular team members. Unrated players, unless assigned ratings (28D), must play on higher-numbered boards than rated players.

TD TIP: The lowest board number is 1 (first position where the highest rated player is seated). This can be confusing since the top players play on this board.

If a player is missing from the lineup, lower-rated teammates must move up to preserve the order by rating, so that if a team forfeits games, they are always on the last (highest-numbered, lowest-rated) boards. Board assignments must always be made as described in the preceding paragraph.

TD TIP: Players missing from a team lineup require special care. The director can announce that individual team members should not start play unless all team members for both teams are present. After a very short time, announced by the director, all players missing from the lineup must be replaced by lower-rated teammates as outlined in 31B or any announced and posted variations of 31B. The individual games may then begin.

A variation on this technique is used in round one, which presents special problems regarding players missing from the lineup. Travel is known to delay a player's arrival. Some directors, if they are confident that the player will arrive in time to complete a game, allow play to start in round one with a player missing from the lineup without enforcing 31B. Those directors often check with site officials, such as the hotel staff, to see if the player has arrived before making this ruling; however, this technique can backfire. For a lot of reasons the missing player may not show up at all. What the director rules at this point has an effect on team match points and team tiebreak points.

Ruling one: The team with the missing player forfeits that board and all boards below it. The actual game result is reported to US Chess for rating purposes but scored as forfeit losses for the team event. This method has a negative impact on the calculation of future tiebreak points.

Ruling two: The team with the missing player forfeits only the missing board. In all future rounds 31B will apply to the team with the missing player. This lessens the negative impact on future calculations of tiebreak points; however, it may cause the team with a full team roster to actually lose the round one match.

Since either ruling directly affects the team with the full roster of players, some directors allow that team to choose which ruling they prefer. Other directors may allow that team to decide before play starts if they prefer the enforcement of 31B or one of the two rulings just outlined here.

31B1. Board prizes.
If individual board prizes are offered, players who play on more than one board are eligible only for the lowest board played. The player's points on all boards combined are credited toward the board prize on the lowest board.

TD TIP: If a player plays in positions 1 and 4, the player's combined points would be credited toward the board prize for position 4.

Variation 31B2. Placement of unrated players in team lineup.
An unrated player may play on any board.

31C. Team ratings.

Teams are ranked in order of the average of individual ratings of the rated regulars, not alternates. Unrated players (28D) do not affect their team's average rating.

Variation 31C1. Unrateds and team ratings.

In calculating the average team rating, an unrated on board four is assigned 50 points below the rating of board three. An unrated on board three is assigned the average of the board two and four ratings. An unrated on board two is assigned the average of the board one and three ratings. An unrated on board one is assigned 50 points above the rating of board two. This system and 31B1 have been used at the Pan-American Intercollegiate.

TD TIP: Pairing software can calculate a team's average rating automatically.

31D. Pairing cards.

Team tournaments use pairing cards similar to those used in individual tournaments, except that there is space to note both match scores and game points. Ideally, a larger pairing card, such as one measuring five-by-eight inches, should be used. These are available from US Chess office.

The front of the pairing card should contain the team name, the team average rating, the round-by-round results of the team, the colors of the team, and the team's opponents. The reverse side should contain the names of the players, their ratings, their US Chess identification numbers, and the name of the team captain, as well as any information about fees and dues paid.

TD TIP: Pairing software can take care of these tasks automatically.

31E. Pairing rules.

Swiss team events should be paired in the same manner as individual events. Teams are grouped by their match points and then ranked within the group by their ratings. Rules governing color allocations apply to the color received by board one. If the first board receives white, for example, so do all teammates on odd-numbered boards, while his or her even-numbered teammates play black. Byes, defaults, lateness, and so forth are treated as in individual tournaments. Scoring is based on match points, without regard to the margin of victory.

In each match of a team tournament, a full match point (1.0) is awarded to the team with the greater game point total, while the opposing team receives no match points (0.0). If the two teams' game point totals are the same, each team receives half a match point (0.5).

TD TIP: Typically to win a match point a team's game point total must be at least one-half point more than the opposing team's game point total for that round (to draw the match both teams' game point totals are the same); i.e., the team with the largest total team game score wins the match or if the team game scores are equal draws the match. In the case of a double forfeit on one or more boards, it is possible for a team to win or draw the match even though its game point total seems insufficient to typically win or draw. For example, with 4-player teams, neither team's 4th board shows up. Team A wins on boards 1 and 2 (two game points) while team B wins on board 3 (one game point). Team A wins the match (and scores 1.0 match point) even though its game score is only 2.0 (typically only enough to draw a 4 board team match). Or, if the games on boards 1 through 3 are all draws, and board 4 is a double forfeit, then teams A and B each draw the match (0.5 match points) even though each team's game score is only 1.5 (typically not enough to draw or win a 4 board team match).

The director or organizer should announce in advance any variation on this procedure, including the minimum number of players (other than a full team) required to be present for a team to be paired or the minimum number of game points required for a team to win or draw a match.

One example variation: in each match of a team tournament, a full match point (1.0) is awarded to the team with the greater game point total only if that game point total is greater than half the available game points for the match; e.g., a team's game point total must be at least 2.5 in a team tournament with four-board teams in order to win. If a team scores exactly half the available game points, then the team receives half a match point (0.5); e.g., a team's game point total must be at least 2.0 in a team tournament with four-board teams in order to draw the match. If a team scores fewer than half the available match points for the match that team receives no game points (0.0); e.g., a team with a game point total equal to or less than 1.5 in a team tournament with four-board teams cannot score a match point.

Under this variation, if two teams with only three players each meet in a four-board match, a game score of 2-1 would lead to one team drawing the match (0.5 match point) and the other team losing the match (0.0 match point), while a game score of 1.5-1.5 would lead to both teams losing the match (0.0 match point).

Note that colors are less important for teams with an even number of boards than they are in an individual tournament, since half the team will have each color in every round.

Variation 31E1. Game point scoring.
Scoring and pairings may be done by game points rather than match points, or by a combination of the two (match points first, then game points if tied).

TD TIP: This is an ideal task for properly set pairing software.

31F. Wall charts.

Swiss team events are unique in that two sets of wall charts are needed: team charts to display team results and individual charts for individual results. The latter, in addition to being informative, are needed for tiebreak and rating purposes.

The individual charts are set up by team so that the highest-average-rated team's players would appear as numbers 1, 2, 3, 4, etc., the second-highest-rated team's players next, and so on down to the lowest-rated team's players. Note that a player on a lower-rated team could have the highest individual rating in the tournament but still be placed far down on the wall charts.

A form that combines individual and team entries on a single wall chart is also possible, as is the use of a separate individual wall chart for each board.

31G. Team captain.

The role of the team captain is:

31G1. Registration.

To register the team with all appropriate information.

31G2. Arrival.

To see that the team arrives on time for each match.

31G3. Lineup.

To see that the team plays the correct opponent, in the correct board order, with the correct colors.

31G4. Draw consequences.

To advise the players, if asked, what the likely consequences of a draw would be for the team, and to respond to such a request without looking at the game of the player making the request.

31G4a. Captain may not impose results.

Each player alone is responsible for the result of his or her own game. The team captain may not impose results upon team members.

31G5. Reporting result.

To report the result of the match to the tournament director in the manner required.

31G6. Wall charts.

To check the wall charts for accuracy and to report any discrepancies to the director.

32. Prizes

32A. Announcement.
Prizes to be awarded and the methods used to allocate them must be announced in pre-tournament publicity if they vary from the standards below. In all cases, these guidelines apply equally to individuals or teams. **See also** 23A1, Obligation to pay guaranteed prizes.

32B. Distribution.

32B1. One cash prize per player.
No winner shall receive more than one cash award. The award may be one full cash prize if a clear winner, or parts of two or more cash prizes if tied with others. Prizes such as *biggest upset*, *best game*, or *brilliancy* are standard exceptions from this rule. Any other special prizes should be announced and designated as such. A clear winner of more than one cash prize must be awarded the most valuable prize. For examples see 32B5, Offering a choice of prizes.

32B2. Ties.
Tied winners of place prizes or tied winners in the same class of class prizes shall be awarded all the cash prizes involved, summed and divided equally; but no more than one cash prize shall go into the division for each winner. For examples see 32B5, Offering a choice of prizes.

32B3. Ties for more than one prize.
If winners of different prizes tie with each other, all the cash prizes involved shall be summed and divided equally among the tied winners unless any of the winners would receive more money by winning or dividing only a particular prize for which others in the tie are ineligible. No player may receive an amount greater from the division of those prizes than the largest prize for which he would be eligible if there were no tie. No more than one cash prize shall go into the pool for each winner. **For examples** see 32B5, Offering a choice of prizes.

TD TIP: The number of prizes in the pool to be split may not exceed the number of players in the tie.

32B4. Priority of identical prizes.
A player who is eligible for both a place prize and a class prize of an identical amount shall receive the place prize. A player who is eligible for more than one class prize of an identical amount shall receive the prize for the highest class involved. A player who is eligible for prizes of identical amounts, with one being a rating-based class prize and the other being a prize for juniors, seniors, etc., shall receive the rating-based class prize. For examples see 32B5, Offering a choice of prizes.

32B5. Offering a choice of prizes.

No player shall ever be offered a choice of which cash prize to accept, as this would allow that player to determine which prizes are available to be awarded to others.

Example 1:

1st prize = $200

2nd prize = $100

3rd prize = $75

Players 1 and 2 tie for 1st and 2nd with 4.5-0.5, players 3, 4, and 5 score 4-1. No other player has more than 3.5 points.

Players 1 and 2 win $150 each (equal shares of 1st and 2nd).

Players 3, 4, and 5 win $25 each (equal shares of 3rd).

Example 2:

1st prize = $400

2nd prize = $200

A prize = $100

B prize = $50

Players 1, 2, 3 (Masters) score 5-0, players 4 (an Expert), 5 (an A), and 6 (a B) are next with 4-1. No other player has more than 3.5 points.

Players 1, 2, and 3 win $200 each (equal shares of 1st-2nd).

Player 4 wins no money.

Player 5 wins $100 (the A prize).

Player 6 wins $50 (the B prize).

Note: If instead of the A prize of $100 and B prize of $50 an *Under 2000* prize of $100 and *Under 1800* prize of $50 had been advertised, players 5 and 6 would win $75 each.

Example 3:

1st prize = $250	1st A = $75
2nd prize = $200	2nd A = $50
3rd prize = $150	1st B = $75
4th prize = $100	

Players 1 and 2 score 5-0. Players 3, 4, 5, 6 score 4.5-0.5, where 4 and 5 are A players and 6 a B player. Player 7 (an A) scores 4-1.

Players 1 and 2 each win $225 (equal shares of $250 + $200).

Players 3, 4, 5, 6 each win $100 (equal shares of $150 + $100 + $75 + $75).

Player 7 wins $50 (second A).

If both monetary and non-monetary prizes are offered, see 33D2 and Variation 33D2a plus the examples following 33D2a.

32C. Payment.
Prizes advertised as guaranteed must be paid promptly and in full. Prize winners may be required to provide ID, social security numbers, tax forms information, etc. before prizes can be issued. Failure to pay guaranteed prizes may result in penalties, including revocation of affiliation or tournament director certification.

32C1. Withdrawals.
Unless the director decides otherwise, players who fail to complete the tournament are not entitled to prizes.

32C2. One player in class.
An announced class prize must be awarded even if only one player in that class completes the schedule, unless otherwise advertised.

32C3. No players in class.
If no player in a class completes the schedule, awarding an advertised prize for that class is not required.

32C4. Based-on prizes.
In tournaments in which prizes are based on entries, if the actual turnout is smaller than the based-on turnout, the following rules apply:

32C4a. Proportional payout.
Each prize must be paid at least in proportion to the turnout.

32C4b. 50% minimum.
If the total advertised prize fund is greater than $500 (all sections combined), at least 50% of each advertised prize must be paid.

32C4c. Multiple-section tournaments.
If separate based-on goals are announced for different sections, then the proportion paid in each section (32C4a) is treated separately. If a common based-on goal is announced for multiple sections, then the proportion paid in these sections is considered together. In either case, 32C4b also applies.

Examples:

1. A tournament advertises $1,000 in prizes if 100 players enter. Only 30 enter. The organizer is required to pay at least $500, each prize being at least half the original projection.

2. A tournament advertises $1,000 in prizes if 100 players enter. Only 70 enter. The organizer is required to pay at least $700 in prizes, each prize to be at least 70 percent of the amount originally advertised.

3. A tournament advertises $400 in prizes if 40 players enter. Only 10 players enter. The organizer is required to pay at least $100 in prizes, each prize to be at least 25% (10/40 = 25%) of the amount originally advertised.

TD TIP: When there are no players eligible for a prize, that prize is simply not awarded. The based-on formula then applies (as it would have been if there were players eligible for all prizes) to the remaining advertised prize money. Directors are not required to redistribute any prize money that players do not qualify for in based-on prize funds; however, be aware that any based-on prize in any tournament that is a also a Grand Prix event is subject to review and adjustment by US Chess.

32C5. Reentry prizes.

Unless announced otherwise, reentries (28S) qualify only for prizes calculated by their latest reentry score. **See also** 28S5, Reentry scores and 34H, Reentry tiebreaks.

32C6. Limited Prizes:

In general, when a player is allowed to enter a given event or section, that player is eligible for the prizes in that section. However, when a player (e.g. an unrated in a lower section) receives a limited prize, the distribution of the remaining prize is to follow the following priority list.

The total dollar amount of all cash prizes announced or computed by "based on" shall be paid:

1. Within the event.
2. Within the section in which the limit was awarded.
3. Within the prize group (e.g. place, class or under) in which the limit was awarded.
4. Within the point group in which the limit was awarded.

See also 33F Unrateds.

32D. Minimum penalty for violation of 32C4.

The minimum penalty shall be disqualification from advertising in *Chess Life* for one year. Additional penalties may be imposed at the discretion of the Executive Director. If a tournament is affected with extreme adverse events, then the organizer may appeal to US Chess. **See also** 21L, Appeal to US Chess.

Organizers are expected to base their prize funds on estimates of player attendance that can be reasonably achieved. An organizer who repeatedly overestimates tournament attendance may be subject to penalties, at the discretion of US Chess.

32E. Partial guarantees.

Sometimes the overall prize fund is based on entries, but some prize(s), most often first overall, is (are) guaranteed. Organizers should realize that, in such cases, they are guaranteeing more than a proportional payment of prizes, and that if the projected prize fund is more than $500, they are also guaranteeing more than 50 percent of the projected prize fund under these circumstances.

For example, if projected prizes are $2,000 based on 60 entries with $500 guaranteed to first, and 30 players enter, the $500 first prize must be awarded and the remaining $1,500 that was projected cannot be lowered below $750 (as each prize must not be less than half of what was projected). So, the actual total guarantee is $1,250 ($500 first place + $750 minimum based on $1500 expected payment based on 32C4), not $1,000.

TD TIP: The TD should realize that in the unique case of multiple players all finishing the tournament with perfect scores (winning the maximum number of games possible in a tournament), the standard tiebreaking systems would not have the same relevance as they would in outcomes where the players finished with less-than perfect scores, and could have otherwise done better. It is impossible to improve on a perfect score. Therefore, in the special case of more than one player finishing with a perfect score, the TD should make every effort possible to have a playoff among all players with perfect scores, to determine the winner of the event. The playoff does not have to be rated, and the time control can be faster than the time control used for the tournament (but should allow at least five minutes per player). A special playoff to break perfect-score ties does not need to be announced in the tournament publicity, but should be announced to the players at the beginning of the tournament.

32F. Trophies.

No player should receive more than one individual trophy or plaque, the most desirable to which he or she is entitled. It is recommended that no class, age, or school grade trophy be as desirable as any of the place trophies. A player should not have a choice of trophies, since such a choice would decide which trophies are available to be awarded to others. **See Also** 33D1 one non-monetary prize per player.

32F1. Tiebreaking.

Unless another method has been announced in advance, tiebreaking (see 34, Breaking ties) will be used to resolve ties for trophies.

TD TIP: One popular announced method is to have a series of speed game playoffs for non-divisible prizes such as trophies. See also 34E12, Speed play-off game(s).

Variation 32F2. School grade or age trophy and place trophy.

The winner of a school grade or age trophy may also win a place or class trophy. This addresses the common problem of young children who consider any first place better than any lower place regardless of the category. The use of this variation should be posted or announced at the tournament before the first round.

32G. Other non-cash prizes.

No player shall receive more than one non-cash, non-trophy prize, the most valuable to which he or she is entitled. **See Also** 33D1 one non-monetary prize per player.

32G1. Tiebreaking.

Unless another method has been announced in advance, tiebreaking (see 34, Breaking ties) will be used to resolve ties for merchandise, memberships, or free entries, to determine which player wins any title at stake or qualifies to advance into another contest, or for any purpose other than the awarding of money prizes.

TD TIP: One popular method is to have a series of speed game playoffs for non-divisible prizes such as trophies. This should be announced in advance. See also 34E12, Speed play-off game(s)

33. Some Notes About Prize Funds

These are recommendations, rather than rules or mandates, but are included since some less-experienced organizers may find them useful.

33A. First prize.

A ratio of about ten to one between first prize and the entry fee is typical for serious tournaments, as opposed to club events or other tournaments organized to provide experience. This ratio should be even greater in an event designed to attract top players.

33B. Place prizes and class prizes.

When there is apt to be a number of players in a rating class competing in an event, it is frequently the case that some sort of class prize is offered. This should be at least as much as the entry fee paid. Generally, place prizes should be higher than class prizes, both to reward the relative excellence of the chess played and to avoid distribution problems.

In major tournaments, the top prizes for classes or rating-based lower sections are often higher than the lower place prizes, but most organizers consider it inappropriate for any class prize or rating-based lower section prize to be as large as the corresponding overall or top section prize.

TD TIP: One correct example: 1st = $1000, 2nd = $700, 3rd = $500, Class X = $400. One problematical example (the class prize equals or exceeds the lowest place prize): 1st = $1000, 2nd = $700, 3rd = $500, Class X= $600 (or even Class X= $500).

33C. Classes.

A common variation on class prizes is the use of *under* prizes for players below a specified rating. There is a difference between a Class A prize and an Under 2000 prize, since only a Class A player may win the former, while a Class A, B, C, D, or E player can qualify for the latter. If a prize is intended for a restricted group, it should be named by the class or by both ratings boundaries, e.g., Class A or 1800-1999.

33D. Non-monetary (indivisible) prizes.

Non-monetary prizes, such as trophies, clocks, medals, and the like are sometimes offered. These are especially popular at scholastic tournaments, where they are offered in place of monetary prizes. In non-scholastic tournaments, these are sometimes offered alone or sometimes with monetary prizes. See Example 4 in 33D2a below, where the A prize is "$100 + clock."

Indivisible prizes present certain problems because they are, well, indivisible. This often necessitates tie-breaking procedures. **See also** 34, Breaking Ties

33D1. One non-monetary prize per player.

No winner shall receive more than one non-monetary award. Prizes such as *biggest upset*, *best game*, or *brilliancy* are standard exceptions from this rule. Any other special prizes should be announced and designated as such. A clear winner of more than one non-monetary prize must be awarded the highest-ranked prize (*ranking* is described below).

33D1a. Ranking of prizes.

Ranking prizes becomes important when a player qualifies for more than one non-monetary prize. This often leads to the question of which non-monetary prize should be awarded to the player and which left for someone else. For instance, is second Under 2000 ranked ahead of first Under 1800, or is any first place higher than any second place?

If each of the prizes also has a monetary component, the choice of rankings is easy: The prize with the higher cash award is ranked higher. If monetary components of prizes are equal (e.g., 3rd place, 2nd Under 2000, and 1st Under 1800 each has a $100 monetary component along with a trophy), the rankings become more difficult. In this situation, it is recommended that all top prizes be ranked first, then all class prizes for the highest class, then all class prizes for the next highest class, etc., but this may be varied. If the rankings are varied from the recommendation, the director should post the actual rankings at the tournament site in advance and include them in pre-tournament publicity if possible. Example: 1st Under 1800 is ranked as a higher prize than 2nd Under 2000.

TD TIP: For scholastic tournaments, age- or grade-based prizes are usually considered equivalent to class prizes when determining the rank of a prize.

33D2. Monetary and non-monetary prizes calculated separately.

If monetary and non-monetary prizes are offered together, such as "$100 + trophy," the monetary and non-monetary prizewinners should be calculated separately. In case of ties, monetary prizes should be combined and divided equally, as described in 32B5, while tie-breaking procedures should be used to award non-monetary prizes, as in 33D. No player should receive more than one non-monetary prize, except for the standard exceptions listed in 33D1.

TD TIP: As in the TD TIP above, for scholastic tournaments, age- or grade-based prizes are usually considered equivalent to class prizes when determining the rank of a prize.

Variation 33D2a. Monetary and non-monetary prizes calculated together.

If monetary and non-monetary prizes are offered together, such as "$100 + trophy," the non-monetary prize must be awarded to the same person who is awarded the monetary prize, or, if there is a tie for the prize, to the player with the greatest tiebreak points qualifying for the prize. TDs who use this variation should do so consistently and post it at the tournament.

Examples of 33D2 and 33D2a:

Example 1:

1st	$200 + trophy
2nd	$100 + trophy
3rd	$50 + trophy
Top A	$40 + trophy

Player 1 (2250)	5 points
Player 2 (2225)	4.5 points, 20 tiebreak points
Player 3 (1940)	4.5 points, 18 tiebreak points
Player 4 (1865)	4 points, 16 tiebreak points
Player 5 (1990)	4 points, 14 tiebreak points

Player 1 gets $200 and the 1st place trophy.

Player 2 gets $75 + the 2nd place trophy ($75 as an equal share of 2nd and 3rd money, plus the 2nd place trophy because 2's tiebreaks are better than 3's).

Player 3 gets $75 + the 3rd place trophy ($75 as an equal share of 2nd and 3rd money, plus the 3rd place trophy because 3's tiebreaks are worse than 2's). This assumes that the director has ranked top prizes ahead of class prizes.

Player 4 gets $20 + the Top A trophy ($20 as an equal share of the Top A money, plus the Top A trophy because 4's tiebreaks are better than 5's).

Player 5 gets $20 ($20 as an equal share of the Top A money; all trophies have been awarded to other players).

Example 2:

1st	$200 + trophy
2nd	$100 + trophy
3rd	$50 + trophy
Top Under 2200	$40 + trophy
Top Under 2000	$30 + trophy

Player 1 (2250)	5 points
Player 2 (2225)	4.5 points, 20 tiebreak points
Player 3 (1940)	4.5 points, 18 tiebreak points
Player 4 (2375)	4 points, 16 tiebreak points

Player 5 (1990)   4 points, 14 tiebreak points
Player 6 (2125)   3.5 points, 19 tiebreak points
Player 7 (1865)   3.5 points, 10 tiebreak points

Player 1 gets $200 + the 1st place trophy.

Player 2 gets $75 + the 2nd place trophy (an equal share of 2nd and 3rd money, plus the 2nd place trophy because 2's tiebreaks are better than 3's). This assumes that the director has ranked top prizes ahead of class prizes. Player 3 gets $75 + the 3rd place trophy (an equal share of 2nd and 3rd money, plus the 3rd place trophy because 3's tiebreaks are worse than 2's). This assumes that the director has ranked top prizes ahead of class prizes.

Player 4 gets nothing (because player 4 does not qualify for the Top Under 2200 prize or the Top Under 2000 prize).

Player 5 gets $40 + the Top Under 2200 trophy ($40 because the money for Top Under 2200 is greater than the money for Top Under 2000, and the Top Under 2200 trophy because Top Under 2200 is ranked higher than Top Under 2000).

Player 6 gets nothing (because the Top Under 2200 prize has already been awarded and 6 is ineligible for the Top Under 2000 prize).

Player 7 gets $30 + the Top Under 2000 trophy.

Example 3:

(Top prizes – already awarded)
1st Under 2000 $200 + trophy
2nd Under 2000 $100 + trophy
1st Under 1800 $200 + trophy
2nd Under 1800 $100 + trophy

Player 1 (1650)   5, 20 tiebreak points
Player 2 (1750)   5, 18 tiebreak points
Player 3 (2020)   4.5, 23 tiebreak points
Player 4 (1675)   4.5,19 tiebreak points
Player 5 (1920)   4.5, 17 tiebreak points
Player 6 (1700)   4.5, 16 tiebreak points
Player 7 (1845)   4.5, 15 tiebreak points

Player 1 gets $200 + the 1st Under 2000 trophy (because 1st Under 2000 is ranked higher than 1st Under 1800).

Player 2 gets $200 + the 1st Under 1800 trophy.

Player 3 gets nothing.

Player 4 gets $50 + the 2nd Under 2000 trophy (because 2nd Under 2000 is ranked higher than 2nd Under 1800).

Player 5 gets $50.

Player 6 gets $50 + the 2nd Under 1800 trophy.

Player 7 gets $50.

This example illustrates the difference between Class prizes and Under prizes. If the Under 2000 prizes were Class A prizes instead, they would go to Players 5 and 7, as both 5-pointers and the 4.5-pointers in Class B would be ineligible for the Class A prizes.

Example 4:

1st prize = $300

2nd prize = $200

A prize = $100 + clock

Player 1 (Expert) scores 5-0, player 2 (A) scores 4.5-0.5, player 3 (A) scores 4-1.

Player 1 wins $300 as a clear 1st place finisher.

Player 2 wins $200 as a clear 2nd place finisher.

Player 3 wins $100 as clear winner of the A prize, since the other A player has already taken 2nd prize.

Who wins the clock depends on which rule is being followed. If mainline rule 33D2 is being followed, Player 2 gets the clock, as the top finisher in Class A. If Variation 33D2a is being followed, Player 3 gets the clock, as the clock follows the money for the Class A prize.

Example 5:

1st Under 2200	$100 + trophy
2nd Under 2200	$50 + trophy
1st Under 2000	$80 +trophy

Player 1 (1900)	4.5, 20 tiebreak points
Player 2 (2100)	4.5, 18 tiebreak points
Player 3 (2150)	4.5, 16 tiebreak points
Player 4 (1900)	3.5, 23 tiebreak points

Player 1 gets $80 and a trophy. The $80 is the 1st under 2000 prize, which is the greatest monetary prize for which Player 1 is eligible. (If all three listed prizes are summed and divided equally, Player 1 would only receive $76.67.)

Which trophy Player 1 receives depends on which rule is being followed. Under mainline rule 33D2, Player 1 gets the 1st Under 2200 trophy, the highest-ranked trophy for which he qualifies. Under Variation 33D2a, Player 1 gets the 1st Under 2000 trophy, because the trophy follows the money and Player 1 received the 1st under 2000 money (see above for explanation).

Player 2 gets $75 and a trophy. The $75 is an equal share of 1st Under 2200 and 2nd Under 2200 money, as the 1st under 2000 money has already been awarded.

Which trophy Player 2 gets depends on which rule is being followed. Under mainline rule 33D2, Player 2 gets the 2nd under 2200 trophy, because the 1st under 2200 trophy has already been awarded and 2's tiebreaks are better than 3's. Under Variation 33D2a, Player 2 gets the 1st Under 2200 trophy because this trophy is still available and 2's tiebreaks are better than 3's.

Player 3 gets $75 and *might or might not get a trophy depending on which rule is being followed.* The $75 is an equal share of 1st Under 2200 and 2nd Under 2200 money.

If mainline rule 33D2 is being followed, Player 3 gets no trophy, because both Under 2200 trophies have already been awarded. If Variation 33D2a is being followed, Player 3 gets the 2nd Under 2200 trophy, because this trophy is still available and 3 has more points than 4.

Player 4 gets no money, as it has all been awarded. If *mainline rule 33D2* is being followed, Player 4 gets the *1st Under 2000 trophy*, as this trophy is still available. If *Variation* 33D2a is being followed, Player 4 gets *no trophy*, as they have all been awarded.

Trophy prizes for Example 5 under the two rules (monetary prizes are the same under the two rules):

	33D2	33D2a
Player 1	1st U2200	1st U2000
Player 2	2nd U2200	1st U2200
Player 3		2nd U2200
Player 4	1st U2000	

TD TIP: *The prize Player 1 received in this example shows how money is taken out of a pool to be split if a player in the tied group would get more money by taking a particular prize, 1st under 2000 in this example, for which others in the tie are ineligible. In this case the $80 is removed from the pool that is split by the remaining players in the tie (Player 2 and Player 3).* **See also** *32B3, Ties for more than one prize.*

33E. Prizes based on points.

Some organizers base prizes on points scored rather than place. Such events often award prizes to all plus scores, a popular feature for players who doubt their ability to win the top-place prizes.

For example, in a 5-round Swiss with an entry fee of $30, it could be announced that 5 points will win $100, 4.5 points will win $50, 4 points will win $30, 3.5 points will win $20, and 3 points will win $10. With a fee of $60, prizes might be 5 points will win $300, 4.5 point will win $150, 4 points will win $90, 3.5 points will win $60, and 3 points will win $30. These levels provide relative safety for the organizer, since even with a poor turnout prizes will often be less than entry fees.

Prizes based on points have proven more popular with Experts and below than with Masters, so organizers should consider not using them in top sections. It is desirable to have such events in sections of no more than two 200-point classes each or to offer supplementary prizes for lower classes unlikely to make plus scores. A separate section for each class is ideal if the expected turnout is sufficient.

The based-on-points method has a unique advantage over prizes that are guaranteed or based on entries. The announced prizes are never reduced, but their total varies according to the turnout. This protects the organizer against financial loss without the player disappointment sometimes caused by prize reduction. **See also** *32C4, Minimum prizes in based-on-entries tournaments.*

33F. Unrateds.

Note that many players who are playing in their first US Chess tournament, although they have no US Chess ratings, are by no means beginners. Some have high ratings or categories in other countries, and not all reveal these to directors as required. Unrated players should generally not be eligible for any prizes of value other than place or unrated prizes. Prizes such as "D/E/Unrated" are not recommended.

When substantial cash prizes are offered in sections for lower-rated players, unrateds are often ineligible to enter or have a prize limit far below that of rated players. **See also** *29J, Unrateds in class tournaments.*

34. Breaking Ties

34A. Introduction.
There is no perfect tiebreak system; each has its faults. In some events, especially large ones, ease and speed of calculation is a concern. In other events where time is not pressing, playoffs provide a better alternative to traditional tiebreak systems. Playoffs are often conducted at a faster time control than the tournament; even five-minute games have been used.

34B. Announcement.
When used, tiebreak systems should be posted at the site before the first round. There are several tiebreak systems that provide good and objective methods for directors to break ties for indivisible prizes.

Frequently, one tiebreak method alone will not break the tie, and it is necessary to use a secondary and sometimes even a tertiary method to produce a decision. Thus, at least the first two tiebreak systems should be posted. The director should be prepared to explain how the tiebreak systems work, as time permits.

34C. Monetary prizes.
Tiebreaks are not used for cash prizes, which are divided evenly among the tied players. An exception is a playoff, which may be used to determine cash prizes if notice of this is given in all detailed pre-tournament publicity. *See also 32B, Distribution.*

34D. Choice of tiebreak methods.
Different systems will yield different results, but the systems discussed here are not capricious or random. Each seeks to discover the *first among equals*, the player who has a somewhat better claim to a prize than those who earned the same score based on the strength of his or her opposition. Which system to choose depends on the nature of the tournament, its traditions, and the qualities required for the specific situations and conditions at hand.

34E. Calculating Swiss tiebreaks.
This section deals with various systems that have been used successfully at all levels of play. For team events see 34G, Team tiebreaks.

Unless a different method has been posted or announced before the start of the first round, players will expect the following sequence of tiebreak systems to be employed as the first four tiebreakers. Any variation to be used within the various systems should be posted also. These systems (and some additional ones) are explained in detail following the list.

1. Modified Median

2. Solkoff

3. Cumulative

4. Cumulative of Opposition

TD TIP: *Pairing software can calculate tiebreaks automatically.*

TD TIP: *The TD should realize that in the unique case of multiple players all finishing the tournament with perfect scores (winning the maximum number of games possible in a tournament), the standard tiebreaking systems would not have the same relevance as they would in outcomes where the players finished with less-than perfect scores, and could have otherwise done better. It is impossible to improve on a perfect score. Therefore, in the special case of more than one player finishing with a perfect score, the TD should make every effort possible to have a playoff among all players with perfect scores to determine the winner of the event. The playoff does not have to be rated, and the time control can be faster than the time control used for the tournament (but should allow at least five minutes per player). A special playoff to break perfect-score ties does not need to be announced in the tournament publicity, but should be announced to the players at the beginning of the tournament.*

34E1. Modified Median
The Median system, also known as the Harkness system for inventor Kenneth Harkness, evaluates the strength of a player's opposition by summing the final scores of his or her opponents and then discarding the highest and lowest of these scores.

In the Modified Median system, players who tie with even scores (an even score is equal to exactly one half of the maximum possible score), have the highest- and lowest-scoring opponents' scores excluded. The system is modified for players with non-even scores to disregard only the least significant opponents' scores: the lowest-scoring opponent's score is discarded for tied players with plus scores and the highest-scoring for tied players with minus scores.

For tournaments of nine or more rounds, the top two and bottom two scores are discarded for even-score ties, the bottom two scores for plus-score ties, and the top two scores for minus-score ties.

These scores are adjusted for unplayed games, which count a half point each, regardless of whether they were byes, forfeits, or simply rounds not played after an opponent withdrew. So an opponent who won the first two games, lost the third, withdrew and did not play rounds four or five would have an adjusted score of 3 points ($1+1+0+0.5+0.5 = 3$). These adjusted scores are used only to calculate the opponent's tiebreaks. The player's own score is not changed.

If the player involved in the tie has any unplayed games, they count as opponents with adjusted scores of 0.

34E2. Solkoff.
The Solkoff system is the same as the Median system (34E1) except that no opponents' scores are discarded.

34E3. Cumulative.
To determine cumulative tiebreak score, simply add up the cumulative (running) score for each round. For example, if a player's results were win, loss, win, draw, loss, the wall chart would show a cumulative score round by round as 1, 1, 2, 2.5, 2.5. The cumulative tiebreak total is 9 ($1+1+2+2.5+2.5 = 9$). If another player scored 2.5 with a sequence 1, 2, 2.5, 2.5, 2.5, the tiebreak points scored would be 10.5 ($1+2+2.5+2.5+2.5 = 10.5$). The latter player's tiebreaks are higher because he or she scored earlier and presumably had tougher opposition for the remainder of the event. One point is subtracted from the sum for each unplayed win or full-point bye (22B); likewise, one-half point is subtracted from the sum for each unplayed draw or half-point bye.

This system is ideal for large events, since it is very fast and easy to use. It also avoids the problem, common in Median and Solkoff, of having to wait for a lengthy last-round game between two non-contenders to end for top prizes to be decided. Another advantage is that last-round scores need not be included in calculating cumulative tiebreak points, since they have no effect on breaking the tie (both tied players will necessarily have the same last round score).

TD TIP: Cumulative tiebreaks can be calculated after the next to last round or while the last round is in progress.

Additional systems choose the stronger player by:

34E4. Median system (not modified).
See 34E1.

34E5. Result between tied players.

Self-explanatory if two tie, but useful only when they were paired and did not draw. If more than two tie, all results among tied players should be considered, with rank according to plus or minus, not percentage. For example, 3-1 (+2) beats 1-0 (+1).

34E6. Most blacks.

Also self-explanatory.

34E7. Kashdan.

This system rewards aggressive play by scoring 4 tiebreak points for a win, 2 for a draw, 1 for a loss, and 0 for an unplayed game. Note that if players with no unplayed games tie, the one with fewer draws will come out ahead.

34E8. Sonneborn-Berger.

See 34F. The disadvantage of using this system in a Swiss is that losses are disregarded, and a player losing to a strong opponent deserves more credit than one losing to a weak opponent. In a round robin, this problem does not exist, since everyone plays the same field.

34E9. Cumulative scores of opposition.

The cumulative tiebreak points of each opponent are calculated as in 34E3 and these are added together.

34E10. Opposition's performance.

This method averages the performance ratings of the players' opposition. Performance ratings are calculated by crediting the player with the opponent's rating plus 400 points for a victory, the opponent's rating minus 400 points for a loss, and the opponent's rating for a draw. Results of tied players against each other should not be included, since this would give one of the players an unfair advantage. After the performance rating for each tied players' opponents has been calculated, they are averaged. Both this system and 34E11 may be difficult to use when unrated players are in the tournament.

Example: A player who wins against a 1400 and a 1500, draws against a 1600, and loses to a 1700 would have a performance rating of 1650: (1400+400) + (1500+400) + 1600 + (1700–400) = 6600; 6600/4 = 1650.

34E11. Average rating of opposition.

This system averages the ratings of players' opponents, the better tiebreak score going to the person who played the highest-rated average field. It sounds fair but has drawbacks. A tied player rated slightly above another will often have a very slightly higher-rated field and win the tiebreak by a statistically insignificant margin.

34E12. Speed play-off game(s).

The speed playoff, an exciting way to wind up a tournament, has been used as the first tiebreak to determine the title at several major events. **See also** 32F1, Tiebreaking and 32F, Trophies.

34E13. Coin flip

This breaks all ties.

TD TIP: One state chess association that has had a comprehensive list of tiebreaks for many years uses (in order): Modified Median; Solkoff; Cumulative; Result between tied players; Most blacks; Kashdan; Sonneborn-Berger; and Coin flip. Having an ordered list that goes this deep can be useful.

34F. Round robin tiebreaks.

The most common method is the Sonneborn-Berger system, also known as the partial-score method. For each player in the tie, add the final scores of all the opponents the player defeated and half the final scores of all the opponents with whom the player drew. Nothing is added for the games the player lost, or for unplayed games. If the tie still remains, the results of the game(s) between the players involved in the tie are used.

34G. Team tiebreaks.

34G1. Game (or match) points.

Since most team events in the United States are scored on match points, the easiest tiebreak is simply the total game points earned by the teams involved. However, it is of questionable value because the teams that face the weakest opposition are more likely to win their matches by large margins. If game scoring is primary, the number of matches won is a simple and fair tiebreak.

34G2. U.S. Amateur Team System.

For each round, the tiebreak points are the final score of the opposing team multiplied by the number of points scored against that team. For example, if Team A scored 2.5-1.5 against Team B, which finished the tournament with 3 match points, Team A's tiebreak for that round is $2.5 \times 3 = 7.5$. This system awards credit for an extra margin of victory without the drawbacks of using straight game points, and is preferable.

34G3. Other systems.

Most of the individual tiebreak systems described in 34E are also suitable for team play, but they have the drawback of making the margin of victory meaningless in match-point scoring. Many players find a team event more exciting when every game can affect the team standings, even after a match has been won or lost.

34H. Reentry tiebreaks.
a. The reentered player must use the announced tiebreaks for the entry determined by 28S5, Reentry scores.
b. The opponents of reentered players can use only the scores of whichever entry (the original entry or one of the reentries) that they played, when calculating the announced tiebreaks.

See also 32C5, Reentry prizes.

TD TIP: Due to the complexity of reentry tiebreaks directors and organizers need to consider very carefully the advisability of having both reentries and non-divisible prizes as options at the same event.

35. Rules for Disabled and Assisted Players

35A. Purpose.
The purpose of these rules for players with temporary or permanent disabilities is to encourage them to play chess. Bearing in mind that there are many kinds of disabled individuals with a wide variety of challenges, the tournament director enjoys considerable discretionary authority to institute special rules.

35B. Equality of treatment.
Players with temporary or permanent disabilities that prevent them from fulfilling certain conditions of the *Official Rules of Chess* shall have special consideration in meeting those rules. Their opponents shall be offered the same, or equivalent in the judgment of the TD, consideration. The tournament director is responsible for seeing that both opponents know about and understand any special rules for that particular game. No player may refuse to play a disabled or assisted human opponent. For rules regarding computers see 36, Rules and Regulations For Computer Participants. For Internet rules regarding disabled players see Rule 14. Players with Disabilities (Chapter 10).

35C. Eligibility for US Chess events.
To be eligible to compete, a player must be able to communicate in some unambiguous manner his or her selection of moves, in a way that does not require prompting of any kind from any person. An interpreter may be employed.

35D. Analogous situations.
When there are doubts concerning provisions to make in the rules for disabled players, the tournament director should consult the following rules for visually impaired players, closely adapted from FIDE's rules for the visually

impaired, and apply them analogously. These rules apply when one or both players are impaired.

35E. Access.

US Chess organizers should make every effort to secure sites for their tournaments that are accessible to disabled players and provided with accessible facilities for their comfort.

35F. Rules for visually impaired and disabled players.

TD TIP: These rules can be applied analogously to any case where a player is disabled. The director might also find it valuable to use these rules as a guide for dealing with cases in which the player has religious, philosophical, or practical concerns. See also 15A1, Players unable to keep score.

35F1. Special chessboard.

A blind, visually impaired, or disabled player is entitled to use a chessboard with securing apertures or other devices designed specifically for use by disabled players even if a non-disabled opponent prefers to use a normal board simultaneously. In a game between two unsighted or disabled players, each is entitled to individually use a separate board.

In a game involving a single disabled player, such player may use an additional special board, while the non-disabled player uses a normal board. In a game between two disabled players, either is entitled to use a special board, but the game may be played on a single special board if both players agree. In cases where there are two boards in use, the game position is maintained on both. A player or his assistant is responsible for physically moving the pieces on any board used by that player.

35F2. Announcement of moves.

Legal moves shall be announced clearly by the player, repeated by the opponent, and executed on the player's board. Failure to announce moves correctly may be penalized by the addition of two unused minutes to the opponent's remaining time.

TD TIP: If a move different from that announced and repeated is executed, the TD or his designee must stop the game and determine if the announced or executed move will be designated as the completed move. See Rule 35F8, Conflict between two positions.

35F3. Touch-move rule.

On the blind, visually impaired, or disabled player's board, a piece shall be deemed *touched* when it has been taken entirely out of the securing aperture or other device on the special chessboard. *See also Rule 10, The Touched Piece and 35F1, Special chessboard.*

35F4. Determination of a move.

A move shall be deemed determined (Rule 9, Determination and Completion of the Move) when all of the following procedures have occurred:

a. A piece is placed into a securing aperture or other device on a special chessboard (35F1).

b. In the case of a capture, the captured piece has been removed from the board of the player who is on move.

c. The move has been announced (35F2).

Only after completing these procedures shall the opponent's clock be started. The move is completed (Rule 9, Determination and Completion of the Move) when the clock is pressed (5H). Pressing the clock before the move has been determined by these procedures may be penalized by the addition of two minutes to the opponent's remaining time.

TD TIP: Often players will press the clock after determining the move on their own board but before announcing the move to the opponent. This would violate the procedures outlined in 35F4 and 35F2. The offending player should be penalized.

35F5. Special clock.

A chess clock made especially for the blind, visually impaired or disabled player shall be admissible for use in that player's game. Rule 16B2a does not apply to such a clock.

35F6. Scorekeeping options.

An unsighted player or disabled player may keep the score of the game in Braille, by using a tape recorder, or by using any other specially-designed device. **See also** 35F10, Optional assistance.

35F7. Correction of erroneously stated move.

A slip of the tongue in announcing a move must be corrected immediately and before starting the clock of the opponent.

35F8. Conflict between two positions.

If different positions arise on the two boards during a game, such differences must be corrected with the assistance of the director and with consultation of both players' game scores. In resolving such differences, the player who has recorded or announced one move but has made another one may be penalized by the addition of two minutes to the opponent's remaining time. **See also** 35F2, Announcement of moves and 35F9, Conflict between positions and game scores.

35F9. Conflict between positions and game scores.

If discrepancies such as those described in 35F8 occur, and the two game scores are also found to differ, the game shall be reconstructed up to the last point of agreement, and the director shall adjust the clocks accordingly.

35F10. Optional assistance.

A blind, visually impaired, or disabled player shall have the right to make use of an assistant, who shall have any or all of the following duties:

a. to make the moves of the blind or disabled player on the board of the opponent;

b. to announce the moves of the non-disabled player;

c. to keep score for the blind or disabled player and to start the opponent's clock;

d. to inform the blind or disabled player, on request, of the number of moves made and the time consumed by either or both players;

e. to claim a win on time for the blind or disabled player or inform the blind or disabled player when the opponent has touched a piece without moving it (effective 1-1-19);

f. to carry out the necessary formalities in cases when the game is to be adjourned;

g. to pause the clock and summon a tournament director at the request of the blind or disabled player (effective 1-1-19).

If the blind, visually impaired, or disabled player uses such assistance, the non-disabled player is entitled to and must provide his or her own parallel assistance should he or she so desire.

TD TIP: Though not required to do so, the TD should do everything possible to help both the disabled and non-disabled players(opponents) to secure assistants. Often spectators or players with byes are willing to act as assistants.

35F11. Assistance for the non-disabled player.

If the blind, visually impaired, or disabled player uses a special chessboard and does not require any assistance, the non-disabled player may make use of an assistant, provided by the non-disabled player, who shall announce either one or both players' moves and make the blind or disabled player's moves on the non-disabled player's board. Note that if acceptable to both players, they may both use the same assistant.

TD TIP: As in the TD TIP above, though not required to do so, the TD should do everything possible to help both the disabled and non-disabled players (opponents) to secure assistants. Often spectators or players with byes are willing to act as assistants. same as tip above.

35F12. Certification of visual impairment.
US Chess accepts a state's certification of a person's legal blindness as sufficient evidence of eligibility for tournaments for the visually impaired and for special considerations under these rules except if that person holds a valid driver's license.

36. Rules and Regulations for Computer Participants

36A. Membership.
The originator or the legal owner of a computer program may register the computer program as a member of US Chess. The dues for computers are the same as for regular members. The rights of computer members are: the right to play in US Chess-rated tournaments, subject to possible restrictions; the right to acquire an official US Chess rating; and a subscription to *Chess Life* magazine. Specific identification and registration procedures shall be determined administratively.

36B. Purchase of membership.
Computer program owners may purchase memberships only directly from US Chess office. Owners are required to sign a statement agreeing to specific rules. The memberships are available only for experimental programs, and owners are required to sign a noncommercial-use agreement.

36C. Computer participation must be advertised in advance.
Computers may not participate in rated tournaments unless that participation is prominently advertised in all pre-tournament publicity. Tournament announcements in *Chess Life* must specify that computers are eligible to participate by using the symbol "C" for computer participation. If this symbol does not appear, computers may not enter. Entries must be arranged in advance with the director's or organizer's consent.

36D. Player may not object.
A player may not object to being paired against a chess-playing computer program in a tournament that advertised computer participation.

TD TIP: Because computer participation must be advertised in advance, players will know before they decide to enter a tournament that there is a possibility that they will be paired against a computer program; therefore, by entering the event they have given their implied consent to being paired against any possible computer program. It would be wise to post this at the site and to give players an opportunity to withdraw from the event if they do not wish to give their consent to such a pairing.

36E. Computer vs. computer.

Computers shall not be paired against each other unless the event is for computers only.

36F. Prize eligibility.

Computers may win only prizes specifically designated for them. Other prizes shall be distributed as though computers were not entered.

36G. Commercial computers.

Commercially available computers and computer programs may acquire ratings only through US Chess's Computer Rating Agency. Interested manufacturers should write to US Chess for details.

36H. Consultation.

Players who consult a computer for advice about their games shall be subject to the same penalties that would be imposed for asking advice from another person. *See also 20D, Use of additional chessboard or computer prohibited.*

36I. Rules for play involving computers.

Following are rules for US Chess-rated tournaments in which one player is a computer. In matters not governed by these rules, play is governed by applicable human rules, as interpreted by the director. In the following, the term *computer* refers to a chess program running on a computer. The term *opponent* refers to the computer's opponent. The term *operator* refers to the person running the computer.

36I1. Parameter settings.

Before play begins, the operator shall do all initial setting up of the computer. At that time, the operator may freely specify any operating parameters, such as rate of play, suggested openings, value of a draw, etc. After play begins, the role of the operator is passive. During the game, the operator is not allowed to alter any parameter settings that might affect the course of the game.

36I2. Communication of moves.

During play, the operator is to communicate the opponent's moves to the computer.

36I3. Execution of moves.

The operator is to execute the computer's specified move on the chessboard. *Touch* rules do not apply to the operator, but excessive handling of pieces may violate other rules, such as those against distracting the opponent. A piece shall be deemed touched by the computer when a move involving that piece has been communicated by the program to its output device, except that displays of moves it is considering shall not be considered communication of a move. A move for the computer shall be deemed completed when the operator, in accordance with normal rules, has executed it on the board.

36I4. The clock.

After the computer's move is executed, the operator is to start the opponent's clock.

36I5. Reconciliation of positions.

If different positions should arise on the playing chessboard and the computer's representation of same, such difference shall be corrected with the assistance of the director. The director may choose either to accept the playing chessboard as official or retrace the moves to the point of departure. If the director chooses to back up the game, then clocks shall be adjusted accordingly. The director shall penalize the computer if the score indicates that the computer or its operator has caused the discrepancy of position.

36I6. Resetting the computer.

If the computer is unable to accept a legal move because of discrepancies, communication trouble, or computer trouble, then the operator may reset the current board position and status on the computer, along with clock times. Other parameters set must be the same as those in effect at the start of the game. The clocks are not stopped during the resetting of the computer nor for any other "down time" (time when the computer is unable to function despite the efforts of its operator).

36I7. Clock times.

There shall be a clock at the chessboard whether or not there is an internal clock in the computer. The operator and the opponent shall use the external clock, which shall be the official timer for the game.

The operator may communicate the clock times to the computer only if the computer initiates the request.

36I8. Memory-unit exchange.

The operator may change or insert memory units when the computer requests this and identifies the unit to be inserted, by description or by generating a coded signal or message with a single, predetermined meaning. Diskettes, disk cartridges, tapes, ROM cartridges ("program modules" in commercial machines), and the like are all considered equivalent forms of memory units.

36I9. Draw offers and resignation.

The operator may offer a draw, accept a draw, or resign on behalf of the computer, either with or without consulting the computer or humans of any playing strength about the decision. Humans so consulted should be disinterested as to the result of the game.

36I10. Time forfeits.

The operator may claim a win on time (13C) if the opponent has exceeded the time limit.

36I11. Adjournments.

The operator shall carry out the necessary adjournment formalities.

36I12. Score.

The operator and/or the computer must keep a score of the game.

36I13. FIDE warning.

An event with a non-FIDE registered computer cannot be FIDE-rated even for humans who are not paired against the computer.

CHAPTER THREE

CHESS NOTATION

37. Introduction

Since 1981, the World Chess Federation (FIDE) has recognized only algebraic notation for its highest-level tournaments and has vigorously encouraged the universal use of this system. US Chess officially supports the use of this single, worldwide notation system, but still recognizes other systems, including the older descriptive notation and the newer computer algebraic. These three systems and some variants are described here, along with international correspondence notation.

38. Notation Systems

38A. Algebraic.
This has become the most widely used system.

38A1. Pieces.
Pieces except pawns are identified by an uppercase letter, the first letter of their names. King and knight start with *K*, so *N* is used for the knight. Pawn moves are indicated by the absence of such an uppercase letter.

The names of the pieces vary from language to language, of course, so the identifying abbreviations vary also. Here is a table of the symbols for the pieces in some major Western languages:

	♔	♕	♖	♗	♘
English	K	Q	R	B	N
German	K	D	T	L	S
Spanish	R	D	T	A	C
French	R	D	T	F	C
Dutch	K	D	T	L	P
Russian	KP	Ф	Л	С	K
Icelandic	K	D	H	B	R

Figure 8

38A2. Squares.
Squares are identified by a small letter and a number (see **Figure 9,** next page), signifying the algebra-like coordinates on the board; thus, the name of the system.

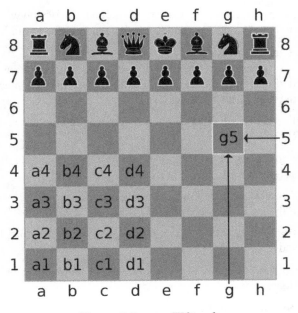

Figure 9 *Image: Wikipedia*

38A3. Files.

The rows of squares going from one player to the other (*up and down*) are files and are labeled with letters *a* through *h*, starting with the row to White's left.

38A4. Ranks.

The rows of squares going from the left to the right edge of the board are ranks and are labeled with numbers 1 through 8, starting at White's side of the board. At the start of the game, therefore, White's major pieces are on the first rank and pawns on the second; Black's are on the eighth and seventh ranks, respectively.

38A5. Moves.

Moves are indicated by combining the symbol for the piece and its arrival square, for example, Bg5, Rh5, Nf6. Pawn moves indicate only the arrival square, for example, e4, c5, g3.

38A6. Captures.

Captures are indicated by inserting an "*X*" or "*:*" (pronounced *takes*) between the piece symbol and the arrival square, for example, Bxe5, N:c6, Rxh5, axb4, Nxf6. Other acceptable forms for indicating capture are Bc6 or ab.

Because there is no abbreviation used for pawns, pawn captures include the original file, the x, and the arrival square, for example, cxd4, exf5, gxh7. In the case of a capture en passant, the arrival square is the one on which the capturing pawn finally rests, and *e.p.* is added to the notation, for example, 14 f4 gxf3 e.p.

38A7. Clarification.

In cases where these brief notations would be ambiguous, clarification is achieved first by adding the original file of the moving piece or second by adding the rank of the moving piece:

a. If rooks on a1 or f1 can move to d1, such moves are written Rad1 or Rfd1.

b. If rooks on a5 or d1 can move to a1, the notation Raa1 or Rda1 is preferred to R5a1 or R1a1.

c. If knights on f3 or f7 can move to e5, adding the f file would be useless, so the move is N3e5 or N7e5.

d. If knights on f3 or c2 can move to d4, the file is the clarifier: Nfd4 or Ncd4.

e. For a capture, the x goes between the piece identifier and the arrival square: Nfxd4.

38A8. Special symbols.

a. O-O castling kingside

b. O-O-O castling queenside

c. x captures or takes (an earlier version of algebraic notation used a colon instead)

d. + check (sometimes *ch*)

e. ++ checkmate (or #)

f. = a pawn promotion, as in f8=Q or d1=N

g. e.p. en passant

38B. Figurine algebraic.

This system is exactly like regular algebraic, except the abbreviations of the pieces are replaced by internationally recognized symbols:

Figure 10

This system is obviously advantageous for publications but not practical for players in the tournament hall.

38C. Long algebraic.

This system is just like normal algebraic, except that it prevents the possibility of ambiguities by indicating departure as well as arrival square for each move. A sample game might start 1. e2-e4 d7-d5 2. e4xd5 Qd8xd5 3. Nb1-c3 Qd5-a5, etc.

38D. Abbreviated algebraic.

This variation of algebraic, designed for quick scorekeeping, omits the capture and check symbols and the ranks of pawns captured by pawns. For instance, the opening moves of 38C would be written 1. e4 d5 2. ed Qd5 3. Nc3 Qa5.

38E. Computer notation.

This variation of long algebraic, used for play with computers without sensory boards, eliminates the abbreviation of the pieces and captures symbols. Written versions generally use capital letters rather than the small ones otherwise associated with squares.

The sample moves of 38C and 38D would be written 1 E2-E4 D7-D5 2 E4-D5 D8-D5 3 B1-C3 D5-A5. Castling is indicated by the departure and arrival squares of the king: E1-G1, E1-C1, E8-G8, or E8-C8.

38F. English descriptive notation.

38F1. Pieces.

Pieces, including pawns, are identified by their initials, as in algebraic. Those that begin the game on the side of the board nearer the king sometimes have a *K* in front of their own initial; those on the queen's side of the board a *Q*.

38F2. Files.

The files are named for the pieces originally occupying them: QR, QN, QB, Q, K, KB, KN, KR.

38F3. Ranks.

The ranks are numbered from each player's point of view, from 1 to 8. White's pieces and pawns begin the game on the first and second ranks from White's point of view, the eighth and seventh ranks respectively from Black's point of view.

38F4. Squares.

Each square has two names, one from each player's point of view. The white QR, for example, starts the game at White's QR1, which is Black's QR8.

38F5. Pawns.

When necessary to distinguish it from other pawns, each pawn is named after its file: QRP, QNP, etc.

38F6. Moves.

A move to a vacant square is indicated by the piece symbol, a hyphen, and the arrival square. To avoid ambiguity, squares are clarified before pieces. N-KB3 is preferred to KN-B3 unless the QN could also reach the KB3 square, for example, from Q2.

38F7. Captures.

A capture is indicated by the abbreviation of the capturing piece, an x, and the abbreviation of the captured piece, for example, BxN, or QRxP (necessary if the KR also attacked a pawn), or NxKBP (necessary if a knight can capture the QBP), etc.

38F8. Further clarification.

If the K and Q prefixes do not clarify an ambiguity, or the pieces have made enough moves so that it is no longer obvious which side of the board they started on, clarity is achieved with a slash and rank number after the piece symbol. For example, if either of two knights may capture a bishop, the notation might be N/4xB.

38F9. Check.

A check (*ch*) may be enough to clarify an ambiguity, for example, B-N5ch even if both bishops could go to N5 squares.

38F10. Other symbols.

Castling kingside is O-O, castling queenside O-O-O, and pawn promotion a slash and the new piece (P-B8/Q or PxR/N).

38G. Spanish descriptive.

English and Spanish are the two major languages in which descriptive notation is sometimes found. Spanish descriptive notation differs from the English version not only in the piece symbols (38A1) but also in the order of symbols. For example, the move P-QB4 in English descriptive is written P4AD in Spanish; this would literally translate into P4BQ.

38H. Sample game.

Here, without further comment, is a sample game fragment written in each of the three common notations:

	Algebraic		Computer		Descriptive	
1	e4	e5	E2-E4	E7-E5	P-K4	P-K4
2	Nf3	Nc6	G1-F3	B8-C6	N-KB3	N-QB3
3	Bb5	a6	F1-B5	A7-A6	B-N5	P-QR3
4	Bxc6	dxc6	B5-C6	D7-C6	BxN	QPxB
5	d3	Bb4+	D2-D3	F8-B4	P-Q3	B-N5ch
6	Nc3	Nf6	B1-C3	G8-F6	N-B3	N-B3
7	0-0	Bxc3	E1-G1	B4-C3	0-0	BxN

If you have played through the notation of your choice accurately, you should have reached the following position on your board:

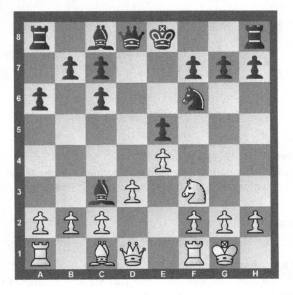

Figure 11

38I. International correspondence notation.

To avoid language problems, including different alphabets, international correspondence players use an all-numeric system that is otherwise very similar to computer notation.

38I1. Squares.

A two-digit number, as indicated below (see **Figure 12,** next page), designates each square. The first digit is a replacement of the a-h files by the numbers 1-8, the second is the conventional rank number.

BLACK

8	18	28	38	48	58	68	78	88
7	17	27	37	47	57	67	77	87
6	16	26	36	46	56	66	76	86
5	15	25	35	45	55	65	75	85
4	14	24	34	44	54	64	74	84
3	13	23	33	43	53	63	73	83
2	12	22	32	42	52	62	72	82
1	11	21	31	41	51	61	71	81
	1	2	3	4	5	6	7	8

WHITE

Figure 12

38I2. Moves.

A move is indicated by a four-digit number that combines the departure and arrival squares without punctuation. For example, 5254 is the same as e4 or P-K4.

38I3. Castling.

Castling is noted as a king move: 5171, 5131, 5878, or 5838.

38I4. Pawn promotion.

The first two digits indicate the departure square, the third the arrival file, and the fourth the new piece (1=Q, 2=R, 3=B, 4=N). For example, 1714 would be the same as the algebraic a8=N.

38J. Telephone and radio notation.

When players or their agents relay moves with their voices, some confusion can arise because b, c, d, e, and g can all sound rather alike. Using algebraic notation with a variation of the military alphabet solves the potential difficulty: able, baker, charlie, david, easy, fox, george, harry.

CHAPTER FOUR

EQUIPMENT STANDARDS

39. Introduction

The three elements of chess equipment---pieces, boards, and clocks---are each discussed in detail below. In general, simple, functional designs are preferred for use in tournaments so players, spectators, and directors are not distracted by ornateness, unusual design, or other aesthetic values. The designer and decorator pieces available today serve good purposes other than as suitable equipment for tournament chess.

39A. Choice of equipment.

If the organizer of the tournament provides equipment conforming to the following standards, the players should expect that the organizer or TD would require the use of that equipment. If the organizer does not provide one or more elements of equipment, the players should agree on any that meets the standards or, failing such agreement, play with Black's choice if it meets the standards. If Black does not provide standard equipment and White does, Black does not have the right to delay the start of the game to search for alternative equipment. The director is the final arbiter of whether the equipment in question is standard. **See also** 42, Chess Clocks; 42C, Standard clocks; 42D, Delay clock preferable in sudden death; and 42E, Increment clock preferable.

TD TIP: *The players of the black pieces sometimes misunderstand this rule when they want to use an analog clock A properly set digital clock is preferred equipment and supersedes Black's choice in cases where White has such a clock and Black does not (5F).*

39A1. Black player late.

If Black is late for the start of a round, White makes the choice of equipment. Unless announced or posted otherwise, White also may choose which side of the board the clock is on and which side of the board to sit on. Black may not object unless White's equipment is non-standard or White has not complied with any special announced or posted stipulations (16L), in which case Black's clock continues to run. Again, the final decision is up to the director in questionable cases.

39A2. Neither player has standard equipment.

If neither player provides standard equipment, the director should rule in favor of the equipment that is the nearest to being standard.

39A3. Non-US Chess play.

For non-tournament or non-US Chess-rated play against opponents not used to popular tournament sets or boards, equipment differing somewhat from these standards is likely to be acceptable.

40. Chess Pieces

40A. Material.
Pieces should be made of plastic, wood, or possibly a material similar in appearance.

40B. Size.
The king's height should be 3⅜ to 4½ inches (8.65 to 11.54 cm). The cross (or other King's finial) should occupy no more than 20 percent of the total height of the King. The diameter of the king's base should be 40–50 percent of the height. The other pieces should be proportionate in height and form. All pieces should be well balanced for stability and comfortable moving.

40C. Form.
The conventional Staunton pattern is the standard. The Staunton design was registered in 1849 and first offered for sale to the general public by John Jaques of London in October of that year. The first 500 sets were hand signed and numbered by Howard Staunton. The design soon became the standard for all serious play. An example of an original Staunton pattern chess set is shown in **Figure 13**. Minor variations in design may be tolerated, especially in sets that are widely used. The king and queen should have clearly different tops, and the bishop's top may have an angled groove.

Figure 13 *Image courtesy of US Chess Federation Sales*

40D. Color.
Pieces should be the colors of naturally light and dark wood (for example, maple or boxwood and walnut or ebony) or approximations of these colors, such as simply white and black.

40E. Examples.
Jaques chess sets are still used for World Championship matches, and are quite expensive. The most commonly used tournament set is US Chess Special,

an inexpensive, plastic set with a 3¾-inch king, also sold elsewhere under various names.

41. Chessboards

41A. Material.
The board must be opaque and fabricated from a smooth material that allows the easy movement of pieces. Satisfactory boards have been made from plastic, wood, paper, cardboard, leather, cloth, and marble.

41B. Color.
Like the pieces, chessboard colors should offer high contrast between the light and dark sections yet remain pleasing to the eye. Good combinations include green or brown with ivory or buff, and walnut or teak with maple or birch. The colors and the finish should allow extended examination without eyestrain.

Squares that do not exactly match the colors of the pieces are popular because they allow ready distinction between empty and occupied squares. For example, the green and buff vinyl roll-up board sold by US Chess and others is the most commonly used at tournaments. Red and black checkerboards are nonstandard.

41C. Proportions.
The pieces should fit comfortably on the board, being neither too crowded nor too isolated on the squares. The king and queen, for example, should be subject to easy placement on a square without touching any edge. Boards for standard sets should have squares of approximately 2 to 2½ inches (5.08 to 6.35 cm). The guideline for determining the proper square size for a Staunton chess set is that the King should occupy around 78 percent of the square. (Dividing the base diameter of the King by 0.78 will yield the proper square size). An acceptable square size may be up to ⅛ inch larger than this number, but not smaller. For example, a set of chessmen having a King with a base diameter of 1¾ inches will play well on a chessboard with 2¼ inch or 2⅜ inch squares. **See also** 35F1, Special chessboard.

41D. Borders.
The width of the border around the squares is a matter of personal taste, so long as it does not affect a player's ability to easily reach the pieces. Some borders include aids to scorekeeping in the form of letters and numbers for algebraic notation and some do not; both designs are acceptable.

41E. Tables.

A table with an inset or otherwise fitted chessboard is very satisfactory. The playing surface should be about 27 to 30 inches from the ground (normal table height). If the board is not fastened to the table, it should remain stationary. The table should provide ample room for the clock, captured pieces, scoresheets, players' elbows or forearms, and water glasses.

42. Chess Clocks

42A. Basic requirements.

Analog chess clocks should be as accurate and silent as possible. They should have a device that clearly signals the end of a time control, such as a *flag* that falls when the minute hand reaches the mark at the figure 12. The flag should be of a size and color so as to be clearly visible to players and directors.

42B. Digital clocks.

Digital clocks with time delay (or Bronstein add back) capability are fully acceptable as tournament equipment. If such clocks are used in competition the providers should, upon request, explain all relevant operational facts to the tournament director and each opponent. Relevant operational facts to be explained include, but are not limited to, the signal at the end of the time control period, any display change from minutes to seconds and any resetting that might occur at the start of a new time control period.

42B1. Signaling devices.

Timers with move counters and flag fall indicators are legal. Move counters, however, should not be relied upon and in cases of a time forfeiture claim only the scoresheets of the players may be used to validate or repudiate the claim.

42B2. Move counters.

Clocks with move counters are legal. The counter offers impartial assistance to both players, but its count may not be used to support or defend against a time-forfeit claim and can sometimes be inaccurate. Players rely on the count at their own risk. Move counters can be useful to a director asked to count moves for the 50-move rule (14F4f). Players using a counter should be aware that if a move is not counted or is double counted, and the players cannot easily adjust the clock to reflect this, the clock should be stopped and the director notified.

42C. Standard clocks in games without sudden death.

See rule 5F3, Standard timer for time controls with neither delay nor increment.

42D. Delay clock preferable in sudden death.

See rule 5F2, Standard timer for delay time controls.

42E. Increment clock preferable in increment time controls.

See rule 5F1, Standard timer for increment time controls.

42E1. Recommended function of an increment clock.

a. The display at all times should show the time available to complete a player's next move (i.e. time added at the completion of a move).

b. In case of passing a time control, a sign on the display must give clear signal time has expired.

c. In case of accumulative or delay timing systems, the clock should not add any additional time if a player passed the last time control.

TD TIP: *Check the clock manufacturer's manual. Ideally clocks add the increment time to a player's side of the clock once he has completed the move by pressing his clock (known as: add-after)—some clocks may work differently. The player's total playing time, including the added increment, should now be displayed. Some clocks wait until their opponent presses their side of the clock for the increment time to be added to the player's display (known as: add-before). The TD TIP for rule 16B2 explains the procedure to use if the increment time is not automatically given at the start of move one. Either function is considered standard, and are, in fact equivalent. If unsure, ask your opponent when the time is added, and observe that function early in the game when the clock is in use. Time expires when the clock reaches 0:00. Most clocks freeze time (do not add the increment) of a player who has expired (always reads 0:00, but continue to run for the player who does not.) This is considered standard. In this case, it is not possible for a player to "unflag", but it is possible for both players to run out of time. **See also** 16T. Both players exceed time control. Clocks that do not freeze time (run negative time or pause at zero), continue to run and adds back the increment at the completion of a move are still considered preferable to a clock that does not have increment capability. This function should be explained to an opponent prior to the game, and claims of expired time should be made in accordance with 13C. In this case, a claim may still be made after the player whose time has expired has completed a move (time added) if the displayed time is equal to or less than the increment. Such a claim (in accordance with 13C5) must be made before the claimant has completed the next move. It is possible, with the next or subsequent moves that the displayed time is greater than the increment without a claim being made. In this case there is no evidence that time has expired, and therefore a player may have "unflagged". With this type of clock function, you lose your right to claim the win on time if you complete your next move and your opponent's clock now show positive time with his own clock running.*

43. Scoresheets.

A scoresheet is any piece of paper, or electronic or mechanical recording device, that allows a player to comply with rule 15A. Electronic scoresheets are subject to certification guidelines as published by US Chess. An electronic scoresheet not so certified is not considered standard and may only be used at the discretion of the tournament director.

Often a pre-printed scoresheet has spaces that indication the players' names, event, other game-related information, spaces for the recording of the moves, result and the signatures of the players.

If a scoresheet is provided by the event, then that scoresheet is the standard used for that event. If an event, even when it provides scoresheets, does not require that a copy of the score be submitted, then the TD may allow the use of any method of keeping score.

A TD may require the use of the provided scoresheet, or may allow non-standard scoresheets to be used even if one is provided.

If a scoresheet is not provided by the event, then any method of keeping score is allowed provided it meets the rules established in 15A.

TD TIP: *Tournament directors are advised to be flexible on the above. Many players have their own scoresheet in the form of notebooks or recording devices, and prefer to keep their games in an orderly fashion within that book. If a player can provide a copy of the score from their notebook, or a printout or downloaded from the electronic scoresheet, this is acceptable. You have the score and the result of the game. Contact the US Chess office regarding the policies and guidelines for electronic scorekeeping devices. A current copy of those guidelines can be found at:*

www.uschess.org/images/stories/scholastic_chess_resources/electronicscoresheet2.pdf

Frank Camaratta contributed to the material in this chapter.

CHAPTER FIVE

PLAYERS RIGHTS
and
RESPONSIBILITIES

All players have the right to expect:

1. That the tournament director is reliable and has knowledge of the laws of chess, as per US Chess standards.

2. That all prizes shall be awarded as advertised.

3. That the director has this US Chess rulebook on the premises and available for consultation during the tournament.

4. That any special rules pertinent to that particular tournament shall be announced and/or posted; e.g., time-forfeit procedure, color allocation, tiebreak system, prize distribution, etc. **See also** 1B1, Notification, and 1B2, Major variations.

5. That the pairing system used is fair and impartial and that it will be administered fairly.

6. That the starting time of the rounds will be posted and that the rounds will start reasonably on time.

7. That conditions such as lighting, space requirements, noise, etc., be at an acceptable level conducive to good competition.

8. That tournament directors be available at all times in the event of questions or problems.

9. That the round results will be posted in a timely fashion.

10. That upon request, a tournament director will initiate the appeals process.

All players are responsible:

1. To conduct themselves in an orderly fashion.

2. To compete in a spirit of good sportsmanship.

3. To be present at the starting time for each round, if possible.

4. To refrain from analysis of games or audible talking in the tournament room while others are playing.

5. To notify the director well in advance of plans to withdraw from the tournament or miss a round.

6. To promptly report game results in the manner required by the director.

7. To read pertinent information posted for the players, usually near the wall charts, including the list of times that the rounds are scheduled to start.

8. To obey the laws of chess.

9. To conform to the US Chess code of ethics. **See also** Chapter 6: US Chess Code of Ethics.

CHAPTER SIX

CODE
of
ETHICS

PURPOSE AND SCOPE

1. The purpose of this code of ethics is to set forth standards to which the conduct of players, tournament directors, sponsors, and other individuals and entities participating in the affairs of the United States Chess Federation (US Chess), including tournaments and other activities sponsored by or sanctioned by US Chess, should conform; to specify sanctions for conduct that does not conform to such standards; and to specify the procedures by which alleged violations are to be investigated and, if necessary, the appropriate sanctions imposed.

2. The standards, procedures, and sanctions set forth in this code of ethics are not equivalent to criminal laws and procedures. Rather, they concern the rights and privileges of US Chess membership, including, but not limited to, the privilege of participating in tournaments, events, or other activities as a member of US Chess.

3. The standards, procedures, and sanctions set forth in this code of ethics shall apply only to actions and behavior by:

   (a) Members of US Chess, that occur in connection with tournaments or other activities sponsored by or sanctioned by US Chess; and

   (b) Individuals and entities acting in an official capacity as officers or representatives of US Chess. This code shall not apply to actions or behavior by employees of US Chess acting in the scope of their duties. Such actions fall instead under the province of the Executive Board.

4. Each member of US Chess and each participant in a US Chess activity shall be bound by this code of ethics.

THE US CHESS ETHICS COMMITTEE

5. The US Chess Ethics Committee is appointed in accordance with procedures consistent with the bylaws of US Chess. The committee exists to consider allegations of unethical conduct at or in connection with events sanctioned by US Chess, and allegations of unethical conduct involving US Chess and its activities, in accordance with the standards and procedures contained in this code. The committee will exercise all other duties as may be assigned by the Bylaws or by action of the US Chess Board of Delegates.

STANDARDS OF CONDUCT

6. The actions and behavior of players, tournament directors, sponsors, and other individuals and entities participating in US Chess activities, or in events sponsored by or sanctioned by US Chess, shall be lawful and in accordance with all US Chess rules and regulations, and consistent with the principles of fair play, good sportsmanship, honesty, and respect for the rights of others. The following is a list of examples of actions and behavior that are considered unethical. The list is not intended to be exhaustive, and any action or behavior that is unlawful or violates US Chess rules and regulations, or is inconsistent with the principles of fair play, good sportsmanship, honesty, and respect for the rights of others, may be considered to fall within the scope of this code of ethics.

    (a) Intentional violations of tournament regulations, or of any other regulations pertaining to US Chess activities and goals, particularly after being warned.

    (b) Cheating in a game of chess by illegally giving, receiving, offering, or soliciting advice; or by consulting written sources; or by tampering with clocks; or in any other manner.

    (c) Deliberately losing a game for payment, or to lower one's rating, or for any other reason; or attempting to induce another player to do so. Deliberately failing to play at one's best in a game, in any manner inconsistent with the principles of good sportsmanship, honesty, or fair play.

    (d) Deliberately misrepresenting one's playing ability in order to compete in a tournament or division of a tournament intended for players of lesser ability; players with foreign ratings are expected to disclose those ratings.

    (e) Participating in a tournament under a false name or submitting a falsified rating report.

    (f) Participating in a tournament while under suspension.

    (g) Purposely giving false information in order to circumvent or violate any rule or regulation or goal recognized by US Chess.

    (h) Attempting to interfere with the rights of any US Chess member, such as by barring someone from entering a US Chess-sanctioned event for personal reasons. Generally, no individual

187

should be barred from a US Chess-sanctioned event for which he or she meets the advertised qualifications, without appropriate due process, and then only for behavior inconsistent with the principles of this code and/or the rules of chess. If a ban on future participation is imposed, the individual should be notified of the ban prior to his attempting to appear at future events.

(i) Violating federal, state, or local laws while participating in activities that are associated with US Chess.

PROCEDURES

7. Any US Chess member may initiate procedures under this code of ethics by filing a complaint in a timely manner with the US Chess Ethics Committee. A good-faith deposit must be submitted by the complainant. The amount of the deposit shall be set by the US Chess Executive Director, who shall review it from time to time in consultation with the Ethics Committee. The deposit shall be returned unless the Committee rules that the case is frivolous. The Committee may determine whether to return the deposit even before it determines jurisdictional and merit questions. The Committee may also, by a two-thirds vote, accept complaints submitted without the deposit. Complaints submitted by a US Chess employee as a result of actions related to official US Chess activities shall not require the payment of the deposit.

In the case of any accusation that does not fall clearly under the Standards of Conduct above, the Ethics Committee shall have the authority to decide whether the alleged conduct is within the scope of the code of ethics. In the case of each alleged violation that is within the scope of the code of ethics, the following steps shall occur in a timely manner:

(a) A factual inquiry shall be made by the Ethics Committee, assisted as necessary by the US Chess staff. Previous findings of the Ethics Committee or other US Chess entities may be included among the evidence considered by the Ethics Committee, if relevant to the circumstances of the present case. As a part of such an inquiry, any person accused of unethical conduct shall have the right to examine the evidence against him or her, the right to respond to the accusation, and the right to produce written evidence in his or her behalf.

(b) When issuing a decision, the Ethics Committee will provide a rationale for its decision to the parties involved and to the Executive Board.

(c) Appropriate sanctions, if any, shall be recommended to the Executive Board by the Ethics Committee. In recommending sanctions, the Ethics Committee may consider any previous ruling or finding of the Ethics Committee, or other US Chess entity, pertaining to the past conduct of the person being sanctioned. In recommending sanctions, the person being recommended for sanctions must be informed of this fact. Any person against whom sanctions have been recommended shall be promptly notified. If appeals are filed, the Ethics Committee shall be promptly notified.

(d) Except as specified in 7(f) sanctions recommended to the Executive Board shall be deemed final unless appealed to the Executive Board by the person or persons upon whom the sanctions have been imposed, or upon the initiative of any member of the Executive Board. Such an appeal must be made within thirty days of the date that notification of recommended sanctions occurred, except that the Executive Board may extend the deadline for appeal if in its judgment an unavoidable delay in communications or other valid cause prevented a timely appeal. If an appeal has not been filed by the deadline the recommended sanctions shall be placed into effect. No appeals shall be permitted in cases where the Ethics Committee has found in favor of the defendant and has recommended no sanctions.

(e) Upon appeal, a review of the facts and the appropriateness of the recommended sanction shall be undertaken by the Executive Board. The person against whom the sanction has been recommended, as well as the person filing the initial complaint, shall be given notice of the time and place the Executive Board will review the case. The person against whom the sanctions have been recommended shall have the right to appear before the Board and present evidence from the record. Any person appearing before the Executive Board upon appeal may be represented by counsel with the permission and at the sole discretion of the Executive Board. In all appeals the recommended sanctions imposed by the Ethics Committee shall not be in effect until the appeal hearing is completed. The recommended sanctions shall be either confirmed, modified, or revoked by the Executive Board.

(f) If the person against whom sanctions have been recommended is a member of the US Chess Executive Board, he or she may not appeal the sanctions to the Executive Board, but may appeal to the US Chess Board of Delegates at its next scheduled meeting.

(g) If any member of the Ethics Committee or of the US Chess Executive Board has a conflict of interest of any kind that might preclude objective participation in the consideration of any case, that person may not act in the capacity of a committee or board member on the case.

SANCTIONS

8. The following are some of the sanctions that may be imposed as a result of the procedures specified above. In unusual cases, other appropriate sanctions may be imposed, or these sanctions may be varied or combined.

(a) Reprimand. A determination that a member has committed an offense warranting discipline becomes a matter of record, but no further sanction is imposed at the time. A reprimand automatically carries a probation of at least three months, or longer if so specified. If the member is judged guilty of another offense during the probation, he or she is then liable to further sanctions for both offenses.

(b) Censure. A determination that a member has committed a serious offense warranting discipline becomes a matter of record, but no further sanction is imposed at the time. Censure automatically carries a probation of at least one year, or longer if so specified. If the member is judged guilty of another offense during the probationary period, he or she is then liable to further sanctions for both offenses.

(c) Suspended sentence with probation. A determination is made that the member has committed an offense warranting discipline. When the discipline is imposed and execution thereof suspended, such suspension shall include probation for at least six months longer than the discipline imposed. If the member is judged guilty of another offense during this period, unless otherwise decreed, the original discipline shall be added to such new discipline as may be imposed for the new offense.

(d) Suspension. Suspension is a determination that the member has committed an offense warranting abrogation, for a specified period of time, of all membership rights and privileges.

(e) Expulsion. Expulsion is a determination that a member has committed an offense warranting permanent abrogation of all membership rights and privileges. An expelled member may be readmitted to membership only by the US Chess Executive Board or by the US Chess Board of Delegates.

(f) Exclusion from events. This is a more selective determination that a member has committed an offense warranting abrogation of the right to participate in certain specified events or activities.

9. If the person being sanctioned is a member of the US Chess Executive Board, the Ethics Committee may recommend to the Executive Board no sanctions other than censure or reprimand, but may also recommend to the Board of Delegates other actions.

10. In the case of every sanction that involves suspension or expulsion, a member may not hold any office in US Chess or participate in any capacity in any event or activity sponsored by or sanctioned by US Chess.

11. The US Chess Business Office shall be informed in writing of all official determinations by the Ethics Committee, and shall record any recommendations of any sanctions. The US Chess Business Office shall inform the Executive Board of any sanctions recommended.

CHAPTER SEVEN

TOURNAMENT DIRECTOR CERTIFICATION

Purpose

US Chess certifies tournament directors in order to standardize procedures and ensure a competent tournament director (TD) for each level of US Chess-rated tournament.

General Qualifications

1. US Chess Membership.

All certified TDs must be current members of US Chess. If a TD allows his or her membership to lapse, his or her TD certification is canceled and is not automatically restored upon payment of membership dues.

2. Established Rating.

Except for the club level, all TDs taking a test for certification must have an established US Chess rating as an over-the-board player. TDs are encouraged to remain active as players to maintain proper perspective when directing.

TD TIP: Currently the Ratings Committee has set the number of games that must be played to obtain an established rating at 26; however, that number is subject to change.

3. Training.

All TDs are encouraged to work with and assist other directors with greater experience and expertise to increase directing knowledge and understanding. All TDs are likewise encouraged to provide opportunities for less experienced directors to share in their philosophical understanding of tournament direction.

4. Rules.

Every TD should own a copy of US Chess's Official Rules of Chess. TDs should become thoroughly familiar with these rules, and any rules changes or rulings by the Rules Committee effectively changing these rules, and administrative procedures regarding the sale of memberships, reporting formats and deadlines, basic rating formulas, and a variety of other subjects.

TD Testing Procedures

5. Exams.

Tests are written by the Tournament Director Certification Committee (TDCC) and administered by the US Chess business office. These tests are generally mailed to qualified applicants to be completed with the assistance of any printed matter, but applicants are bound by honor not to discuss specific questions with other persons. Applicants must return all testing materials within two months. An applicant must first satisfy all experience requirements for the

TD certification for which they are applying before taking an exam for that level of certification. The applicant may apply to the TDCC for a variance on this procedure.

6. Applicants.

Applicants for promotion of TD certification level shall provide the technical director with the names, dates, and number of entrants of the tournaments that satisfy the experience requirements. Upon request, applicants will present written verification of their claimed experience requirements.

TD TIP: Tournament categories are backwards compatible for TD credit. For example: A five round Category C tournament (or a single Category C section of a tournament) with 55 players can be used to meet a Category D TD requirement; being the chief assistant at a 180-player five round Category B event can be used to meet a Category D or Category C chief assistant TD requirement.

7. Unsuccessful Senior, Local And Renewing Applicants.

Applicants who fail the test for local or senior level of TD certification must wait two months before taking the test a second time. Applicants who fail the second attempt must wait six months before taking the test a third or subsequent time. The same form of the same examination may not be taken more than once by any applicant.

8. Unsuccessful ANTD And NTD Applicants.

Applicants who fail the test for associate national or national level of TD certification must wait three months before taking the test a second time. Applicants who do not pass the second attempt must wait one year before taking the test a third or subsequent time. The same form of the same examination may not be taken more than once by any applicant.

9. Documents And Tests.

All documents, including completed tests, shall be submitted to the US Chess Federation via e-mail.

Chief TDs, Assistant TDs, and Tournament Aides

10. Chief TD.

The Chief TD has the ultimate authority and responsibility for the tournament. The Chief TD of an event is expected to be physically present during tournament play. If the Chief TD must be absent for short periods of time, another certified TD shall be present on-site. The Chief TD should not himself be a player in the tournament. **See also** 21E, The playing director.

11. Co-Chief TD.

In unusual circumstances two directors may jointly function as co-Chief TDs. Each co-chief receives US Chess credit for one tournament with one-half the total number of entries.

12. Assistant TD.

An assistant TD serves under the Chief TD performing assigned tasks relevant to tournament direction. Assistant TDs gain US Chess credit for their experience when their duties include pairings and rules enforcement. Such credit is limited to 1 assistant per 50 players or fraction thereof. Assistant TDs must be certified TDs. A chief assistant TD is distinguished from a regular assistant TD by added duties and responsibilities as assigned by the Chief TD.

13. Tournament Aides.

Tournament aides serve under the Chief TD performing primarily clerical tasks, such as entering results on pairing cards and wall charts. Aides do not possess the authority to make pairings or enforce rules, and they do not need to be certified TDs.

Tournament Categories

14. Category I.

A Tournament held in the United States that will be submitted to both FIDE and US Chess for rating.

a. FIDE events that award title norms for GMs, IMs, WGMs and WIMs and will be submitted to FIDE for rating must be directed by an onsite International Arbiter (IA) or FIDE Arbiter (FA).

b. U.S. events that are also FIDE rated should be directed by an onsite US Chess Senior TD or higher, or IA/FA that meets US Chess requirements for Senior TD and for the expected size of the event.

c. Effective January 1, 2014, no tournament will be rated by FIDE without the arbiter being licensed which applies to FIDE Arbiters and International Arbiters. A new category was introduced called the National Arbiter. In US Chess, the National Arbiter must be a SrTD or higher and apply/pay the license fee through the US Chess office in order to direct FIDE rated events.

TD TIP: When a tournament is dual FIDE and US Chess rated the National Arbiters, FIDE Arbiters and/or International Arbiters must be licensed by FIDE and currently certified as US Chess TDs with the chief TD/Arbiter being the appropriate level to direct the tournament for the event to be rated by FIDE and US Chess; i.e., all TDs of dual rated FIDE/US Chess tournaments (or the FIDE/US Chess rated sections of a tournament) must be certified by both FIDE and US Chess.

15. Category N.

An over-the-board tournament that awards a national title. *It is strongly recommended that for these types of tournaments, TDs have experience with computer pairing programs, back room pairing procedures, and on site player contact, or "floor," problem solving procedures.*

> **Subcategory N1:** Any national tournament that averages over 150 players in the previous five-year period plus the U. S. Championship, U. S. Women's Championship, and U. S. Junior Championship.

> **Subcategory N2:** Any national tournament that averages 150 or fewer players in the previous five-year period, excluding the U. S. Championship, U. S. Women's Championship, and U. S. Junior Championship.

> **Subcategory N3:** One section of a N1 tournament where the TD is limited to solving problems and making rulings on the floor only (floor TD). Examples: The K-3 section of the National Elementary Championship or any section of the National Open.

> **Subcategory N4:** One section of a N1 tournament where the TD is limited to the duties of pairings in a backroom capacity using a pairing program (backroom TD). Examples: The K-3 section of the National Elementary Championship or any section of the National Open.

16. Category A.

A US Chess-rated over-the-board Swiss system tournament or section of a tournament, except Category I or N, that regularly draws more than 300 entrants and awards $5,000+ in cash prizes. Examples: World Open, New York Open, Atlantic Open, and Chicago Open. Such tournaments may be directed by associate national TDs. *It is strongly recommended that for these types of tournaments, TDs have experience with computer pairing programs, back room pairing procedures, and on site player contact, or "floor," problem solving procedures.*

> **Subcategory A1:** A Category A tournament, or any one section considered as a stand-alone event, of any tournament,

that by itself meets the Category A requirements, where the TD is limited to solving problems and making rulings on the floor only (floor TD) for the entire tournament or any one section, of any tournament, that by itself meets the Category A requirements.

Subcategory A2: A Category A tournament, or any one section considered as a stand-alone event, of any tournament, that by itself meets the Category A requirements, where the TD is limited to the duties of pairings in a backroom capacity using a pairing program (backroom TD) for the entire tournament or any one section, of any tournament, that by itself meets the Category A requirements.

TD TIP: A, A1 or A2 TD experience credit can be claimed for an entire tournament meeting the requirements of a Category A tournament or for any tournament section (of any category tournament) that by itself, as a stand-alone section, would qualify as a Category A tournament.

17. Category B.

A US Chess-rated over-the-board Swiss system tournament or section of a tournament, except Category I, N, or A, drawing 100 or more entrants. **See also** 32, Limitations. *It is strongly recommended that for these types of tournaments, TDs have experience with computer pairing programs, back room pairing procedures, and on site player contact, or "floor," problem solving procedures.*

Subcategory B1: A Category B tournament, or any one section considered as a stand-alone event, of any tournament, that by itself meets the Category B requirements, where the TD is limited to solving problems and making rulings on the floor only (floor TD) for the entire tournament or any one section, of any tournament, that by itself meets the Category B requirements.

Subcategory B2: A Category B tournament, or any one section considered as a stand-alone event, of any tournament, that by itself meets the Category B requirements, where the TD is limited to the duties of pairings in a backroom capacity using a pairing program (backroom TD) for the entire tournament or any one section, of any tournament, that by itself meets the Category B requirements.

TD TIP: B, B1 or B2 TD experience credit can be claimed for an entire tournament meeting the requirements of a Category B tournament or for any tournament section (of any category tournament) that by itself, as a stand-alone section, would qualify as a Category B tournament.

18. Category C.

A US Chess-rated over-the-board Swiss system tournament or section of a tournament, except Category I or N, drawing 50 to 99 entrants. Such tournaments or sections of tournaments may be directed by local TDs. For more information see 28, Limitations. *It is strongly recommended that for these types of tournaments, TDs have experience with computer pairing programs, back room pairing procedures, and on site player contact, or "floor," problem solving procedures.*

> **Subcategory C1:** A Category C tournament, or any one section considered as a stand-alone event, of any tournament, that by itself meets the Category C requirements, where the TD is limited to solving problems and making rulings on the floor only (floor TD) for the entire tournament or any one section, of any tournament, that by itself meets the Category C requirements.

> **Subcategory C2:** A Category C tournament, or any one section considered as a stand-alone event, of any tournament, that by itself meets the Category C requirements, where the TD is limited to the duties of pairings in a backroom capacity using a pairing program (backroom TD) for the entire tournament or any one section, of any tournament, that by itself meets the Category C requirements.

TD TIP: C, C1 or C2 TD experience credit can be claimed for an entire tournament meeting the requirements of a Category C tournament or for any tournament section (of any category tournament) that by itself, as a stand-alone section, would qualify as a Category C tournament.

19. Category D.

Any US Chess-rated over-the-board Swiss system tournament or section of a tournament, except Category I or N, drawing fewer than 50 entrants. Club TDs may direct such tournaments or sections of tournaments. **See also** 24, Limitations.

> **Subcategory D1:** A Category D tournament, or any one section considered as a stand-alone event, of any tournament, that by itself meets the Category D requirements, where the TD is limited to solving problems and making rulings on the floor only (floor TD) for the entire tournament or any one section, of

any tournament, that by itself meets the Category D requirements.

Subcategory D2: A Category D tournament, or any one section considered as a stand-alone event, of any tournament, that by itself meets the Category D requirements, where the TD is limited to the duties of pairings in a backroom capacity using a pairing program (backroom TD) for the entire tournament or any one section, of any tournament, that by itself meets the Category D requirements.

TD TIP: D, D1 or D2 TD experience credit can be claimed for an entire tournament meeting the requirements of a Category D tournament or for any tournament section (of any category tournament) that by itself, as a stand-alone section, would qualify as a Category D tournament.

20. Category R.

A US Chess-rated round robin tournament of six or more rated entrants with a mean rating of at least 1400, with the mean being calculated by using the ratings of the players in the applicable ratings supplement on the starting date of the event.

21. Category T.

A US Chess-rated team-vs.-team, or individual/team, Swiss system tournament involving at least fifty players. *It is strongly recommended that for these types of tournaments, TDs have experience with computer pairing programs, back room pairing procedures, and on site player contact, or "floor," problem solving procedures.*

The Club Director

22. Experience Requirement.

An applicant for club TD accreditation must sign a statement indicating that he or she has read, has access to, and will abide by the rules contained in US Chess's Official Rules of Chess.

23. Testing Requirement.

None for the first three year term. Each three-year term thereafter an objective test of moderate difficulty must be passed at the 70% level.

24. Limitations.

A club TD may not be the Chief TD for US Chess Grand Prix, Category N or Category I tournaments and should not be the Chief TD of Category A, B, or C tournaments, which includes any tournament, or section of a tournament, expected to draw more than 50 players. Computer assisted club TDs can be the Chief TD of any tournament, or section of a tournament, expected to draw up to 60 players with the aid of one assistant TD. IA and FA experience credit of any kind is unavailable at Category I tournaments.

25. Expiration.

Three-year renewable term. Every three years, the club TD may apply to extend the Club TD Certification for an additional three years. This three-year renewal requires that the applicant pass an objective test of moderate difficulty designed to measure the applicant's knowledge of basic rules at the 70% level. Except for the first exam, which may not be waived, the testing requirement for re-certification is waived for a Club TD with satisfactory performance as the chief or chief assistant TD of three tournaments or a minimum of a single section at three different tournaments during the three-year term. Club TDs meeting the rating and directing experience requirements are encouraged to take the Local TD exam. Club TDs passing the Club TD exam at the 80% level that also meet the experience and rating requirements for Local TD certification may have their Club TD certification automatically upgraded to a Local TD certification.

The Local Director

26. Experience Requirements.

a. A total of three Category D tournament experience credits are required, as listed below in a1– a3, with the total number of players for all three tournaments summed together being 50 or greater:

a1. Satisfactory performance as Chief TD of one Category D tournament. No substitutions are allowed for this TD credit.

a2. Satisfactory performance as a Chief TD or chief assistant TD of a second additional Category D tournament of at least three rounds. No substitutions are allowed for this TD credit.

a3. Satisfactory performance as a Chief TD or chief assistant TD of a third additional Category D tournament of at least three rounds. A one-time substitution for this single TD experience credit is allowed as outlined in b1 – b4 below.

b. Any of the following may be substituted for the tournaments in requirement a3 as per the limitations imposed by sections b1 –b4:

b1. Satisfactory performance as a TD at either a Category D1 or D2 tournament can be used as a single one-time substitute for a requirement (a3) category D tournament.

b2. Satisfactory performance as a TD at any combination of two (2) Category D, D1, or D2 tournaments can be used as a single one-time substitute for a requirement (a3) category D tournament.

b3. Attendance at any TDCC, or US Chess approved, problem solving and discussion workshop (not a TDCC business meeting workshop) typically, but not exclusively, offered at a U.S. Open Championship. This TD credit can be used as a single one-time substitute for a requirement (a3) category D tournament.

b4. Satisfactory performance as a TD at an online Swiss tournament, or section of a tournament, of at least three rounds can be used as a single one-time substitution for a requirement (a3) category C tournament.

b5. For any applicant who takes and passes the local TD test (closed book) under supervision at a Category N tournament, the sole experience requirement is satisfactory performance as a Chief TD at one Category D tournament, requirement (a1), of at least three rounds. No substitutions may be made for the Category D tournament. Applicants must contact US Chess two weeks in advance of the tournament to request this option.

c. Only one experience credit as a section chief or chief assistant section chief or assistant section chief is allowed in multiple sectioned tournaments. Multiple tournaments held at the same site on the same dates may be defined as sections of the same tournament. Dual rated tournaments count as Regular rated, not Quick rated, for TD experience credit.

27. Testing Requirement.

Objective test of moderate difficulty designed to measure the applicant's knowledge of basic rules; or, if the Local TD experience requirements (a-c) are met by a Club TD, scoring 80% or higher on a Club TD test.

TD TIP: The passing grade for all TD exams at all levels, except for Club, is 80%. For more information on how a Club TD automatically is upgraded to a Local TD, see paragraph 25.

28. Limitations.

A local TD may not be the Chief TD for Category N or Category I tournaments and should not be the Chief TD of Category A or B tournaments, which includes any tournament, or section of a tournament, expected to draw more than 100 players. Computer assisted local TDs can be the Chief TD of any tournament, or section of a tournament, expected to draw up to 120 players with the aid of one assistant TD.

TD TIP: For Local TDs, neither FA nor IA norm experience credit is available at Category I tournaments.

29. Expiration.

Four-year renewable term: The testing requirement for re-certification is waived for a local TD with satisfactory performance as the chief or chief assistant TD of four tournaments or a minimum of a single section at four different tournaments during the four-year term.

The Senior Director

30. Experience Requirements.

a. A total of ten Category C tournament experience credits, as listed below in a1 – a3, are required with the total number of players for all ten tournaments summed together being 400 or greater:

   a1. Satisfactory performance as Chief TD of five Category C tournaments of at least four rounds; no substitutions are allowed for these five TD credits.

   a2. Satisfactory performance as Chief TD or chief assistant TD of one Category C tournament of at least four rounds; no substitutions are allowed for this TD credit.

   a3. Satisfactory performance as Chief TD or chief assistant TD at four Category C tournaments of at least four rounds; substitutions for each of the four TD experience credits is allowed as outlined in (b) below.

b. Any of the following may be substituted for the tournaments in requirement a3 as per the limitations imposed by sections b1 –b9:

   b1. Attendance at any TDCC, or US Chess approved, problem solving and discussion workshop (not a TDCC business meeting workshop) typically, but not exclusively, offered at a U.S. Open Championship. This TD credit can be used as a single one-time substitute replacing only one of the four requirement a3 category C tournaments.

   b2. Satisfactory performance as a chief assistant TD to a national TD or associate national TD at one Category A, A1, A2, B, B1, or B2 tournament of at least four rounds. This type of TD credit can be used as a substitute only twice replacing only two of the four requirement a3 category C tournaments.

   b3. Satisfactory performance as a chief assistant TD to a national TD or associate national TD at any combination of two Quick/Blitz

Chess Category A, A1, A2, B, B1, or B2 tournaments of at least four rounds. The two Quick/Blitz Chess events count as only a single TD credit. This type of TD credit can be used as a substitute only twice replacing only two of the four requirement a3 category C tournaments.

b4. Satisfactory performance as a Chief TD or chief assistant TD at any combination of two Category C1 or C2 tournaments of at least four rounds. The two Category C1 or C2 tournaments together count as only one single TD credit. This type of TD credit can be used as a substitute only twice replacing only two of the four requirement a3 category C tournaments.

b5. Satisfactory performance as a Chief TD or chief assistant TD at any combination of four Quick/Blitz Chess Category C, C1 or C2 tournaments of at least four rounds. The four Quick/Blitz Chess Category C, C1 or C2 tournaments combined count as only one single TD credit. This type of TD credit can be used as a substitute only twice replacing only two of the four requirement a3 category C tournaments.

b6. Satisfactory performance as a Chief TD or chief assistant TD at any combination of regular rated or Quick/Blitz Chess Category D, D1 or D2 tournaments of at least four rounds. The total number of players combined for the entire Regular rated and/or the entire Quick/Blitz Chess Category D, D1, D2 tournaments must be at least 100 players. The entire number of Regular rated or Quick/Blitz Chess Category D, D1 or D2 tournaments combined count as only one single requirement a3 Category C tournament TD credit. This type of TD credit can be used as a substitute only once as a replacement for a single requirement a3 category C tournament.

b7. Satisfactory performance as Chief TD of one Category R tournament. this type of TD credit cannot be used if a b8 TD Credit has already been used. This TD credit can be used as a substitute only once as a replacement for a single requirement a3 category C tournament.

b8. Satisfactory performance as Chief TD of two Quick/Blitz Chess Category R tournaments; this TD credit cannot be used if a b7 TD Credit has already been used. This type of TD credit can be used as a substitute only once as a replacement for a single requirement a3 category C tournament.

b9. Satisfactory performance as a TD at an online Swiss tournament, or section of a tournament, of at least four rounds and having at least 50 entrants, can be used as a single one-time substitute for a requirement (a3) category C requirement. This type of TD credit can be used as a substitute no more than twice, replacing nor more than two of the four a3 category C requirements. If it is used twice then two different online events must be used.

b10. For any applicant who takes and passes the Senior TD test (closed book) under supervision at a category N tournament, experience requirements are reduced to satisfactory performance as a Chief TD at three category C tournaments of at least four rounds (either a Category C1 or C2 tournament may be substituted for one of the three Category C tournaments, or two Quick/Blitz Chess Category C, C1 or C2 tournaments may be substituted for one of the three Category C tournaments) and three additional Swiss system tournaments of at least four rounds (two Quick/Blitz Chess Swiss system tournaments may be substituted for one of the three additional Swiss system tournaments) with at least 2 tournaments, of any size, having been successfully submitted for a rating online. Applicants must contact US Chess two weeks in advance of the tournament to request this option.

c. Only one experience credit as a section chief is allowed in multiple sectioned tournaments. Multiple tournaments held at the same site on the same dates may be defined as sections of the same tournament. Dual rated tournaments count as Regular rated, not Quick rated, for TD experience credit.

d. At least 3 tournaments, of any size (including substitutions), having been successfully submitted for a rating online.

e. A current International arbiter (IA) or FIDE arbiter (FA) meets Senior TD experience requirements if:

1. The IA or FA status is verified by FIDE.

2. The IA or FA states they are relocating to the United States from a foreign country.

3. The IA or FA is an US Chess member.

4. The IA or FA is at least certified as a US Chess Club TD.

5. The IA or FA has satisfactorily assisted at a minimum of three US Chess Category C tournaments under the supervision of a Senior TD totaling at least 200 players.

6. The IA or FA has been the chief of at least one Category D tournament and satisfactorily submitted the rating report online.

7. The IA or FA has an established US Chess rating.

31. Testing Requirement.

Difficult objective examination designed to evaluate the applicant's knowledge and judgment in situations not clearly addressed by the rules.

TD TIP: The passing grade for all TD exams at all levels, except for Club, is 80%.

32. Limitations.

A senior TD may not be the Chief TD for Category N tournaments and should not be the Chief TD of Category A tournaments, which includes any tournament, or section of a tournament, expected to draw more than 300 players. Computer assisted senior TDs can be the Chief TD of any tournament or section of a tournament (excluding category A or category N tournaments) expected to draw up to 360 players with the aid of one assistant TD.

33. Expiration.

Five-year renewable term: The testing requirement for re-certification is waived for a Senior TD with satisfactory performance as the chief or chief assistant TD of five tournaments or a minimum of a single section at five different tournaments during the five-year term.

The Associate National Director (ANTD)

34. Experience Requirements.

a. FIRST, a total of ten Category B tournament experience credits, as listed below in a1 – a4, are required:

a1. Satisfactory performance as Chief TD at four Category B tournaments; no substitutions are allowed.

a2. Satisfactory performance as Chief TD at one Category B tournament which awarded $1000+ in cash prizes; no substitutions are allowed.

a3. Satisfactory performance as Chief TD or Chief Assistant TD at two additional Category B tournaments which each awarded $1000+ in cash prizes; substitutions are allowed.

a4. Satisfactory performance as Chief TD at three Category B tournaments; substitutions are allowed.

b. Any of the following may be substituted for the tournaments in requirements a3-a4 as per the limitations imposed by sections b1 –b3:

b1. Satisfactory performance as Chief TD at one Category C, C1, C2, B1 or B2 tournament (or any combination of two Quick/Blitz Chess Category C, C1, C2, B1 or B2 tournaments that can be combined to count as only one TD credit) which each awarded $1000 in cash prizes. This type of TD credit can be used as a substitute only twice, replacing at most two of the requirement a3 category B tournaments.

b2. One TD experience credit can be earned with the satisfactory performance as Chief TD at any combination of three Category C, C1, C2, B1 or B2 tournaments (or any combination of six Quick/Blitz Chess Category C, C1, C2, B1 or B2 tournaments that can be combined to count as only one TD credit). This single type of TD credit can be used as a substitute only three times, replacing at most three of the requirement a4 category B tournaments.

b3. One TD experience credit can be with the satisfactory performance as a TD at an online Swiss tournament, or section of a tournament, of at least four rounds and having at least 100 entrants. This single type of TD credit can be used as a substitute no more than twice, replacing no more than two of the three a4 category B requirements. If it is used twice then two different online events must be used.

c.   SECOND, satisfactory performance as Chief TD or Chief Assistant to a national TD at a Category N, N1, N2, N3, N4, A, A1, or A2 tournament or any combination of two Quick/Blitz Chess Category N, N1, N2, N3, N4, A, A1, or A2 tournaments.

d.   THIRD, satisfactory performance as Chief TD of a Category R tournament or two Quick/Blitz Chess Category R tournaments.

e.   At least 4 tournaments, of any size (including substitutions), must have been successfully submitted for a rating online.

f.   Only one experience credit as a section chief or chief assistant section chief or assistant section chief is allowed in multiple sectioned tournaments. Multiple tournaments held at the same site on the same dates may be defined as sections of the same tournament. Dual rated tournaments count as Regular rated, not Quick rated, for TD experience credit.

35. Testing Requirement.

Essay examination of substantial difficulty designed to measure the applicant's understanding of the rules as they relate to complex problems. An experienced national TD grades the examination. If the NTD gives the exam a failing grade, the applicant may request that the exam be regraded by two additional experienced NTDs. A regrade will automatically occur if the applicant scored between 70%-79%. The final result of the grading process will then be the result given by at least two of the three graders. The same form of the same examination may not be taken more than once by any applicant.

TD TIP: The passing grade for all TD exams at all levels, except for Club, is 80%.

36. Limitations.

An associate national TD may not be the Chief TD of Category N1 tournaments.

37. Expiration.

Six-year renewable terms: The testing requirement for re-certification is waived for an ANTD with satisfactory performance as the chief or chief assistant TD of six tournaments or a minimum of a single section at six different tournaments during the six-year term.

The National Director (NTD)

38. Experience Requirements.

a. FIRST, a total of fifteen Category B tournament experience credits, as listed below in a1 – a4, are required:

a1. Satisfactory performance as Chief TD at eight Category B tournaments; no substitutions are allowed.

a2. Satisfactory performance as Chief TD at one Category B tournament which awarded $1000+ in cash prizes; no substitutions are allowed.

a3. Satisfactory performance as Chief TD or Chief Assistant TD at two additional Category B tournaments each which awarded $1000+ in cash prizes; substitutions are allowed.

a4. Satisfactory performance as Chief TD at four Category B tournaments; substitutions are allowed.

b. Any of the following may be substituted for the tournaments in requirements a3-a4 as per the limitations imposed by sections b1 –b3.

b1. Satisfactory performance as Chief TD at one Category C, C1, C2, B1 or B2 tournament (or any combination of two Quick/Blitz Chess Category C, C1, C2, B1 or B2 tournaments that can be combined to count as only one TD credit) which each awarded $1000 in cash prizes. This type of TD credit can be used as a substitute only twice, replacing at most two of the requirement a3 category B tournaments.

b2. One TD experience credit can be earned with the satisfactory performance as Chief TD at any combination of three Category C, C1, C2, B1 or B2 tournaments (or any combination of six Quick/Blitz Chess Category C, C1, C2, B1 or B2 tournaments that can be combined to count as only one TD credit). This single type of TD credit can be used as a substitute only four times, replacing at most four of the requirement a4 category B tournaments.

b3. One TD experience credit can be earned with the satisfactory performance as a TD at an online Swiss tournament, or section of a tournament, of at least four rounds and having at least 100 entrants. This single type of TD credit can be used as a substitute no more than twice, replacing no more than two of the four a4 category B requirements. If it is used twice then two different online events must be used.

c. SECOND, Satisfactory performance as Chief Assistant to a national TD at a Category N1 tournament (the following may be substituted for one Category N1 tournament: a combination of one Category N3 tournament plus one Category N4 tournament).

d. THIRD, Satisfactory performance as Chief TD or Chief Assistant to a national TD at an additional Category N1, N2, N3, N4, A, A1, or A2, or satisfactory performance as Chief TD or Chief Assistant to a national TD at any combination of two additional Quick/Blitz Chess Category N1, N2, N3, N4, A, A1, or A2 tournaments.

e. FOURTH, Satisfactory performance as Chief TD of a Category R tournament or satisfactory performance as Chief TD at two Quick/Blitz Chess Category R tournaments.

f. FIFTH, Satisfactory performance as Chief TD or Chief Assistant to a national or associate national TD at a Category T tournament of at least four rounds, or satisfactory performance as Chief TD or Chief Assistant to a national or associate national TD at two Quick/Blitz Chess Category T tournaments of at least four rounds.

g. Only one experience credit as a section chief or chief assistant section chief or assistant section chief is allowed in multiple sectioned tournaments. Multiple tournaments held at the same site on the same dates may be defined as sections of the same tournament. Dual rated tournaments count as Regular rated, not Quick rated, for TD experience credit.

h. At least 5 tournaments, of any size (including substitutions), must have been successfully submitted for a rating online.

39. Testing Requirement.
A rigorous essay examination designed to measure the applicant's understanding of the philosophies behind the rules. An experienced national TD grades the examination. The same form of the same examination may not be

taken more than once by any applicant. If the NTD gives the exam a failing grade, the applicant may request that the exam be regraded by two additional experienced NTDs. A regrade will automatically occur if the applicant scored between 70%-79%. The final result of the grading process will then be the result given by at least two of the three graders. The same form of the same examination may not be taken more than once by any applicant.

TD TIP: *The passing grade for all TD exams at all levels, except for Club, is 80%.*

40. Limitations.
None.

41. Expiration.
Life.

The International Arbiter (IA) and FIDE Arbiter (FA)

42. Title.
The titles of international arbiter and FIDE arbiter are awarded by the World Chess Federation (FIDE).

TD TIP: FIDE has other titles and licenses, such as national arbiter (NA).

43. Qualifications.
US Chess will submit a title application for the International arbiter and FIDE arbiter titles for current US Chess members who are certified at the Senior, ANTD, or NTD level and meet all the following requirements. FIDE requires that an IA applicant must already hold the title of FA. Applicants will pay all fees regarding this process:

a. Thorough knowledge of the *Laws of Chess* and the FIDE Regulations for chess competitions;

b. Absolute objectivity, demonstrated at all times during his or her activity as an arbiter;

c. Sufficient knowledge of at least one official FIDE language for FA and obligatory knowledge of the English language, minimum at conversation level, and of chess terms in other official FIDE languages, for IA.

d. Experience: US Chess Senior TD and chief or deputy arbiter in at least four category I events documented by the appropriate title norm certificate signed by a current IA or FA and governed by the FIDE Laws of Chess and Rules of Play such as the following:

d1. The final of the National Adult Championship (not more than two);
d2. All official FIDE tournaments and matches;
d3. International title tournaments and matches;
d4. International chess festivals with at least 100 contestants.

TD TIP: All applications for titles and licenses must meet FIDE requirements and go through (be submitted by) US Chess.

44. Testing Requirement.
Contact US Chess.

45. Limitations.
International Arbiters may direct all Category I tournaments. In order to submit the tournament as a US Chess rated tournament, the IA must also have a level of US Chess TD certification appropriate to the US Chess Category into which the tournament fits.

TD TIP: Contact the US Chess office BEFORE any FIDE tournament is run to make sure all US Chess/FIDE current requirements for both the tournament and TD qualifications (experience requirements, fees,...) are met. Category I tournaments have arbiter limitations and qualifications set by FIDE that must be met before they can be submitted to FIDE.

46. Expiration.
The expiration of IA certification is determined by FIDE. Currently (as of the adoption of these standards), International arbiters are certified for life.

Waivers

47. Special Consideration.
The TDCC reserves the right to give special consideration to applicants in extraordinary situations. Requests detailing the extraordinary circumstances must be submitted in writing to the TDCC chairperson through the technical director.

Certification Restrictions

48. Restrictions.
US Chess may impose restrictions on a TD's certification upon documentation of technical incompetence, partiality, professional misconduct, or inefficiency.

49. Due Process.
Allegations of these offenses will be investigated by the TDCC or the executive director. The accused will be afforded due process. In every investigation the TDCC or executive director will consider the past accomplishments of the TD in service to chess and other substantiated complaints against the TD.

50. Penalties.
Imposed restrictions may include warnings, probations, requirements of additional experience or testing to maintain or advance level, demotions of level, limitations on the types of tournaments that may be directed, temporary suspensions of directing certification, or permanent de-certifications.

51. Appeals.
Any imposition of TD restrictions made by the executive director may be appealed to the TDCC. Any decision made by the TDCC may be appealed to the Executive Board. Any decision made by the Executive Board may be appealed to the Board of Delegates. All appeals should be filed within 30 days of notice of action taken. Restrictions will generally remain in effect during the appeals process.

Uniform Code of Discipline

52. Technical Incompetence.
In cases in which technical incompetence on the part of the TD has been demonstrated, the TDCC will normally impose additional testing requirements for the TD to maintain his or her level of certification. In extreme cases the TDCC may demote the TD's level of certification or suspend his or her certification until greater competence is demonstrated. Technical incompetence is typically demonstrated by gross misapplication of US Chess's Official Rules of Chess.

53. Partiality.
In cases in which partiality on the part of the TD has been demonstrated, the TDCC will normally impose a suspension of directing privileges for a period not less than three months and not greater than three years. In extreme cases the TDCC may recommend permanent de-certification to the Executive Board.

Bribery, fraudulent reports, deliberately unfair pairing or scoring practices, deliberately inconsistent rules enforcement, and even minor irregularities that benefit the TD as a player in an event in which he or she is eligible for a prize typically demonstrates partiality.

54. Professional Misconduct.

In cases in which professional misconduct on the part of the TD has been demonstrated and reconciliation between the complainant and the TD cannot be achieved, the TDCC will normally issue a warning to the TD. Extreme cases of professional misconduct, especially when representing US Chess at a national tournament, may warrant certification demotion or suspension. Professional misconduct is typically demonstrated by denigration of a player, arrogance, rude behavior, and failure to respond to official inquiries by the executive director, his or her designee, or the TDCC.

55. Inefficiency.

In cases in which inefficiency has been demonstrated as the cause of a poorly directed tournament, the TDCC will normally issue a warning to the TD. In extreme cases certification may be suspended until the TD demonstrates improved procedural techniques. Inefficiency is typically demonstrated by lack of adherence to an announced tournament schedule, untimely or inaccurate posting of pairings and results, and untimely or inaccurate calculation of tournament-prize distributions.

CHAPTER EIGHT

The
US CHESS RATING SYSTEM

Editor's Note: The material in this chapter is a mix of ever-changing ratings formulas, ratings policies, and rules changes. This chapter does not reflect the exact system used to calculate ratings. It uses simulated data and procedures to demonstrate the ideas behind the Ratings System. For the exact current formulas, policies, and rules please contact US Chess directly.

The rating system described here is for over-the-board competition only. Those interested in correspondence ratings should contact the US Chess office to request the correspondence chess pamphlet describing that system. For those interested in Online ratings see Rule 2. The US Chess Online Rating System (Chapter 10).

The basic theory of the US Chess's rating system is that the difference between the ratings of players is a guide to predicting the outcome of a contest between those two players.

A specific formula has been worked out according to statistical and probability theory and is available from US Chess. No rating, however, is a precise evaluation of a player's strength. Instead, ratings are averages of performances and should be viewed as approximations.

US Chess
Rating Classification

Senior Master	above 2399
Master	2200-2399
Expert	2000-2199
Class A	1800-1999
Class B	1600-1799
Class C	1400-1599
Class D	1200-1399
Class E	1000-1199
Class F	800- 999
Class G	600- 799
Class H	400- 599
Class I	200- 399
Class J	Under 200

US Chess Rating Regulations

1. Rated games.
All games played in US Chess-rated events are rated, including games decided by time-forfeit, games decided when a player fails to appear for resumption after an adjournment, and games played by contestants who subsequently withdraw or are not allowed to continue. Games in which one

player makes no move are not rated. There are three separate rating systems. A player's Blitz rating is calculated if he or she participates in events with total playing times of G/5 – G/10. A player's *Quick* rating is calculated if he or she participates in events with a total playing time greater than 10 minutes and less than 30 minutes. A player's *Regular* rating is computed if he or she enters a tournament with the total playing time of G/30 or slower. Games with total playing times of G/30-G/65 are used to calculate both *Regular* and *Quick* ratings at the same time. For an explanation of how to calculate total playing time, **See also** 5C, Ratable time controls.

An established rating is a rating based on at least 26 games. A provisional rating is a rating based on fewer than 26 games. In order to be published in a rating supplement, a rating must be based on at least four games.

2. Time controls.
Time controls must be announced in advance. Sudden-death time controls require that all remaining moves, no matter how many, be completed within a fixed time. Increment time controls add a specific amount of time, usually in seconds, for every move a player makes. **See also** 5B1, Delay and increment.

3. Order of ratings.
Normally, events are rated in chronological order by their ending dates. New ratings produced by each event are used for the next calculation, and so forth. Published ratings are those current as of the closing date of a given monthly rating list.

4. Matches.
A match is inherently different than other types of chess events, because it is an arranged contest between two players, generally involving multiple games. This affects the statistical assumptions upon which the US Chess rating system is based, namely that ratings are based upon a large number of games against a diverse group of opponents. There are also numerous opportunities for manipulation of ratings via matches. As a result, US Chess treats matches differently than other ways to pair players, such as the Swiss System, Round Robin, randomly paired or ladder events, both in terms of who may play in a match and what ratings changes may result from that match.

For US Chess purposes, a match is defined as any event in which all or substantially all of the games are between two individuals who choose to play each other or are chosen to play each other multiple times, such as a multi-game team-on-team match. That definition would exclude any games from events that arise as a result of specific pairing situations during a tournament, such as extra games involving a house player, poor turnout in a section, etc. Since the players didn't enter the event with the intention of playing one person multiple times, the rules regarding participation in a match should not apply. The limitations on ratings changes from match play given below may still apply. Playoffs to decide place prizes in a tournament may be treated as matches. In validating events, sections in which all the players have just one opponent and at least one of those pairs of players play each other more than once will be considered matches. An event which would otherwise be considered a match between two players but with an extra round in which one or both of the players in the match play another person will also be considered a match

a. Matches can be as short as one game or as long as 32 games. They can be rated under the regular US Chess rating system, quick rated, or rated under both systems, depending upon the time control.

b. Both players in a match must have established and published ratings, and those ratings must be no more than 400 points apart as of the most recent published ratings for those players when the match is held. Under the US Chess ratings system, matches are not eligible for bonus points. A player may gain or lose no more than 50 rating points in a match. Also, a player may only have a cumulative gain or cumulative loss of up to 100 rating points through match play during any 180 day period, and may only have a cumulative gain or cumulative loss of up to 200 rating points through match play during any three year period.

c. Matches must be coded properly when they are submitted to US Chess for rating, either by clearly noting it as a match on the rating report form and crosstable when sending the rating report to US Chess via USPS mail, or by coding the event as a match when submitting the event online using US Chess's TD/Affiliate Support Area.

d. If a certified TD is not submitting the match results, both players must sign a notarized statement that the match conformed to US Chess match rules and other conditions for US Chess rated play.

e. During validation of an event, any section involving just two players that is two or more games long will be considered an error if it is not coded as a match, as will other sections that appear to be a match. TDs are asked to identify as matches any one-game sections they submit that were intended as matches between those two players (i.e., the two players chose to play each other.)

f. In the event that some sections in a tournament appear to be matches based on the above definition but are not, the chief TD will have to contact US Chess to explain the circumstances before US Chess will rate the event. The US Chess office will decide if the circumstances warrant an exception to the rules regarding the ratings of the players separately from whether the restrictions on ratings changes should apply to that event.

g. US Chess may, at its discretion, apply the match rules to any section in which two players face each other more than twice, either before rating the event or after it has been rated. TDs may be asked to identify any such sections in advance and explain why they should not be treated as matches. US Chess may also choose to combine multiple sections or multiple events and treat them as a match.

h. Match results may not count towards qualification for invitational events.

i. Matches are not eligible for Grand Prix or Junior Grand Prix points.

j. Finally, any player who plays in a match and who is either at his or her floor or reaches his or her floor as a result of that match will be considered to have submitted a request to have that floor lowered by 100 points. The US Chess ratings department will review the player's tournament history to decide if the floor should be lowered.

Events which in the US Chess's judgment are intended to flaunt or circumvent these match rules may be classified as a match, and may also result in sanctions against the submitting TD, the sponsoring affiliate and/or the players involved. **See also** Rule 3C, Match Play Limitations (Chapter 10).

5. Rating floor.

Each rated player has a rating floor. Every player has a personal absolute floor between 100 and 150. A player with an established rating may have a rating floor higher than the absolute floor. In most cases, floors are calculated by subtracting 200 points from the individual's highest rating achieved and setting the last two digits to zero. If a player's highest rating achieved is greater than or equal to 1400 but less than 1500, the individual's floor is 1200. If the highest rating achieved by a player is below 1400, then the individual's floor is the same as his or her absolute floor. No floor can be above 2100 or below 100, except that a player who achieves the Original Life Master (OLM) title is given a floor of 2200. The OLM title is earned by playing 300 games, not necessarily consecutive, with an established rating of 2200 or higher.

A person's rating floor can also change if he or she wins a large class prize. The dollar limit is set by the Executive Board and may change due to economic conditions or periodic updates. The current floor will be listed on the US Chess Federation official web site. The minimum post-tournament rating of players winning such a prize shall be the lowest rating which would not be eligible for the section or class prize the player won.

A player with a substantial history of not being competitive in a floored class may request that the US Chess office consider lowering this floor.

Rating floor examples

Example 1: If Jack's highest rating achieved is 1830, his floor is 1600.

Example 2: If Joe's highest rating achieved is 1599, his floor is 1300.

Example 3: If Sharon won an Under-1900 prize of $2,010 and her pre-tournament rating was 1853, her post-tournament rating and floor would be at least 1900. Thus, Sharon would be ineligible to win an Under-1900 prize in future events. If Jack won an Under-1500 prize of $2,200, his floor would be set to 1500.

6. Rating entire events.
In General, these are the steps US Chess takes when a tournament gets rated.

a. Set the initial ratings for unrated players.
b. Compute first-pass ratings for unrated players.
c. Calculate a rating for everyone.
d. Based on the opponents' ratings from (c), recalculate a rating for everyone.

7. Imposed rating adjustments.
The US Chess Executive Director may review the rating of any US Chess member and make the appropriate adjustments, including but not limited to imposition of a rating *ceiling* (a level above which a player's rating may not rise).

8. Lifetime titles.
The rating system also calculates players' lifetime titles. One can earn permanent titles by achieving good performances or norms in events of at least four rounds. Technical information on lifetime titles is available on request from the US Chess office.

9. Rating system adjustments.
Occasionally, but not always, the rating system needs to be adjusted when the theoretical model is not reflected in practice. To find out which adjustments, if any, are currently being applied to the rating system, please contact US Chess.

10. Estimating your approximate rating.
From Bill Smythe we have the following explanation of how to estimate your US Chess rating after each tournament. There are two formulas, the Special formula and the Standard formula.

If you are a new player, or have played fewer than 9 previous tournament games, use the Special formula. Players with 9 or more previous games should use the Standard formula.

10A. Special formula.

The Special formula is used for players with fewer than 9 tournament games, not including the current tournament.

Add the ratings of all your opponents, including those from previous tournaments. Add 400 for each win, subtract 400 for each loss, including wins and losses in previous tournaments. Divide by the total number of games. The result is your rating.

You cannot gain rating points by losing a game. If you lose all your games, your new rating is 400 points below the rating of your lowest-rated opponent. For young players, initial ratings of players with all losses may be further reduced based on age (up to age 20). No player's rating is allowed to drop below 100.

Examples

Example 1: You play five games in your first rated event, defeating a player rated 1350, losing to players rated 1700 and 1400, drawing with one rated 1600, and losing to one rated 1450. Your performance ratings are **1750** (1350 +400=1750), **1300** (1700-400=1300), **1000** (1400-400=1000), **1600** (1600+0=1600), and **1050** (1450-400=1050). Dividing the sum of these (6700) by the number of games (5) gives 1340, your initial provisional rating.

Example 2: You play three games in your next rated event. You beat a player rated 1400, lose to one rated 1580, and draw with one rated 1200. Again, there are two easy ways to calculate:

Your old rating (1340) times five (for proper weighting) plus these performances divided by eight, which is the total number of games:

$$((1340 \times 5) + 1800 + 1180 + 1200) / 8 = (6700 + 1800 + 1180 + 1200) / 8 = 10880 / 8 = 1360$$

10B. Standard formula.

The Standard formula is used for players with 9 or more games in previous tournaments. For the exact formulas and procedures used please contact US Chess.

TD TIP: The Standard formula is a mixed bag of the rating difference between you and your opponents, the result(s) of the game(s), the expected result of the game(s), a player's expected score for the number of rounds they played (the K factor), and possibly bonus points. Bonus points are added to a player's rating for having a much better final score at a tournament than was statistically predicted. For a detailed explanation, or even a semi-detailed explanation, of the ratings formulas, please check out the links at the end of this chapter.

10C. Unrated opponents.

If any of your opponents are unrated, you must first calculate their ratings using the Special Formula. These ratings may then be used to calculate your own.

10D. Other considerations.

The approximate rating that is calculated, based on these examples or the US Chess approximate ratings calculator, may differ slightly from the rating computed by US Chess. The major reasons for such differences are as follows:

10D1. Updated ratings.

Your calculations, or those using the US Chess's approximate ratings calculator, are based on your opponent's ratings as shown on the tournament wall chart or listed in the last-published US Chess rating list. US Chess's calculations, on the other hand, are based on updated ratings, reflecting tournaments not yet rated when the wall chart ratings were published. Usually, inaccuracies in computation caused by not knowing your opponents' exact ratings are much larger than the inaccuracies resulting from the use of approximations and simplifications.

The entire official list of rating changes are published in the *Ratings Supplement,* available as a download, every month and used for pairing, prize, and wall chart purposes. Players may also view their individual rating, and any official (plus unofficial) rating changes, by accessing the "Players & Ratings" (Membership Services Area, or MSA) located on US Chess's web site (www.uschess.org).

10D2. Simplifications.

The methods described here are based on approximations and rounding, compared to those used by the US Chess computer. The most significant approximation occurs in the determination of the K-factor (a variable determined in part by a formula based on your expected results in the event you played in).

A more precise description of approximate rating calculations can be found at:

http://glicko.net/ratings/approx.pdf

A more technical version can be viewed at:
http://glicko.net/ratings/rating.system.pdf

Currently there is an online approximate ratings calculator at:
http://www.uschess.org/content/view/9177/679/

Dr. Mark Glickman and Bill Smythe contributed to the material in this chapter.

CHAPTER NINE

OFFICIAL US CHESS CORRESPONDENCE CHESS RULES

These rules superseded previous versions and apply to all Correspondence Chess tournaments and matches starting after December 31, 1991.

Your Pledge

"I undertake to conform to the rules and objectives of US Chess Correspondence Chess, to respond promptly to all chess correspondence and to maintain a high standard of courtesy, sociability, and good fellowship at all times in my contacts with other members. I also understand that I have a responsibility to complete my games."

Your Responsibilities as a Player

1. You must be a US Chess member for the duration of your play in any tournament. You must abide by the latest edition of the US Chess Federation's Official Rules of Chess, except when inappropriate for correspondence play. In case of conflict, correspondence rules take precedence. You are responsible for knowing the rules. By entering correspondence events, you agree to follow directions of the correspondence chess director (CCD), to respond to any legitimate inquiry, and to provide requested information. Players must enter tournaments only in their own names, unless approval for other action is granted by the CCD. A player who withdraws may be denied entry to new events. If you withdraw without proper notice to your opponent and the CCD, it will be the decision of the CCD as to whether or not you will be allowed to play in another CC event.

2. You are expected to act courteously toward opponents. The CCD will forfeit players who use abusive or insulting language or who are disruptive. In case of conflict, you should try to come to an agreement with your opponent.

3. You may consult chess books and periodicals but not other players. You cannot use a computer or computer program (chess playing algorithms) to evaluate a game, but you may use computers for record keeping and databases.

4. In case of appeals, retain all game records (including move cards) for at least four months after receiving notice of a game result. Otherwise, you may find yourself without a defense to an opponent's claim.

Reflection Time

5. Every day counts as reflection time including Sundays and holidays. For each 10 moves (1-10, 11-20,...) you have 30 days of reflection time.

You may carry unused time over into the next 10-move series. Reflection time is calculated for postal from the date the move is received until the date it is posted. For email it is calculated from the date your opponent's posts his/her move to the date you post a reply. You are charged a day of reflection time for each 24-hour period from the time the move was posted. Example, if your opponent posts a move at 11:50 PM on March 22nd, you have until 11:49 PM March 23rd to post a reply without being charged a day's reflection time. If your reply is posted at 11:55 PM on March 23rd, you are charged with one day of reflection time. If you post a reply at 11:55 PM on March 24th, you are charged with two days reflection time, etc. If you post or send your reply at 11:48 PM March 24th, you are charged with one day of reflection time. There is no transit time in email games

6. You must advise the CCD and your opponents of address changes in advance or at the latest within seven days of vacating previous premises. Also email address changes. If you don't, five days will be charged as reflection time.

Transmitting Moves

7. You must use English algebraic notation unless you and your opponent agree on another system. All games shall be conducted using written or typed correspondence unless otherwise indicated. Transmitted moves, including conditional moves, are binding if the moves are legal. If an illegal or ambiguous move is transmitted as part of a conditional move set, the moves immediately preceding the illegal or ambiguous move are binding. Missing or mistaken announcement of check, capture, or "e.p." does not invalidate a move. Diagrams or commentary have no significance in disputes over move legality.

8. You can purchase convenient postcards for sending moves through the mail from US Chess sales.com. Your move card must contain:

a. Names and addresses of both players;

b. Section and game numbers;

c. The previous move sent and your response;

    d. For conditional moves, the move sent immediately prior to the conditional move(s), all conditional moves you accept, and your response;

    e. Receipt and postmark dates of your opponent's previous move and the date of your reply;

    f. Time used on current move by you and your opponent;

    g. Current reflection time totals. If you do not include "f." and "g." with your moves, you cannot claim a win on time.

In the Golden Knights Finals, Absolute Championship, and other events deemed appropriate by US Chess, there is also a five-day reflection time penalty for:

    a. Impossible, ambiguous or illegible move(s);

    b. Failing to confirm your opponent's last move.

An impossible move is a move which cannot be played as recorded. Notify your opponent immediately of your finding. An impossible move or an illegible move in no way obliges the player to move the piece in question. In a case of an ambiguous move, the ambiguous move must be clarified and executed. For example, if your opponent writes Nd2 and either Nbd2 or Nfd2 can be made, the person writing the ambiguous move must execute Nbd2 or Nfd2. Clerical errors are binding and once posted, can in no way be taken back.

9. To offer conditional moves, send them as a series of consecutively numbered moves. To accept conditional moves, acknowledge them as you would other moves. You can accept a series of conditional moves in whole or in part. Conditional moves are binding only until the next reply.

Example: you are responding to your opponent's second move, 2. Nf3. You want to reply 2. ... Nc6 and offer two conditional moves. Your card should have the following appearance:

    1. e4 e5 2. Nf3 Nc6

    If 3. Bb5, then 3. ... a6

    If 3. Bc4, then 3. ... Nf6

A typical opponent's reply might be:

2. Nf3 Nc6 3. Bb5 a6 4. Bxc6 ... (or 4. Bc6 ... or 4. B:c6 ...)

There is no penalty for misrecording an "if" move by the sending player.

10. If you intend to use more than 10 days on a single move, you must tell your opponent within one week of receiving his move. If you don't receive your opponent's reply within normal transmission time plus 10 days, send a repeat. Repeat moves must be labeled as such and must include all information from the original move. If no reply after one repeat see Rule 13.

Loss on Time Overstep

11. In Golden Knights Finals, the Absolute Championship, and other events deemed appropriate by US Chess, if a player oversteps the time control (rule #5), he or she will forfeit the game. In Golden Knights Preliminary and Semi-final rounds and all other US Chess Correspondence Chess events (excluding the Golden Knights Finals, the Absolute Championship, and other events deemed appropriate by US Chess), a player who oversteps the time control on the first occurrence will be given a warning and penalized five days reflection time on the succeeding 10 moves/30 day time control. If a player violates the time control the second time, he or she will forfeit the game.

The following is an example of calculating a player's reflection time after a time control overstep: A player has 30 days to make moves 1-10 inclusive, 60 days to complete moves 11-20, 90 days to complete moves 21-30. A player makes move 18 but uses 61 days, thus overstepping the second time control. He or she is penalized five days reflection time. The five days are added to the reflection time he or she has used (61+5) and the player has 24 days to make moves 19-30.

Excused Time

12. You may take up to 30 days of excused time a calendar year. Additional emergency time may be granted at the discretion of the CCD. You must take excused time for all games in a section. To take excused time, simply notify your opponents and the CCD in advance. If you send a move, your excused time ends immediately. If your opponent takes excused time, you should respond to unanswered moves normally because your reflection time is still counted.

Submitting Time Complaints

13. You may submit a time complaint when your opponent has exceeded his or her allotted reflection time or has failed to respond to a repeat move within 10 days, excluding transmission time. Time complaints should include a full explanation of the facts.

14. Any dispute you cannot resolve or any claim of repeated or willful rule violation must be submitted to the CCD. Relevant evidence must be included. Whenever possible, continue play while the complaint is being considered. Your complaint should include:

> a. Section and game numbers;

> b. Names, ID numbers, and addresses of both players;

> c. Game score;

> d. Supporting documentation (photocopies are acceptable unless the CCD asks for originals). Any complaint must be postmarked within seven days of the time a person becomes aware of the alleged infraction. Failure to comply with the above, including a, b, c, and d, negates your claim.

Reporting Game Results

15. The winner must report the result to the CCD immediately upon conclusion of the game. In case of draws, White must report result. It is a good idea for the other player to submit the result, labeling it "duplicate report." Reports must include section and game numbers as well as the names and ID numbers of both players.

Thirty-Month Limit and Adjudications

16. A US Chess correspondence game must end after thirty (30) months from when the event begins. Either player may submit the game for adjudication postmarked one week after the tournament's end date. The player submitting the adjudication must provide the following to the CCD:

a. The score of the game;

b. Diagram of the position before adjudication;

c. Claim of win or draw;

d. Any analysis to support claim (optional). If neither player submits the adjudication material within one week after the tournament's end date, the game is scored as a ratable draw.

The CCD is not required to provide the basis for the adjudication result.

Ratings

17. Once play begins, games are rated whether they conclude normally or by forfeit. If your rating decreases by one or more rating classes as a result of forfeits or withdrawals, you will be required to enter prize tournaments in the rating class you occupied before the forfeits.

Penalties

18. The CCD may assess penalties for violations of these rules. Penalties include, but are not limited to, informal reprimands, warnings, reflection time reduction, forfeitures, or withdrawal. Warnings are usually issued before more severe penalties but the CCD may skip this step. Smooth and timely completion of games is the main consideration. Penalties will be assessed as necessary to accomplish this purpose.

Appeals

19. You may appeal the CCD's ruling to the Executive Director. Your appeal must be made in writing within seven days of the ruling. US Chess, Attn: Carol Meyer, Executive Director, PO Box 3967, Crossville, TN 38557.

Player Replacements

20. A withdrawn player may be replaced at the option of the CCD. There will be no replacement for a withdrawn player against whom a win, loss, or draw has been scored in actual play. A withdrawn player will not be replaced 60 days after the tournament start date.

GLOSSARY

adjudication: A judge's determination of a game's result, based on best play by both sides.

ambiguous move: A move in which two chess pieces of the same kind can be transferred to a new square and the player does not specify which chess piece. Example, knights on b1 and f3 can be moved to d2. The move "Nd2" is ambiguous because it does not specify which knight is being transferred. The correct transmission is either "Nbd2" or "Nfd2."

conditional or "if" moves: An attempt to save time and postage by offering a plausible continuation beyond the required response. Conditional moves are binding if the recipient accepts the continuations. The game must then follow the indicated continuation or any part accepted in sequence.

correspondence chess director (CCD): Official responsible for the supervision and direction of a correspondence chess tournament.

English algebraic: Conventional algebraic notation with abbreviations of the English names for the pieces : for example, Nf3 or Ng1-f3 or Bc1-f4; "x" or ":" for capture is standard. A full explanation of this system is available from the US Chess office. Please enclose a stamped, self-addressed envelope.

excused time: Time-outs when play is suspended for leaves or for special circumstances with the approval of the CCD.

illegal move: A move which violates the rules of chess.

impossible move: A move which cannot be played as recorded.

Official Rules of Chess: Seventh edition, Chief Editor: Tim Just

reflection time: The time between a player's receipt of a move and the postmarking of his response.

time control: Each player must make 10 moves in 30 days of reflection time. Time saved in a control carries forward. Unusual delays within this limit warrant advanced notice to the opponent(s).

transmission time: The time a move is in the custody of the Postal Service, that is, from the postmark date to date of delivery at the recipient's address.

CHAPTER TEN

INTERNET CHESS

1. Introduction.

1A. Purview.

The rules in this chapter supplement the rules for over-the-board (OTB) play found in the seventh edition of the *Official Rules of Chess*. These rules aim to account for the unique playing situations that arise during online play and to ensure a fair playing environment for all participants.

1B. Online Tournaments and Matches.
Online tournaments and matches are defined as chess games played for US Chess rating purposes using the internet, a local area network, or equivalent. Players may be in the same location during game play, gathered at several designated local or regional playing sites, or playing from many separate sites including their homes. Games played using voice communication (some examples: radio, cell phone, telephone) or other forms of communication including email are not considered online play.

2. The US Chess Online Rating System.
Except as specified below, player rating calculations for online play follow the rules of Chapter 8, The US Chess Rating System.

2A. Online Ratings and Over-The-Board (OTB) Ratings.
The rating reports for games played, submitted and accepted by US Chess for rating as online play are rated only as "Online Ratings". Online game results do not contribute to a player's over-the-board rating.

2B. Ratable Time Controls for Online Play.
US Chess shall maintain three categories of online ratings—Online Regular, Online Quick, and Online Blitz. In non-sudden death time controls, the time unused by a player during one control accumulates and is added to the player's available time for the next control. In online play no games shall be "dual rated". The time control formulas mentioned in this chapter conform to the format provided in Rule 5C, Ratable Time Controls (Chapter 1).

Online Regular: Total playing time for each player is 30 or more minutes ($mm+ss \geq 30$).

Online Quick: Total playing time for each player is more than 10 and less than 30 minutes ($10 < mm+ss < 30$).

Online Blitz: Total playing time for each player is from 5 to 10 minutes inclusive ($5 \leq mm+ss \leq 10$).

TD TIP: Examples of ratable time controls:

Total Playing Time	Minutes per Player	Online Time Control
30/75 20/30 SD/15 d10	130 minutes	Regular, 3 components
40/90 SD/30 inc/30	150 minutes	Regular, 2 components
G/120 inc/30	150 minutes	Regular, 1 component
30/90 SD/15 d/10	115 minutes	Regular, 2 components
30/30 SD/30 inc/10	70 minutes	Regular, 2 components
G/45 d/5	50 minutes	Regular, 1 component
G/30 d/0	30 minutes	Regular, 1 component
G/25 d/5 or inc/5	30 minutes	Regular, 1 component
15/15 SD/9 d/5 or inc/5	29 minutes	Quick, 2 components
G/25 d/4 or inc/4	29 minutes	Quick, 1 component
G/15 d/5 or inc/5	20 minutes	Quick, 1 component
G/10 d/3 or inc/3	13 minutes	Quick, 1 component
G/10 d/0 or inc/0	10 minutes	Blitz
G/8 d/2 or inc/2	10 minutes	Blitz
G/5 d/0 or inc/0	5 minutes	Blitz
G/3 d/2 or inc/2	5 minutes	Blitz

2C. US Chess Rating System and FIDE Rating System.

Unless FIDE rules change, the US Chess rating reports for online play cannot be submitted to FIDE.

2D. Calculating Player Ratings.

For players who already have an online regular, quick or blitz rating US Chess shall apply the same rating formulas to calculate online ratings that are used to generate over-the-board ratings. US Chess procedures for initializing online ratings for regular, quick and blitz are found in a document maintained by the US Chess Ratings Committee and warehoused at this link: https://new.uschess.org/sites/default/files/media/documents/the-us-chess-rating-system.pdf.

2E. Assigning Ratings to Unrated Players.

Under the auspices of Rule 28E, Assigned Ratings for Rated Players (Chapter 2) directors running online events have the option to assign ratings to players for the purposes of pairings and awarding of prizes.

TD TIP: TDs should remind unrated players that ratings assigned to them by the TD do not initialize or otherwise count toward their rating calculated by US Chess.

3. Tournament Formats.

3A. Acceptable Formats.
Any of the formats described in the *Official Rules of Chess* are allowed—for example. Swiss, Round-Robin, Quads, or Match Play. Team events paired as fixed-roster teams or paired as individual Swiss events also are allowed.

3B. Unacceptable Formats.
Other online formats and variants are not ratable. Examples include arena, blindfold chess, Chess-960, computer-assisted chess, odds games (for example: piece, time, or draw odds), one player vs many players (for example: simuls, tandem chess), and variants with partners (like. Bughouse).

3C. Match Play Limitations.
The number of match play games shall adhere to the limitations given in <u>Rule 4, Matches</u> (Chapter 8).

4. The Chief TD and Assistant TDs.
TDs for online events are subject to the limitations of <u>Rule 21E, The Playing Director</u> (Chapter 1).

4A. The Standard for TD Presence during Online Play.
Ideally, a US Chess-certified director (the Chief TD or an Assistant TD) shall be physically present, in person, at every location from which online play originates. TDs must be able to directly witness players' actions for all games and all rounds. This standard not only ensures enforcement of the *Official Rules of Chess*, but also minimizes potential for violations of fair play.

4B. Authorized Variations from the Standard.
The variations described below are a hierarchy of preferred options in priority sequence. Their use, alone or in combination, is authorized in lieu of or as a supplement to the standard rule (Rule 4A above). If any variation is used, the organizer and Chief TD shall ensure the pre-event publicity provides specific instructions to players for contacting a member of the TD staff if there is a problem during the event. If the Chief TD cannot fulfill the conditions of Rule 4A (above) or any of the three variations below, then the Chief TD cannot submit the event to US Chess for rating.

4B1. Variation 1: Use of Remote Observation Technologies to Monitor Players and Games.
The Chief TD, alone or with Assistant TDs, observes all players and their games from an off-site location using video cameras or other player monitoring technologies. This approach may be supplemented by either variation described below.

4B2. Variation 2: Use of Fair Play Algorithms and/or Technology to Monitor Players and Games.

The Chief TD uses one or more fair play method(s) that are endorsed in writing by US Chess. It relies on the game service provider applying an algorithm to monitor each player's moves during game play or afterwards.

TD TIP: These algorithms, which usually are proprietary to the vendor, compare the player's moves to the best moves calculated by well-known chess engines, as well as, player behavior patterns such as time used per move. The process appraises a player's actual move accuracy against the level of precision statistically expected out of a player with the same rating (e.g. whether a 1400-rated player is playing like a 1400 should play). Cameras, microphones and other technologies that monitor and evaluate players' head and eye movements, their cursor activity, and ambient sounds during games are additional technology-based fair play screening methods. Algorithms and technology may be used separately or in parallel.

4B3. Variation 3: Post-game Analysis by the Director and/or Other Third Parties

This variation relies exclusively on post-game analysis by the tournament staff or other third parties arranged by the director in advance (e.g. other players or external expertise that are exclusive of the service provider). It is the least preferred variation when used alone because it is labor intensive and often depends on player complaints or TD observations to detect violations of fair play. The result is that this variation has the highest risk of cheating going undetected.

TD TIP: In view of the risks a director should use this variation only for match play or for events where the total number of games is 10 or less, or all the players are well-known to the director.

5. The Host System, Software and Hardware for Online Play.

All games in an online event rated by US Chess shall be played using the same host system or game service provider.

TD TIP: This rule exists because allowing the pre-planned use of multiple platforms for a single ratable event complicates the ability of fair play methods to compare the results of multiple games played by a player.

TD TIP: In a situation where Rounds one and two of a five-round event were played on "Host System A" which has crashed for an indefinite period, the director is not forced to cancel Rounds 3-5 just to comply with Rule 5. Rather, in this emergency situation, the director has the authority to apply discretion by moving the remaining rounds to another platform and perhaps adjusting those rounds' start times. **See also** <u>*Rule 1C2, Director discretion*</u> *(Chapter 1) and* <u>*Rule 17C, Changes in round times*</u> *(Chapter 1).*

5A. The Game Software Interface.

All players in an event shall use a software interface provided or authorized by the game service provider. As part of reviewing candidate vendors' systems for hosting online events, organizers and Chief TDs must consider how the game interface allows players or TDs to have appropriate control over the game play.

*   **TD TIP:** *All TDs need to be familiar with the features offered by the service provider's software so they can answer players' questions about features such as: pawn promotion, pre-moves, safe-moves, illegal moves, drawn positions, how to offer a draw or resign, etc. In addition, TDs are reminded that service providers routinely update their software to include new features, or change/remove existing features.*

5B. Use of Other Chess Software.

While a game is in progress, other chess playing software or game analysis software shall not be used by either player, regardless of whether the software is resident on the player's device or being accessed through the internet or another external system.

5C. Acceptable Game Hardware.

Players may use any hardware they are comfortable using except when the hardware (console, interface, device) is specified by the event rules or is provided by the organizer. When players use their own devices they are responsible for the ramifications of their decisions on what device they choose to use.

*   **TD TIP:** *Organizers and Chief TDs need to carefully consider what devices the players can use in an event and should consider specifying acceptable device types in their event rules. Devices with small screens (e.g. many cell phones) have a limited amount of display space. This can cause unwelcome difficulties for players when entering their moves, trying to read the time remaining on their clocks, and ensuring they see the same information their opponents are seeing.*

5C1. Graphical Display Required.

Every players' game platform shall have a graphical display with the screen being of a size the player is comfortable using. Displays may be color or monochrome and can use touch-screen technology. Players may connect multiple displays to the same device.

5C1a. Orientation and Color of the Graphical Chess Board.

The graphical chessboard shall be oriented in the same manner described in Rule 2C, Placement for over-the-board play (Chapter 1). Each player's color shall be at the bottom of the display, with the opponent's color at the top. The names (or User IDs) of both players shall be shown adjacent to the board. The service provider's default settings for the color of the squares shall parallel the specifications of Rule 41B, Color (Chapter 4). It is permitted for the numbers (1-8) and letters (A to H) to appear along the perimeter of the chessboard. If the service provider allows a player to select alternate color schemes or to customize the squares, those options shall not change the opponent's settings.

5C1b. Advertisements and Other Images.

Advertisements or other images are not allowed within the boundaries of the chessboard.

5C1c. Graphical Representation and Color of the Pieces.

It shall be obvious from the colors used for the pieces who is playing White and who is playing Black. The display shall show the pieces in figurine form in a manner similar to Figure 1 and Figure 2 of Chapter 1, Rule 3B. If the service provider allows a player to select alternate pieces or to customize the pieces, those options shall not change the opponent's settings. **See also** 40C, Form (Chapter 4); and 40D, Color (Chapter 4)

5C2. Hardware for Making Moves.

To make their moves or select menu options, players may use voice activation, a keyboard, mouse, trackball, stylus, their finger, or a similar pointing device. During play the two players opposing one another, or an authorized game assistant for a player with a disability (Chapter 10, Rule 14A, Game Assistants), are the only persons permitted to use the move-input hardware except when a TD is summoned or intervenes to resolve a claim or address an issue.

Unless the games are played under conditions specified in Rule 4B, Authorized Variations from the Standard (Chapter 10), Variation 4B1, Variation 1: Use of Remote Observation Technologies to Monitor Players and Games (Chapter 10), or as is permitted for players with disabilities under Rule 14A, players cannot make their moves using an electronic chess board connected to their primary device.

TD TIP: *In practice, some directors have been allowing players to use a non-electronic board "on the side" so players can make their moves on that board, then transfer them to the chessboard on the screen. Directors should be cautious when allowing this and consider limiting it to conditions described in Chapter 10 Rules 4B or Variation 4B1.*

5C3. Cameras for Game Monitoring.

Organizers have the option to specify requirements for cameras positioned to monitor every game. These capabilities may be supplied by the organizer (e.g. when the event is held at designated hub sites), or the cameras may be required of players participating from their locations of choice. When the event rules require players to provide any hardware, organizers and Chief TDs shall provide clear and sufficient instructions in pre-event announcements.

TD TIP: *Using cameras to monitor game play can enhance fair play, but it may impose additional logistical requirements on the organizer and tournament staff (e.g. a separate network, troubleshooting compatibility or other hardware issues, and additional staff to facilitate game monitoring). If this capability can be integrated into the host system's platform, that may be the best option.*

5D. Time for Players to Test their Game Hardware.

Organizers and Chief TDs shall provide players adequate time before the beginning of play to test their devices with the designated host system/game service provider.

TD TIP: *Allowing adequate time for these tests and practice games may require an organizer or Chief TD to select a deadline for entries considerably earlier than the cut-off time most players are accustomed to when entering over-the-board events. Setting a registration deadline that is too close to the event start time, or allowing "walk-ins" after the deadline, may not be practical except for a house player or someone already familiar with the host system. Even when the organizer is providing the players' game devices, the players still need time to become familiar with them.*

6. Event-specific Rules and TLAs for Online Events.

6A. Event Rules.

Organizers and Chief TDs shall collaborate to create and distribute event-specific rules necessary for all players entering their online tournaments.

TD TIP: *TLAs for online events can contain considerably different instructions than their over-the-board counterpart announcements. US Chess encourages organizers and Chief TDs to keep online event TLAs as simple as possible by referring interested players to a common web site for detailed instructions.*

TD TIP: *The examples below are unique to online chess, but they are not all-inclusive. The TD needs to consider not only the format of the event, but also the experience level of the players. Your event's rules also should address certain topics common to any event (e.g. event format, number of sections, prize structure, required fees, rules regarding unrated players, etc.).*

1. *Thorough registration and tournament access instructions and player eligibility criteria (if any).*
2. *Addresses for any authorized playing sites (if applicable).*
3. *The name of the system that will host all games, and the internet address for the game service provider.*
4. *Allowable hardware and software players can use (if there are any restrictions).*
5. *Instructions that describe how players may "test" their hardware with the host system, including the ability to play practice games before the tournament.*
6. *Deadline for registration and optional byes (to allow time for players to test their equipment and for organizers to verify players' identity, US Chess membership, and online account information).*
7. *Criteria for playoff games to determine certain prizes (if this option is used).*
8. *Describe the method the Chief TD shall use to create each round's pairings (e.g. by using the host system's pairing capability or external pairing software).*
9. *Publish the event schedule including mandatory pre-tournament check-in to officially join the tournament (for example: 1 hour before the start time), the start time for Round 1 and consecutive round times, or asap pairing schedule (round is paired as soon as all the games are finished in the previous round). Base all times on a single time zone—e.g. Eastern Daylight, Central Standard. Time zone of the organizer is recommended.*
10. *Where to find and view a list of all registered participants.*
11. *Where to find and view the pairings, standings and wall charts.*
12. *How a round begins and how a player's game starts—e.g. if you or your opponent must invite one another to play the game, or if the games are paired and begin automatically.*
13. *What tiebreak systems shall be used and in what order of priority.* ***See also*** *Rules* <u>34D, Choice of tiebreak methods</u> *(Chapter 2) and* <u>34E, Calculating Swiss tiebreaks</u> *(Chapter 2).*
14. *Procedures for making a claim during game play, what types of claims will be allowed and will not be allowed.*
15. *Procedures for disruptions in internet connectivity.*

241

16. *Player identification requirements, especially post-event where the tournament has significant cash or other prizes that may be reportable to the government.*
17. *Instructions for players with disabilities and their needs for a Game Assistant, including any requirements for players to provide the name and contact information for their Game Assistant.*
18. *A statement notifying players, and requiring them to acknowledge, that all games will be monitored for fair play.*
19. *If the host site automatically posts winners, the organizer/director may want to issue a qualifying statement that the results are "tentative" until reviewed and approved by the Chief TD.*

6B. Event Rules Available to All Players.

Organizers and Chief TDs shall ensure their event rules are available to each player at the time they register for the tournament, including players who register at one of the designated playing locations (if this option is offered).

7. Event Registration and Identities of the Players.

7A. Registration System and Process.

The organizer or Chief TD shall ensure players are able to view a list of all registered players and the ratings being used to pair them for the tournament. This service shall be provided either by the host system or the organizer/Chief TD.

TD TIP: Make the registration process as easy as possible for your players by using a single site for registration and payment of required fees (entry, US Chess memberships, Vendor fees, etc.). Coordinate with the selected game service provider early to determine what their registration system can (and cannot) do. This will inform your decision on how to design and set up registration for your event.

7B. Player Identification.

The Chief TD is responsible for verifying the identities of the players, with Assistant TDs helping at their respective locations.

TD TIP: Directors and organizers need to be familiar with the federal "Children's Online Privacy Protection Act (COPPA)" and its implications on registration of players under the age of 13.

TD TIP: Some third-party event registration sites can generate secure codes or "keys" as part of the registration process, providing a copy of the code/key only to the player and the organizer. Such measures help, but cannot ensure, verification of player identity. As a result, some organizers or directors may opt to wait until after the event to verify identities at the time they award prizes.

8. Pairings, Standings, Wall Charts and Bye Requests.

Every player has the right to know the real names, usernames, and US Chess ID numbers for all other players in the event.

8A. Pairing Method, Ratings Used and Tiebreaks.

Either the game service provider or the TD shall pair the players. All games shall be paired in accordance with the *Official Rules of Chess* or a close approximation of the rules, including FIDE's pairing rules. Chief TDs shall inform players in their pre-event publicity about the pairing method, ratings and tiebreaks being used for the event (e.g. generated by the service provider using the provider's method, or created by the TD according to the *Official Rules of Chess*).

8B. Pairings, Standings and Wall Charts.

The Chief TD is responsible for ensuring all players have equal ability to see the pairings, standings and wall chart. The preferred option is for the Chief TD to make them available to players on the service provider's system.

8C. Bye Requests.

The rules for an event shall specify if half-point or zero-point byes are allowed. When byes are permitted, the event rules shall instruct players how to request them and the deadline for requests.

8D. Games Not Played or Not Completed.

8D1. Games Not Played (Unplayed Games).

Games not played, regardless of the reason, shall be scored in accordance with Rule 28P, Unplayed games (Chapter 2). These games shall not affect either player's rating. Event rules should specify how the Chief TD will handle a player who misses a round without having requested a bye.

8D2. Games Not Completed.

Unless specified otherwise in the event rules, games not completed for any reason shall be scored as losses for players who abandoned their games. Players are responsible for ensuring they have reliable internet connections and that their equipment functions properly when connected to the game service provider. **See also** 5D, Time for Players to Test their Game Hardware (Chapter 10); and 11B, Failure of the Player's Hardware or Network Connection (Chapter 10).

TD TIP: Organizers and directors are strongly encouraged to include, as part of their event rules, how a director will handle a player who could not complete a game.

9. Online Chess Clock.

Both players must use the same time control. Any game where the two players did not use the same time control cannot be submitted for rating.

9A. Time Keeping.

The official time (chess clock) for each player shall be the time displayed on each player's screen, console or device as maintained by the host system used for the online event. Players are not allowed to use separate chess clocks at their locations to keep the official time for their games.

9B. Time Forfeit.

The flag fall on the player's screen, console or device, as transmitted by the host site, shall be considered official. Most host systems will automatically award the game result once one of the players' flags has fallen.

10. The Drawn Game.

10A. Drawn Positions.

Many service providers automatically rule games drawn under several game situations, or they alert the player that the position is drawn. Such assistance is allowed in online play because all players are using the same host system/game interface and, as a result, are afforded the same assistance during their games. When a service provider's automatic rulings differ from US Chess rules, organizers and directors shall include these differences in their pre-event publicity.

*TD TIP: Before playing in an online event, players are strongly advised to ensure they understand the service provider's procedures on drawn positions, especially in those situations where the player is required to claim the draw. **See also** TD TIP, Rule 5D, Time for Player's to Test their Game Hardware (Chapter 10).*

TD TIP: A director or organizer who is concerned about confusion among the players should consider selecting a vendor that closely follows US Chess Rules.

10A1. Platforms that Adhere to US Chess Rules.

Automatic rulings or notifications by the host system for stalemate, triple occurrence of position, insufficient material to continue, insufficient material to win on time, and the 50-move rule—as specified in Chapter 1, Rules 14A, 14C, 14D, 14E and 14F—are permitted. These rulings end the game.

Platforms that adhere to FIDE Rules also are permitted. Games played on these systems are ratable as US Chess online play. An automatic ruling on a drawn position made by a FIDE-compliant system shall end the game.

TD TIP: FIDE and US Chess rules differ significantly on adjudicating positions with few pieces on the board when one of the player's flag falls. Under FIDE rules, if a player's flag falls the game is drawn if the position is such that the opponent cannot checkmate the player's king by any possible series of legal moves.

10B. Drawn by Agreement.
Online games may be drawn upon agreement by both players in accordance with Rule 14B, Agreement (Chapter 1).

TD TIP: Most game platforms automatically start the opponent's clock immediately upon determination of a move. On such platforms, players cannot replicate the over-the-board draw offer procedure given in Rule 14B1, proper timing of draw offer (Chapter 1)—e.g. move, offer your draw, then press the clock. Therefore, online players should become accustomed to extending their draw offer before moving in accordance with Rule 14B3, Draw offer before moving (Chapter 1).

10C. Game Platform declares Draw due to Lack of Progress.
Some platforms are programmed to automatically declare a draw in a manner similar to Rule 14K, Director declares draw for lack of progress (Chapter 1) for one or both of the scenarios listed below. Draws adjudicated by these host systems shall be considered valid.

1. The same position has appeared for at least five consecutive alternate moves by each player. **See also** Rule 14C, Triple occurrence of position (Chapter 1).
2. Any consecutive series of 75 moves has been completed by each player without the movement of a pawn and without any capture. If the last move resulted in checkmate, that shall take precedence.

11. Interrupted Games.
Any loss of signal for an ongoing game, regardless of the cause or duration of that break, can frustrate players and undermine their confidence in the tournament or online play in general. Organizers and directors are responsible for selecting a reliable game service provider. In a similar way, players are responsible for minimizing the potential for interruptions by selecting a stable

network service and taking advantage of opportunities to test their game hardware on the event service provider's system well before the start of tournaments.

When an interrupted game impacts the start time for the next round, the director shall keep players informed of the revised start time using all reasonably available means (event web site, email, text message, chat or message sent via the host system, etc.).

11A. Failure of the Game Service Provider's System.

The game service provider's server may experience a complete or partial failure. When the director can verify that the service provider is causing the interruption, the interruption shall not cause a player to lose their game. The results of games finished before the system fails shall stand. After the round begins, the director has four options, in the priority shown in Rule 11A1 below, for games that are in progress.

11A1. Allow the Unfinished Games to Continue from the Last Saved Position.

This is the standard rule during a service interruption. Game clocks and positions on the board shall be restored automatically by the game service provider to the last position saved by the server and indicate which player is on move. If the restored position represents a position earlier in the game, neither player is obligated to make the same moves they had made before the general system failure. If this standard cannot be achieved, the director may use any of the following three variations.

11A1a. Variation 1: Director Restores Position agreed upon by Both Players.

This variation shall be used only when the service provider allows the director to restore a position, the player and opponent agree to the position, the director is able to adjust clocks, and there are enough directors available to provide this service to all affected players in a timely manner.

11A1b. Variation 2: Last Known Position is not Available for Some Games.

This variation occurs when all move data for some of the unfinished games has been lost by the server. As soon as possible, the director shall re-start these games from move one, with players given the full time control for the round and not obligated to make the moves they made in the prior game. Games for which all moves have not been lost shall continue in accordance with Rules 11A1 or 11A1a, Variation 1 above.

11A1c. Variation 3: Game or Move Data for All Unfinished Games is not Available.

As soon as possible, the director shall restart all games from move one with the players paired according to the round's original pairings. All players shall have the full time control and are not obligated to make the moves made in their prior game.

TD TIP: *In those situations where the director is capable of resetting board positions and adjusting players' clocks, taking such action may only be practical in a very small event, when the ratio of directors to players enables it, and when there is no dispute about the position between a player and opponent.*

TD TIP: *Unless the service provider's system collects game data so that all moves made by the players have been recorded, Rule 11A1, Variations 1, 2 or 3 above, may not be practical or possible in events with short time controls (e.g. Blitz).*

TD TIP: *Despite a TD's best efforts to verify the technical cause of a game disruption, it may not be clear whether the disruption was caused by failure of the service provider's or the player's equipment. Also, all platforms may not allow TDs to restart affected games from move one. In such cases, the director should use their discretion when ruling on the outcome of abandoned games, up to and including use of* Rule 18G, Adjudications *(Chapter 1), which may generate split results.*

11B. Failure of the Player's Hardware or Network Connection.

A game interrupted by a loss of signal on the player's end shall not stop the clock for that player. After the player restores their game signal, the player's clock shall automatically reflect the amount of time remaining. If the game cannot continue before the player's time expires, then the result shall be a loss for that player. Such games shall be rated unless the player's loss of signal occurred before both players completed their first move.

11C. General or Partial Failure at a Designated Playing Site.

If the organizer requires players to play at a designated site (this does not include playing at home), the loss of internet signal shall not cause any player to lose their game. The results of games finished before the site failure shall stand. Once a round begins, the director shall apply the principles and variations shown in Rule 11A above in an effort to allow play to continue in an equitable manner for the affected players.

12. Special Online Move Situations.

The chess interface provided by game service providers vary on how they handle the situations defined in this rule. In most cases, a player's move is not transmitted to the opponent until the player makes a legal move on their display chessboard. The definition of when a piece is "touched" can vary based on the capabilities of the host platform (see Rule 12B below), but the time a move is transmitted by the system defines the time the move is both "determined" and "completed." Move completion shall automatically stop the player's clock and start the opponent's clock. The special online move situations described below in Rules 12C, 12D and 12E shall be player settings that can be adjusted.

TD TIP: When permitted by the game software, players may select their preferred settings. However, the consequences of those choices by players are binding.

TD TIP: Organizers and directors should take steps to ensure players are aware of how the host system handles the situations described in this rule. One way is to include this information in pre-event publicity.

12A. Illegal Moves.

Host systems shall be programmed to not allow players to make illegal moves. A piece picked-up and placed on an illegal square shall be returned automatically by the host software to its square at the start of the move. **See also** Rule 12B, Touch-Move (Chapter 10).

12B. Touch-Move.

In online games, players are not allowed to claim touch-move violations as defined in Rule 10B, Touch-move rule (Chapter 1).

12B1. Variation: Host Platform Programmed to Enforce Touch-Move.

If the host platform is programmed to automatically enforce touch move when a player selects a piece, the host shall not allow a player to select and move a different piece.

12C. Pre-Moves.

A pre-move occurs when a player makes a move on the opponent's time before the opponent has completed their previous move. If a player makes a legal pre-move, the host system shall execute it immediately upon completion of the opponent's move. An executed pre-move shall be considered a completed move. If a player's pre-move is not legal under the *Official Rules of Chess*, the host system shall not allow it to occur.

12D. Smart-Moves.

A smart-move occurs when the player on move has only one possible legal move with a piece and the host system is programmed to automatically execute that move at the time the player selects (clicks-on) that piece.

12E. Automatic Promotion.

Automatic promotion occurs when a player moves a pawn to the last rank and the host system automatically promotes the pawn to a Queen. The player's move is completed when the piece appears on the chessboard.

12E1. Variation: Host System not Programmed for Automatic Promotion.

If the host system is not programmed for automatic promotion, the system shall present the player a choice of pieces to which the player can legally promote the pawn. The host system shall not allow the player to change the selected piece after it appears on the promotion square.

12F. Mouse-Slips.

A mouse slip occurs when a legal move transmitted by the player is not the move the player intended to make. In online play, mouse-slips shall be considered completed moves. **See also** Rule 14A, Game Assistants (Chapter 10).

TD TIP: *To help avoid mouse slips players should consider:*

1. *Using "two click mode" on their mouse instead of dragging the piece (e.g. click on the piece to move, then click on the destination square).*
2. *Investing in a quality gaming mouse.*
3. *Typing their move in algebraic notation on a keyboard (if allowed by the host system).*
4. *Activating the option to "confirm moves" (if offered by the host system).*

13. Scorekeeping and .PGN Files.

13A. Scorekeeping.

13A1. Host System Automatically Keeps Score.

During a game, the host system shall automatically keep score for both players using one of the notation systems described in Rule 38, Notation Systems (Chapter 3).

249

13A2. Previous Moves Visible to Both Players.

At a minimum, the host system shall indicate each player's last move on their display screen. The host system also shall provide each player an option to display all previous moves in the game.

13A3. Manual Notation cannot be used to Make Claims.

Players are allowed to take notation during their games; however, they are not allowed to use their notation to make claims during online play.

13B. PGN Files.

The host system shall record the moves for all games played in the event and make them available in .PGN or another format in order to be shareable among the players, directors, and spectators.

14. Players with Disabilities.

Rule 35, Rules for Disabled and Assisted Players (Chapter 2) applies to online chess.

TD TIP: The "US Chess Guidelines for Accessible Chess Events," which is posted on the US Chess website, provides practical advice for organizers and TDs who anticipate having players with disabilities in their events.

TD TIP: As part of pre-event registration create a free text area on your entry form where players can answer this question, "Do you require any special accommodation to play in the event?"

14A. Game Assistants.

Players with disabilities may participate in online events using a "Game Assistant" (GA) to make their moves. Such players may either observe the on-screen board, or use a separate chessboard, to determine and announce their moves to the GA.

For events where the Chief TD or an assistant TD is available at every playing location, the tournament staff can help the player with a disability find a GA. When an event is being played from multiple sites without TDs, players with disabilities are responsible for arranging their own GA who is subject to the approval of the Chief TD. In all cases, a player using a GA must agree that the actions of their GA on the game platform are considered the player's own actions.

TD TIP: Directors should prepare an instruction sheet they can provide to players with disabilities at the time of registration, and to their GA, so it is clear what the assistant is and is not allowed to do during a game.

TD TIP: To help ensure a GA does not make the wrong move, a player using a GA should consider having the GA verbally confirm the move being made to the player before making the move. For example, the player says, "f6." The GA should respond with, "f6, correct?" The player then answers, "Yes." In addition, players with disabilities should review the TD TIP to <u>Rule 12F, Mouse-Slips</u> (Chapter 10) and consider:

1. *Ensuring their GA is an experienced chess player and familiar with the playing site.*
2. *Turning on speech synthesis in order to make moves (if the host system has this option).*

15. Submitting Event Results to US Chess.

15A. Maximum Time to Submit the Rating Report.
A director has up to three weeks to submit the rating reports for an online event.

TD TIP: The rules for online play deliberately allow directors more time to submit rating reports compared to over-the-board play for at least two reasons. First, generating the rating report may be more complex, depending on the service provider. Second, the Chief TD needs time to review the output produced by the fair play process for the event, including any claims of fair play violations made by players. In general, the rating reports for small events can be turned in almost as quickly as comparably sized over-the-board events. Larger tournaments, or events with substantial prizes and/or suspected fair play issues, may take more time.

TD TIP: Directors are advised to handle accusations of cheating as serious matters and with the greatest discretion.

1. *When an accusation arises, the director should take all steps necessary to control the situation. This includes advising the accuser(s) not to mention the allegations to other players or persons via word-of-mouth, phone calls, texting, internet, email or social media, as well as instructing others not to spread rumors.*

2. *The most likely ways to identify suspected violations of fair play depend on the nature of the tournament. Events with directors at every playing site normally uncover suspected cheating in a manner similar to how it is found at an over-the-board competition—e.g. direct observation by a director, or a claim by another player. However, when directors are not at every site with the players, the ability to detect fair play issues relies almost exclusively on the use*

251

of statistical algorithms by the game service provider, remote monitoring technologies specified in the event rules, post-event analysis of suspect games, and/or claims made by opponents of an accused player.

3. *Paragraph 6 of the US Chess Code of Ethics, states:*

*"**The actions and behavior** of players, tournament directors ... and other individuals ... participating in US Chess activities, or in events sponsored by or sanctioned by US Chess, **shall be** lawful and in accordance with all US Chess rules and regulations, and **consistent with the principles of fair play, good sportsmanship, honesty, and respect for the rights of others."** [emphasis added]*

4. *For an accusation to become a formal Ethics Complaint, the primary accuser must be an active member of the US Chess Federation. When considering whether to file an ethics complaint, one should bear in mind that the burden of proof will be on the complainant and that US Chess does not investigate complaints. The Ethics Committee will rule only on the evidence submitted to the committee by the complainant and will not seek other evidence, even if a complainant includes in their complaint a "witness list" or a description of where to find additional evidence. It is entirely up to the complainant to gather all evidence and submit it with the complaint. When evaluating the quality of the evidence, the fair play standard and variations described in Chapter 10, Rule 4 of this chapter represent a hierarchy. In other words, Rule 4A in this chapter is better than Variation 4B1, which is better than Variation 4B2, which is better than Variation 4B3. Using these options in combination—e.g. the standard in Rule 4A supported by Variations 4B1 and 4B3—would add greater weight to the complaint.*

15B. Prepare and Submit the Rating Report.

After completing all game reviews, the Chief TD or designated Assistant TD shall prepare the rating report and submit it to US Chess in the same manner used for an over-the-board event. The TD shall indicate that the tournament was conducted online. If the report the director has submitted contains game results that are or may be in dispute, the director shall contact US Chess for guidance on handling the situation.

TD TIP: There are different types of "disputed results" including a ratings report with an incorrect game result, to a report with results of one or more games for players involved in an alleged fair play violation. When results were incorrectly reported, the TD should contact US Chess (by email) and ask for guidance on how to best correct the report. By comparison, a rating report containing games in dispute due to alleged violations of fair play is a more serious situation. In such a case, the office may advise the director to file an official complaint to US Chess as explained in the second TD TIP in Rule 15A above.

15C. Certify the Rating Report.

The Chief TD's or authorized Assistant TD's act of submitting the rating report to US Chess means that the director certifies to the best of their knowledge that all games were played according to the rules in this chapter and the *Official Rules of Chess.*

CHAPTER ELEVEN

BLITZ CHESS

Blitz Chess (also known as Speed Chess, 5-minute Chess, Lightning Chess (2-minute), and Bullet Chess (1-minute)) is a variant defined as a single, sudden death time control from 1 to 10 minutes. Blitz games typically are set at five minutes and do not use time delay. Since each game takes only about 10 minutes, it has long been popular for fun games where time is limited, such as lunch breaks or between rounds of other tournaments. Some clubs will host Blitz events that may have as many as 20 rounds in a single evening.

Information regarding FIDE Blitz chess can be found in the FIDE Handbook: E.01. Laws of Chess appendix B:

http://www.fide.com/fide/handbook.html

Take note that Blitz is not Quick Chess with a 5 minute time control (which follows standard sudden death rules.)

Editor's Note: Most of the US Chess rules for regular and quick chess also apply to blitz chess. This chapter covers the rules that are different for blitz and also restates some of the fundamental rules that apply to all three forms of chess and that are important to blitz.

Blitz rating system: Blitz has its own rating system. To be rated, the time controls require from 5 to 10 minutes total playing time, and have a minimum primary time control of 3 minutes. All rounds must use the same time control. Hence G/3 inc/2 is rated under the Blitz system. Currently, Lightning and Bullet are not included in any rating system. *See also 5C. Ratable time controls.*

US Chess Blitz Rules

1.) Each player must make all his moves in the time specified for the game.

1a.) Standard time control (TC) for blitz is G/5 with no delay.

1b.) Time controls, including the use of delay or increment, are to be stated in any advance publicity and must also be announced or posted at the site.

TD TIP: Non-standard time controls should be set keeping in mind the spirit and intent of Blitz Chess (rapid play, quick, fun chess). Total game time should not exceed 10 minutes per player per game.

2.) All the clocks must have a special device, usually called a "flag," either a regular flag or some device on a digital clock that indicates a flag fall.

Standard timer for Blitz chess:

2a.) Whatever timer is used (analog or digital), a standard timer must continue to run for both sides even if one side's time has expired (See 8c).

2b.) A digital timer (given it meets the requirements of 2a) is preferred over an analog timer due to the precision of setting and the accuracy of timing. If no digital timer is available, then an analog timer may be considered standard.

2c.) The player with the black pieces chooses the standard timer.

3.) Before play begins, both players should inspect the position of the pieces and the setting of the clock, since once each side has completed a move the position on the board and the time on the clock remain as set.

3a.) If the king and queen are set up incorrectly, it is legal to castle short on the queenside and long on the kingside.

3b.) If an illegal position is created or an illegal move made without the opponent making a claim, the position stands and a claim not allowed when the opponent has determined a next move.

4.) Each player must press the clock with the same hand that moves the pieces, using one hand to both move the pieces and to press the clock.

TD TIP: This rule, the use of one hand in all blitz moves, also applies to castling and captures.

5.) The tournament director may state at the start of the event the direction the clocks are to face, and the player with the black pieces then chooses the side of the table on which to sit.

6.) Except for pressing the clock, neither player should touch the clock except:

6a.) To straighten it.

6b.) If a player knocks over the clock a penalty may be assessed.

6c.) If your opponent's clock does not tick you may press his side down and re-press your side;

however, if this procedure is unsatisfactory, please call for a director.

6d.) Each player must always be allowed to press the clock after their move is made.

6e.) A player should not keep a hand on or hover over the clock.

7.) Defining a win:

A game is won by the player:

7a.) Who has legally mated his opponent's king.

7b.) Whose opponent resigns.

7c.) Who correctly points out that the opponent's flag has fallen first, at any time before the game is otherwise ended, provided the player has mating material.

Mating Material consists of (at a minimum) two minor pieces, a pawn, a rook, or a queen provided it isn't a position where one could claim a draw under rule 8. If a player who claims a time forfeit states the claim with claimant's flag still up, but then fails to stop the clock in time to avoid also exceeding the time limit, the claim will be void, unless the flag fall was observed by a director or independent witness.

7d.) Who, after an illegal move is completed by the opponent, takes the king (if the king is in check) or claims the win and stops the clock, before the player determines a move and provided the player has sufficient mating material as defined in rule 7c. A player who moves his king adjacent to the opponent's king and then attempts to claim a win under this rule based on the opponent's failure to notice the check shall lose the game.

7e.) An illegal move doesn't negate a player's right to claim on time, provided it is made prior to the opponent's claim of an illegal move. If the claims are simultaneous, the player who made the illegal move loses.

8.) Defining a draw.
Except as listed here, draw claims allowed under the regular rules are also allowed under the blitz rules.

A game is a draw:

8a.) If one of the kings is stalemated.

8b.) By agreement between the players.

8c.) If the flag of one player falls after the flag of the other player has already fallen and a win has not been claimed, unless either side mates before noticing that both flags are down.

8d.) If one player has insufficient mating material when the opponent's flag falls or makes an illegal move. "Insufficient Losing Chances" (ILC) claims are not allowed.

TD TIP: Blitz tournaments allowing "Insufficient Losing Chances" (ILC) claims should be advertised and announced in advance. The TD should be aware that common practice has shown that in addition to the official Blitz rules that "Insufficient Losing Chances" claims are upheld only:

1.) If both players each have just one identical piece and if neither side can show a forced win.

2.) In K+bishop vs. K+bishop of opposite colors, with only 1 pawn on the board, provided there is no forced win.

3.) K+rook pawn vs. K can be claimed as a draw once the defender is on the rook file in front of the pawn. K+pawn vs. K can be claimed as a draw once the defender is immediately on the square directly in front of the pawn as long as it's not on the 7th rank.

4.) K= + rook+rook pawn vs. K+rook is a draw if the pawn is blockaded by the king and there is no immediate win.

5.) The claimant has a significant material and positional advantage.

9.) If a player accidentally displaces one or more pieces, they shall be replaced on the player's own time. If it is necessary, the opponent may press the clock without making a move. If the player presses the clock after displacing pieces, then a penalty may be assessed.

10.) If a player touches one piece, then moves another; and presses the clock, the opponent may press the player's clock to force the player to move the piece touched, or may stop the clock to claim a violation. A penalty may be assessed.

11.) In case of a dispute either player may stop the clock while the tournament director is being summoned. In any unclear situation the tournament director will consider the testimony of both players and any reliable witnesses before rendering a decision.

12.) The tournament director shall not pick up the clock except in the case of a dispute when it is necessary to do so in order to assess penalties or adjust time.

13.) Spectators and players in another game are not to speak or otherwise interfere. If a spectator interferes in any way that may affect the result of the game (e.g. calling attention to a flag fall or an illegal move), the tournament director may cancel the game and rule that a new game be played in its stead and expel the offending party from the playing room. If the offending party is participating in the event, penalties at the discretion of the tournament director may be assessed up to expulsion from the event.

14.) A player who has played an illegal move must retract it and make a legal move with the piece touched prior to pressing the clock. If no legal move exists with that piece then he may make any legal move. Illegal moves unnoticed by both players cannot be corrected afterwards. An illegal move is completed when the player presses the clock.

15.) A legal move is completed when the hand leaves the piece.

16.) If a player is promoting a pawn and the desired piece is not available, the player may stop both clocks in order to locate the piece and place it on the board. It is improper for the player to press the clock to start the opponent's time with the pawn still on the last rank. If this is done, the opponent may immediately restart the player's clock without moving.

17.) Standard penalty for first offense is to add one minute to the opponent's clock. There may be circumstances where a penalty assessed may not be standard (e.g. repeat offenses, unsporting behavior, etc...) and is left to the discretion of the tournament director.

TD TIP: *Illegal moves for any reason lose instantly if claimed correctly. The one-minute penalty does not apply to illegal moves. The standard penalty of one minute applies to other Blitz rules infractions.*

18.) The decision of the tournament director is final.

TD TIP: *This rule's intent stated more accurately could be: "The decision of the chief tournament director is final." Many Blitz events have a staff of TDs. The decision of a floor TD can obviously be appealed to the chief TD. An "appeals committee" or a "special referee" would unnecessarily delay the tournament. Players may appeal directly to US Chess, via their appeals process, after the event is over.*

CHAPTER TWELVE

ROUND ROBIN PAIRING TABLES

The following pairing tables are used for round robin tournaments. The player with the first number in each pairing has the white pieces. Pairing numbers are assigned by lot at the beginning of the event, unlike Swiss tournaments in which pairing numbers are determined by ratings.

The advantage of these Crenshaw-Berger tables over other tables is that they allow the reduction of the distortion of color assignments in cases when a player withdraws in the first half of a tournament with an even number of players. In such an event, players are already assigned unequal blacks and whites, and the withdrawal of one player could mean, for example, that some competitors would actually play two more blacks than whites.

The Crenshaw-Berger system for color equalization minimizes these inequities. The general principles are as follows:

If no one withdraws before playing at least half the scheduled games, there are no color changes. (*Half* is always rounded up, so, for example, 6 is half of 11.)

If one player withdraws before playing half the schedule, some colors are reversed in the last rounds.

The maximum number of color changes is two for any player.

The tournament director may reschedule any games provided that the games in the starred (*) rounds--those involving color reversals--are played after all players have completed half their games.

Each of the following charts applies to an odd and even number of players. If the number of competitors is an odd one, the final position in the tournament is a bye, but the player scheduled for the bye does not get a scoring point for that round. If there is such a bye in a tournament, no color reversals should be made. (See next page.)

Table A 3 or 4 Players

Round	Pairings		Withdrawn Player	Reversals
1	1-4	2-3	1	none
2	3-1	4-2	2	4-3
3	1-2	3-4	3	2-1
			4	none

Colors in the third round are determined by toss, unless one player has withdrawn after the first game. In that case, the director assigns colors in the third game so that each remaining player has at least one black and one white in the tournament.

Table B 5 or 6 Players

Round	Pairings			Withdrawn Player	Reversals	
1	3-6	5-4	1-2	1	5-2	4-3
2	2-6	4-1	3-5	2	4-3	
3	6-5	1-3	4-2	3	none	
4	6-4	5-1	2-3	4	6-1	5-2
5*	1-6	2-5	3-4	5	6-1	
				6	none	

Color reversals should be made in the fifth round if someone withdraws before playing three games:

Table C 7 or 8 Players

Round	Pairings				Withdrawn Player	Reversals			
1	4-8	5-3	6-2	7-1	1	7-2	5-4		
2	8-7	1-6	2-5	3-4	2	6-3			
3	3-8	4-2	5-1	6-7	3	5-4	7-2	2-1	
4	8-6	7-5	1-4	2-3	4	6-3	3-7	7-2	
5*	2-8	3-1	4-7	5-6	5	8-1	7-4	4-6	6-3
6*	8-5	6-4	7-3	1-2	6	8-2	5-4		
7*	1-8	2-7	3-6	4-5	7	8-1	6-3		
					8	none			

Color reversals should be made in the last three rounds if someone withdraws before playing four games:

Table D 9 or 10 Players

Round	Pairings				
1	5-10	6-4	7-3	8-2	9-1
2	10-9	1-8	2-7	3-6	4-5
3	4-10	5-3	6-2	7-1	8-9
4	10-8	9-7	1-6	2-5	3-4
5	3-10	4-2	5-1	6-9	7-8
6	10-7	8-6	9-5	1-4	2-3
7*	2-10	3-1	4-9	5-8	6-7
8*	10-6	7-5	8-4	9-3	1-2
9*	1-10	2-9	3-8	4-7	5-6

* Color reversals should be made in the last three rounds if someone withdraws before playing seven games (see chart next page:

Withdrawn Player	Reversals				
1	9-2	7-4			
2	8-3	6-5			
3	7-4	9-2	2-1		
4	6-5	8-3	3-9	9-2	
5	9-2	7-4	2-1	4-8	8-3
6	10-2	8-5	5-7	7-4	
7	10-1	6-5	9-4	4-8	8-3
8	10-2	7-4			
9	10-1	8-3	6-5		
10	none				

Table E 11 or 12 Players

Round	Pairings					
1	6-12	7-5	8-4	9-3	10-2	11-1
2	12-11	1-10	2-9	3-8	4-7	5-6
3	5-12	6-4	7-3	8-2	9-1	10-11
4	12-10	11-9	1-8	2-7	3-6	4-5
5	4-12	5-3	6-2	7-1	8-11	9-10
6	12-9	10-8	11-7	1-6	2-5	3-4
7	3-12	4-2	5-1	6-11	7-10	8-9
8	12-8	9-7	10-6	11-5	1-4	2-3
9*	2-12	3-1	4-11	5-10	6-9	7-8
10*	12-7	8-6	9-5	10-4	11-3	1-2
11*	1-12	2-11	3-10	4-9	5-8	6-7

Color reversals should be made in the last three rounds if someone withdraws before playing six games:

Withdrawn Player	Reversals						
1	11-2	9-4	7-6				
2	10-3	8-5					
3	9-4	7-6	11-2	2-1			
4	8-5	10-3	3-11	11-2			
5	7-6	11-2	2-1	9-4	4-10	10-3	
6	10-3	3-11	11-2	8-5	5-9	9-4	
7	12-1	11-4	4-10	10-3	9-6	6-8	8-5
8	12-2	7-6	10-5	5-9	9-4		
9	12-1	8-5	11-4	4-10	10-3		
10	12-2	9-4	7-6				
11	12-1	10-3	8-5				
12	none						

Table F 13 or 14 Players

Round	Pairings						
1	7-14	8-6	9-5	10-4	11-3	12-2	13-1
2	14-13	1-12	2-11	3-10	4-9	5-8	6-7
3	6-14	7-5	8-4	9-3	10-2	11-1	12-13
4	14-12	13-11	1-10	2-9	3-8	4-7	5-6
5	5-14	6-4	7-3	8-2	9-1	10-13	11-12
6	14-11	12-10	13-9	1-8	2-7	3-6	4-5
7	4-14	5-3	6-2	7-1	8-13	9-12	10-11
8	14-10	11-9	12-8	13-7	1-6	2-5	3-4
9	3-14	4-2	5-1	6-13	7-12	8-11	9-10
10	14-9	10-8	11-7	12-6	13-5	1-4	2-3
11*	2-14	3-1	4-13	5-12	6-11	7-10	8-9
12*	14-8	9-7	10-6	11-5	12-4	13-3	1-2
13*	1-14	2-13	3-12	4-11	5-10	6-9	7-8

Color reversals should be made in the last three rounds if someone withdraws before playing seven games (see chart next page:

Withdrawn Player	Reversals							
1	13-2	11-4	9-6					
2	12-3	10-5	8-7					
3	13-2	2-1	11-4	9-6				
4	12-3	3-13	13-2	10-5	8-7			
5	13-2	2-1	11-4	4-12	12-3	9-6		
6	12-3	3-13	13-2	10-5	5-11	11-4	8-7	
7	13-2	2-1	11-4	4-12	12-3	9-6	6-10	10-5
8	14-2	12-5	5-11	11-4	10-7	7-9	9-6	
9	14-1	13-4	4-12	12-3	11-6	6-10	10-5	8-7
10	14-2	12-5	5-11	11-4	9-6			
11	14-1	13-4	4-12	12-3	10-5	8-7		
12	14-2	11-4	9-6					
13	14-1	12-3	10-5	8-7				
14	none							

Table G 15 or 16 players

Round	Pairings							
1	8-16	9-7	10-6	11-5	12-4	13-3	14-2	15-1
2	16-15	1-14	2-13	3-12	4-11	5-10	6-9	7-8
3	7-16	8-6	9-5	10-4	11-3	12-2	13-1	14-15
4	16-14	15-13	1-12	2-11	3-10	4-9	5-8	6-7
5	6-16	7-5	8-4	9-3	10-2	11-1	12-15	13-14
6	16-13	14-12	15-11	1-10	2-9	3-8	4-7	5-6
7	5-16	6-4	7-3	8-2	9-1	10-15	11-14	12-13
8	16-12	13-11	14-10	15-9	1-8	2-7	3-6	4-5
9	4-16	5-3	6-2	7-1	8-15	9-14	10-13	11-12
10	16-11	12-10	13-9	14-8	15-7	1-6	2-5	3-4
11	3-16	4-2	5-1	6-15	7-14	8-13	9-12	10-11
12	16-10	11-9	12-8	13-7	14-6	15-5	1-4	2-3
13*	2-16	3-1	4-15	5-14	6-13	7-12	8-11	9-10
14*	16-9	10-8	11-7	12-6	13-5	14-4	15-3	1-2
15*	1-16	2-15	3-14	4-13	5-12	6-11	7-10	8-9

Color reversals should be made in the last three rounds if someone withdraws before playing eight games (see next page):

Withdrawn Player	Reversals								
1	15-2	13-4	11-6	9-8					
2	14-3	12-5	10-7						
3	13-4	11-6	9-8	15-2	2-1				
4	12-5	10-7	14-3	3-15	15-2				
5	11-6	9-8	15-2	2-1	13-4	4-14	14-3		
6	10-7	14-3	3-15	15-2	12-5	5-13	13-4		
7	9-8	15-2	2-1	13-4	4-14	14-3	11-6	6-12	12-5
8	14-3	3-15	15-2	12-5	5-13	13-4	10-7	7-11	11-6
9	16-1	15-4	4-14	14-3	13-6	6-12	12-5	11-8	8-10	10-7
10	16-2	9-8	14-5	5-13	13-4	12-7	7-11	11-6	
11	16-1	10-7	15-4	4-14	14-3	13-6	6-12	12-5	
12	16-2	11-6	9-8	14-5	5-13	13-4			
13	16-1	12-5	10-7	15-4	4-14	14-3			
14	16-2	13-4	11-6	9-8					
15	16-1	14-3	12-5	10-7					
16	none								

The Scheveningen System

The Scheveningen is a system for pairing team matches. The idea is that each member of a team contests a game with each member of the other team.

Pairing tables follow, with the teams called A and B, board numbers indicated by the subscript, and the white player indicated first in each pairing.

Tables for the Scheveningen System

Match on Four Boards

Four Boards			
Round 1	Round 2	Round 3	Round 4
A1–B1	B2–A1	A1–B3	B4–A1
A2–B2	B1–A2	A2–B4	B3–A2
B3–A3	A3–B4	B1–A3	A3–B2
B4–A4	A4–B3	B2–A4	A4–B1

Match on Six Boards

Six Boards					
Round 1	Round 2	Round 3	Round 4	Round 5	Round 6
B1–A1	B2–A1	A1–B3	A1–B4	B5–A1	A1–B6
B5–A2	A2–B1	A2–B2	B6–A2	B4–A2	A2–B3
A3–B4	B3–A3	B1–A3	A3–B5	A3–B6	B2–A3
A4–B2	B4–A4	B6–A4	A4–B1	B3–A4	A4–B5
A5–B3	A5–B6	B5–A5	B2–A5	A5–B1	B4–A5
B6–A6	A6–B5	A6–B4	B3–A6	A6–B2	B1–A6

Match on Eight Boards

Eight Boards							
Rd. 1	Rd. 2	Rd. 3	Rd. 4	Rd. 5	Rd. 6	Rd. 7	Rd. 8
A1-B1	B2-A1	A1-B3	B4-A1	A1-B5	B6-A1	A1-B7	B8-A1
A2-B2	B3-A2	A2-B4	B1-A2	A2-B6	B7-A2	A2-B8	B5-A2
A3-B3	B4-A3	A3-B1	B2-A3	A3-B7	B8-A3	A3-B5	B6-A3
A4-B4	B1-A4	A4-B2	B3-A4	A4-B8	B5-A4	A4-B6	B7-A4
B5-A5	A5-B6	B7-A5	A5-B8	B1-A5	A5-B2	B3-A5	A5-B4
B6-A6	A6-B7	B8-A6	A6-B5	B2-A6	A6-B3	B4-A6	A6-B1
B7-A7	A7-B8	B5-A7	A7-B6	B3-A7	A7-B4	B1-A7	A7-B2
B8-A8	A8-B5	B6-A8	A8-B7	B4-A8	A8-B1	B2-A8	A8-B3

CHAPTER THIRTEEN

The
US CHESS
FEDERATION

The US Chess Federation (US Chess) is the official governing body and nonprofit 501(c)(3) educational organization for chess players and chess supporters in the United States. Its mission is to empower people, enrich lives, and enhance communities through chess. Its vision is that chess is recognized as an essential tool that is inclusive, benefits education and rehabilitation, and promotes recreation and friendly competition.

US Chess represents the United States in the World Chess Federation (FIDE), connecting our members to chess players around the world. Founded in 1939 with the merger of the American Chess Federation and the National Chess Federation, US Chess has grown to serve over 90,000 members and 1,200 affiliated chess clubs and organizations today.

Every year, US Chess sanctions over 11,000 tournaments and rates over 820,000 games. The organization conducts over 25 National Championships and awards titles to both amateurs and professionals, ranging from elementary school students to world-class players.

What Is US Chess?

US Chess provides a framework for American chess players by providing representation with FIDE (the World Chess Federation), by maintaining a rating system, and by publishing *Chess Life* and *Chess Life Kids*. As a federation, there are member state associations and thousands of dedicated volunteers who form the core of the organization that supports everyone from the casual player to world championship candidates. The national office is headquartered in Crossville, Tennessee.

US CHESS CORE VALUES

- **Education:** Chess is an educational tool aiding in the learning of planning, cause and effect relationships, pattern recognition, and research, all key skills for success in STEM (Science, Technology, Engineering, Mathematics).
- **Customer Service:** We strive to be responsive, adaptive and proactive in providing services to our customers.
- **Excellence:** We recognize the value of excellence both in chess as an activity and the services we provide to our customers.
- **Communication:** We will continually inform and be responsive to our members and customers.
- **Integrity:** We respect and maintain good relationships with our customers and stakeholders as well as the game of chess itself.

- **Accessibility:** Chess can and should be enjoyed by individuals regardless of social or economic status or physical or developmental capability.
- **Love of the Game:** Chess is a historic and iconic game, and we celebrate its history, growth and evolution in our activities and services.
- **Outreach:** We work to extend the knowledge and appreciation of chess.

US CHESS GOALS

- Increase the use of chess in education.
- Expand the social, recreational, and rehabilitative applications of chess.
- Develop the depth and breadth of our partnerships.
- Use chess to increase opportunities for under-represented segments of society.
- Continuously improve internal operations and member services.

A Short History US Chess

The US Chess Federation began in 1939 with the merger of the Western Chess Association and the National Chess Federation. The new national organization had the general aim of promoting the game of chess in the U.S. and the specific purpose of organizing the tournaments of both precursors: the invitational U.S. Championship and the U.S. Open.

The new group began with perhaps 1,000 members and an annual yearbook. In 1946, the yearbook became the twice-monthly newspaper *Chess Life*, improving communication among players and organizers. In 1952, US Chess took its next big step forward with the institution of a national rating system. This provided the foundation for membership-required tournaments and led to the establishment of a central office to administer services.

Throughout the 1950s US Chess grew steadily under a succession of dynamic presidents such as Jerry Spann, Fred Cramer, and Ed Edmondson, and membership grew to 4,000.

By the 1960s, membership growth led to rapid expansion of the business office. Under the leadership of Executive Director Ed Edmondson, the Federation moved to larger quarters first in Newburgh, New York, then to its own building in New Windsor, New York. Membership had reached 12,000 when Fischer burst on the scene. In 1961 *Chess Life* assumed the monthly magazine format it has kept to this day.

Bobby Fischer's conquest of the World Championship in 1972 led to a vast expansion of chess in the United States and within the Federation, popularly known as the "Fischer Boom." Membership swelled to almost 60,000, services expanded exponentially, and *Chess Life* merged with *Chess Review,* the other major U.S. chess magazine. But the post-Fischer letdown brought a time of troubles.

When Fischer failed to defend his title in 1975, many of those he had drawn to the game fell away. US Chess met this challenge with improved services, promotion, and outreach to the untapped pool of casual players. A solid groundwork was laid for the new opportunities of the 1980s.

The 1980s ushered in a new period of growth, due in large part to the progress and spread of chess-playing computers. US Chess took full advantage of the new situation, with an aggressive program of promotion and expansion, finding new ways to spread the word of chess while continuing to serve the loyal core of tournament players. By the end of the decade, membership again approached the peak of the Fischer Boom. In the last decade of the 20th century, membership shot past all previous levels as a result of well-developed, popular programs.

The first two decades of the 21st century led to a professionalization of the organization. *Chess Life Kids* was born as an independent publication in 2006 (having evolved from *Schoolmates,* which was part of *Chess Life*). In 2012 *Chess Life* became a full-color publication for the first time. Finances were stabilized and in 2014 a fundamental shift took place when US Chess went from being a 501(c)(4) to a 501(c)(3) organization with an educational mission. Membership reached 90,000 for the first time.

Amid these changes, US Chess remains fully committed to its traditional goals and programs, balancing education, excellence, growth, and service to its members.

Benefits of Joining US Chess

Members of US Chess are entitled to the following benefits, among others:

- USChess.org: Members have access to additional content on the official website such as archival editions of our print publications. The website is the source for daily information for members and the public about the latest news in the chess world. Play through the latest games with our interactive game player, see videos, and find out about upcoming tournaments that you can play in, listen to podcasts, and stay up-to-date with all that is happening in the US Chess world. Much of the website is also available to non-members.

- *Chess Life* magazine: Premium Adult members receive a print copy of *Chess Life* magazine every month, while Regular members receive online-only access to the digital editions. Each issue is packed with instructional articles, personality profiles, human interest stories, and annotated games which give the reader insights into winning strategy. The Tournament Life section shows you where you can play rated chess tournaments around the country.

- *Chess Life Kids* magazine: Premium Scholastic members receive a print copy of *Chess Life for Kids* magazine every two months, while Regular Scholastic members have online-only access to the digital editions. Each issue has news, puzzles, games, and instruction tailored for beginning chess players. Columns such as "My First Move" show how your chess heroes got their start when they were *Chess Life* kids! Upcoming tournaments across America are also listed.

- Tournament play: Hundreds of tournaments are held each year where US Chess members meet and socialize. They play for a weekend or just an evening. Some of these tournaments are attended by hundreds of players competing for large prize funds; while other events are smaller, usually held on weeknights at local clubs. There are even online-only rated events through our partners at *Chessclub.com (Internet Chess Club)* and at *Chess.com*.

- Get rated: You can trace your steady improvement with the US Chess' rating system for tournament play. From beginner (rated under 1000) through grandmaster (rated over 2500 by FIDE), you can view your current rating by accessing the Membership Services Area (MSA) at *uschess.org*. This internationally-recognized service allows you to compare your current level of skill against other chess players.

- Chess product discounts: As a member you will receive promotional discounts from US Chess Sales at *uscfsales.com*, where you can find books, equipment (such as clocks, sets, and boards), and DVDs.

- Play chess locally: Meet people of your playing ability for over-the-board casual or tournament play. With over 1,200 affiliated chess clubs all over the country, there's one near you.

- Build your mind: Whatever your age, as you play chess, you'll continue to hone your critical thinking skills. Children often find more academic success and senior adults often find increased mental acuity.

- Help us grow the game: Get the satisfaction of supporting a growing national sport while you have fun!

Affiliation

US Chess affiliates form a team of 1,200 chess clubs nationwide that support chess in the U.S. These affiliates are the cornerstone of growth for chess in our country. Any group of chess players may affiliate with US Chess for a small annual fee. The benefits include the right to sponsor officially rated tournaments and free promotional materials for use in local outreach. For all of the benefits of affiliation, please click on the "Join" button at *uschess.org*.

Next Steps

Are you ready to get started? Please visit *uschess.org* and click on the "Join" button to find a membership option that is right for you. You can also support chess in the United States by making a tax-deductible donation to US Chess by clicking on the "Donate" button. Whether you join, donate, or do both, you will make a difference in your own life and the life of others.

Daniel Lucas contributed to the material in this chapter.

INDEX

Index

Index

Index

Index

Index

Index

Index

Index